Benjamin Constant's
Philosophy of Liberalism

Benjamin Constant
Courtesy of Bibliothèque Nationale

Benjamin Constant's Philosophy of Liberalism

A Study in Politics and Religion

GUY HOWARD DODGE

The University of North Carolina Press *Chapel Hill*

© 1980 The University of North Carolina Press

Manufactured in the United States of America

Library of Congress Cataloging in Publication Data
Dodge, Guy Howard.
  Benjamin Constant's philosophy of liberalism.

  Bibliography: p.
  Includes index.
  1. Constant de Rebecque, Henri Benjamin,
1767–1830—Political science. 2. Liberalism.
I. Title.
JC229.C8D62   320.5'12'0924   79-26784
ISBN 0-8078-1433-4

For Dorothea always

Contents

Preface

The purpose of this study is to assess for the first time in English Henri Benjamin Constant de Rebecque as a political philosopher, both in his own age and in the continuity of political thought. Although there are a few other works on Constant in English, they are either biographical or so general in nature that they do not treat Constant's political theory in any detail.[1] This volume also includes the most complete bibliography in print on the subject.

To this day, Constant is still much more recognized for such literary efforts as *Adolphe*, *Le cahier rouge*, and *Journaux intimes*, which are autobiographical, than for such political writings as *De l'esprit de conquête et de l'usurpation*, *Réflexions sur les constitutions*, and *Principes de politique*. Furthermore, his political philosophy, as far as it has been noticed at all, has been much neglected in the twentieth century, especially in America and England. This is probably due in part to the contemporary mood, which looks unfavorably upon liberalism after all the sustained attacks on it by the exponents of conservatism, Marxism, Freudianism, existentialism, and the New Left, who have pointed out, among other defects, its shallow and superficial view of man and society.[2]

The historical importance of liberalism, however, is unquestioned. This study, which is rooted in history, will attempt to demonstrate that so significant were Constant's contributions to this

1. There are two biographies of Constant in English: Elizabeth Schermerhorn, *Benjamin Constant, His Private Life and His Contribution to the Cause of Liberal Government in France, 1767–1830* (New York, 1924), and Harold Nicolson, *Benjamin Constant* (London, 1949). Reference should also be made to two short studies of Constant's thought as a whole: William W. Holdheim, *Benjamin Constant* (London, 1961), and John Cruickshank, *Benjamin Constant* (New York, 1974).

2. See Robert P. Wolff, *The Poverty of Liberalism*. For recent analyses of liberalism see D. J. Manning, *Liberalism*, Harvey C. Mansfield, Jr., *The Spirit of Liberalism*, and Massimo Salvadori, *The Liberal Heresy: Origins and Historical Development*.

philosophy that he deserves at last to be ranked alongside its classic theoretical expounders from the seventeenth to the nineteenth centuries, such as John Locke, the Baron Montesquieu, Wilhelm von Humboldt, Jeremy Bentham, Alexis de Tocqueville, John Stuart Mill, Lord Acton, Herbert Spencer, and Thomas Hill Green.[3]

In scope, this book goes beyond merely studying Constant's work and thought. The method employed is to relate him specifically to the liberalism of Montesquieu and Tocqueville in France, Mill and Acton in England, and Lieber in America. In addition, Constant is presented as the focus of the liberal reaction to Rousseau and the French Revolution in the nineteenth century, which has not heretofore received as much attention as has the conservative critique.[4] This procedure involves comparisons and parallels of Constant with such thinkers as Jean Joseph Mounier and Jacques Mallet du Pan in the eighteenth century and Madame de Staël, Jean Charles Simonde de Sismondi, Prosper de Barante, Pierre Paul Royer-Collard, François Guizot, François A. Saint-Marc Girardin, and Edouard Laboulaye in the nineteenth century.

Most of the previous examinations of Constant's political theory have analyzed his various definitions of liberty and individual rights, but they have not, by and large, considered his political ideas in the entire framework of his philosophy of history, law, ethics, and religion. This study attempts to do just that, because it is felt that only then can Constant's contributions to liberalism be adequately understood.

Finally, this volume is based much more on Constant's published works, of which there is yet no complete edition, than on the manuscript sources. The reasons are threefold. First, the manuscripts recently made available, like the Oeuvres manuscrits de 1810, have

3. Since Constant was greatly influenced by Montesquieu, the interpretation of the latter's political theory is of special importance. Although Montesquieu was depicted as a feudal reactionary by A. Mathiez in his article, "La place de Montesquieu dans l'histoire des doctrines politiques du XVIIIᵉ siècle," pp. 97–112, the most recent studies follow Elie Carcassonne, *Montesquieu et le problème de la constitution française au XVIIIᵉ siècle*, in describing him as a liberal, either aristocratic or democratic and civic. See Melvin Richter, *The Political Theory of Montesquieu*; Mark Hulliung, *Montesquieu and the Old Regime*; and Thomas Pangle, *Montesquieu's Philosophy of Liberalism*.

4. For contrasting interpretations of Rousseau, especially his "force-freedom" paradox, see my *Jean-Jacques Rousseau*.

already been extensively utilized by Olivier Pozzo di Borgo in *Benjamin Constant: Ecrits et discours politiques* (Paris, 1964), and by Paul Bastid, *Benjamin Constant et sa doctrine* (Paris, 1966), which are both fine additions in French to our knowledge of Constant as a political thinker.[5] Second, although the manuscripts show that Constant's mature political writings were not just the polemical reactions to events by a political journalist or pamphleteer but instead the carefully conceived efforts of a serious political theorist, historian, sociologist, and moralist that had been germinating for years, they have not changed in essence what has been at our disposal in print for a long time as the basis for the main outlines of his political philosophy.[6] Third, it was through his publications alone that Constant was judged, not only by his contemporaries but also by such subsequent political thinkers as Georg Hegel and Lord Acton, whom he influenced.[7]

I am indebted to the United States Department of State for two Fulbright Fellowships to France in 1949–50 and in 1963–64, which enabled me to pursue my research in the Bibliothèque Nationale in Paris. I also wish to thank the American Philosophical Society for a grant in 1949–50, which made it possible for me to work in the Bibliothèque Cantonale et Universitaire in Lausanne, Switzerland, where Constant was born, and in the Bibliothèque Publique et Universitaire in Geneva. I am also grateful to Brown University for sabbatical leaves and financial assistance, which allowed me to continue and complete this project.

I also wish to express my appreciation to Madame Albert Le

5. Constant produced a huge work in manuscript on the principles of politics between 1806 and 1810 from which large parts of three of his published writings were extracted—*De l'esprit de conquête et de l'usurpation dans leurs rapports avec la civilisation européenne*; *Réflexions sur les constitutions, la distribution des pouvoirs et les garanties dans une monarchie constitutionnelle*; and *Principes de politique applicables à tous les gouvernements représentatifs*.

6. Ephraim Harpaz is publishing an important collection of Constant's political articles. When the entire corpus of his work is considered, it should be noted that there is a great deal of repetition and self-plagiarism, which makes some of his writings monotonous.

7. Georg Lasson has said that "Hegel began reading Benjamin Constant (at Berne) to whom he gave attention to the very end of his life and to whom he owes a good part of his monarchial liberalism" (quoted in Carl J. Friedrich, *The Philosophy of Hegel*, Introduction, p. xxiii). For Lord Acton see his *Lectures on Modern History*, p. 342.

Guillard for permitting me to consult the family Archives d'Estournelles de Constant in the Chateau de Créans at Clermont-Créans in the Department of the Sarthe in France. Also I remember with gratefulness the late Comtesse Jean de Pange, a direct descendant of Madame de Staël, who granted me access to her private library in Paris. I likewise owe a debt to Jean Jacques Chevallier, professor emeritus of the Faculté du Droit of the University of Paris, for his many kindnesses while I was in Paris both of those years.

It was a remark of my beloved teacher many years ago, the late Charles H. McIlwain of Harvard University, to the effect that "the greatest delusion of the modern political world is the delusion of 'popular sovereignty'" that led me to study two French Protestant thinkers—first Pierre Jurieu and then Benjamin Constant—both of whose political theory was centered around that concept.[8] Another esteemed teacher, Carl J. Friedrich, professor emeritus of Harvard, should also be mentioned, because he particularly encouraged me to study Constant.

I should like to pay special tribute to my wife, Dorothea Zantiny Dodge, without whose devoted support I never would have completed this monograph in my own retirement from Brown University. Thanks also to my colleague and former student William T. Bluhm, of the University of Rochester, who kindly read the proof for me when I was ill.

Naples, Florida
June 1979

Guy Howard Dodge

---

8. See my *The Political Theory of the Huguenots of the Dispersion,* republished in 1972 with a new preface, which shows how Pierre Jurieu's theory of popular sovereignty was cited in the nineteenth century in France by both conservatives and liberals, only to be repudiated.

Benjamin Constant's
Philosophy of Liberalism

Je voudrais au moins avoir fini deux ouvrages en politique et en religion pour laisser après moi quelques traces.

Je veux qu'on dise après moi que j'ai contribué à fonder la liberté en France.
—Benjamin Constant

Chapter I
Introduction

BENJAMIN CONSTANT has had a long line of detractors right down to our own time.[1] Let us begin with some of the hostile opinions of his contemporaries.[2] Jacques Mallet du Pan referred to him in 1797 as "the most perverse of the men younger than thirty."[3] Sir James Mackintosh, Constant's old friend from his student days at Edinburgh, the center of the Scottish Enlightenment, wrote in 1814 that "few men have turned talent to less account than Constant. His powers of mind are very great but as they have always been exerted on the events of the moment . . . they have left only a vague and faint reputation, which will scarcely survive the speaker or writer. No man's character could be at more variance with his situation."[4] To Jeremy Bentham, the most famous and

1. Henri Guillemin, *Benjamin Constant muscadin, 1795–1797*, portrays Constant as an unscrupulous *arriviste* during the Directory, who profited personally from the sale of "les biens nationaux."
2. See the following chansonette published in M. et Mme William de Sévery, *La vie de société dans le pays de Vaud à la fin du dix-huitième siècle*, 1:171:

On demande un gouvernement
V' la ce q' c'est que d'être monarchique
Aristocratique
Ou democratique
N'importe j'en serai content
V' la ce q' c'est d'être constant

Je fus républicain ardent
V' la ce q' c'est que d'être constant
Mais sous son pouvoir despotique
L'oppression inique
De la république
Reçut mes voeux et mes serments
V' la ce q' c'est que d'être constant

Le dix-neuf mars, publiquement
V' la q' c'est que d'être constant
Sur Bonaparte, avec outrance
Je criai vengeance
Mais bientôt la France
M' vit le Benjamin du tyran
V' la ce q' c'est que d'être constant

Je trouvai le poste amusant
V' la q' c'est que d'être constant
Mais lorsqu' en ce monde où tout passe
Une auguste race a repris sa place
Je me suis fait indépendant
V' la ce q' c'est que d'être constant

3. *Correspondance inédite de Mallet du Pan avec la Cour de Vienne (1794–1798)*, 2:307.
4. Sir James Mackintosh, *Memoirs of the Life of the Right Honorable Sir James Mackintosh 1767–1832*, 2:412.

influential liberal of the age, he was "the inconstant Constant" ("sola inconstantia constans"), a judgment shared by many, both then and now.[5]

The estimates of two other contemporaries are in the same vein as they reflected on Constant's career. François Guizot remembered him as a "man with an *esprit* infinitely varied, facile, extensive, clear, *piquant*, superior in conversation and in the pamphlet, but sophist, skeptical, mocking, without conviction."[6] Louis Blanc saw Constant as a "man of singularly vigorous intellect, of a feeble temperament, and a cold heart." He was led to the conclusion that "there is in him, in spite of his profession of Liberalism, a great stock of indifference, often manifested by glaring contradictions."[7] Later on, Alfonse de Lamartine labeled Constant as "that equivocal man," who was "without principles," whereas Anatole France thought that he "professed liberty without believing in it."[8]

Powerful as these criticisms are, it was the great nineteenth-century literary critic, Charles Augustin Sainte-Beuve, who really created the Constant legend of the perfect *girouette*—skeptical, cynical, blasé, disillusioned, bitter, sarcastic, egotistic, mocking, indifferent, hesitant, indecisive, timid, procrastinating, two-sided, impulsive, inconstant, vacillating, contradictory, and opportunistic.[9] This extreme indictment has been so persuasive that it has hardly been erased even to this day. William James concluded that Constant was an "extraordinary instance of superior intelligence with inferior character."[10]

Sainte-Beuve's most devastating political attack on Constant was made in his review of Edouard Laboulaye's collection of Constant's political writings, which appeared in 1861.[11] Sainte-Beuve concentrated, in particular, on the two most controversial parts of

5. Jeremy Bentham, *Works*, 10:467.

6. François Guizot, *Mémoires pour servir à l'histoire de mon temps*, 2:143.

7. Louis Blanc, *The History of the Ten Years 1830–1840 or France under Louis Philippe*, 1:344–45.

8. Alfonse de Lamartine, *Cours familier de littérature*, 9:110–13; Anatole France, "Le journal de Benjamin Constant," 1:48–58.

9. For example, in his *Journaux intimes*, pp. 399, 401, in an entry for 11 March 1814, he writes: "Pas vu le Prince [Bernadotte]. Il faut sauter sur une autre branche." On 16 April 1814, he commented: "Servons la bonne cause et servons nous."

10. William James, *The Varieties of Religious Experience*, p. 259.

11. Sainte-Beuve, "Benjamin Constant," 1:411–37. Sainte-Beuve should be com-

Constant's political career.[12] First, he cited Constant's justification during the Directory of the coup d'état of the 18th fructidor in a *Discours prononcé au cercle constitutionnel le 9 ventôse an VI* (1798); he then contrasted it with Constant's impassioned condemnation of *l'arbitraire* and all illegality in two other works written at about this time (1797)—*Des réactions politiques* and *Des effets de la terreur*. He then taunts Laboulaye for not including this *Discours* in his edition of Constant's political writings, an omission made significantly enough by Constant himself in his own edition of his published writings at a time (1818–20) when he tried to draw a veil over this very disputable time of his life.[13]

Constant's much debated role in the last two years of the Directory must now be considered. In the elections of 20 May 1797, the Right was victorious, which meant that the Directors were faced with a hostile legislative body, not to be legally dissolved.[14] As a result, there was a coup d'état on the 18th fructidor in which two Directors and two hundred legally chosen representatives were removed from office. Constant not only defended but praised this coup d'état on the 30th fructidor (1797) in a *Discours prononcé au cercle constitutionnel pour la plantation de l'arbre de la liberté* and on the 9th ventose (1798) in the *Discours*, just cited, before the same society.[15] Furthermore, in his unsuccessful campaign for elec-

pared with Th. Fadeville, *B. Constant jugé par ses discours et ses écrits*, who outlined the same unfavorable estimate earlier.

12. There are other illustrations. In 1798, during the Directory, Constant had denounced the English Restoration and supported the Republic. In the Restoration, he praised the legitimacy of kings and denounced usurpers: "Il célébrait la légitimité des princes et maudissait l'usurpation en termes qu'un habitué de Coblentz n'aurait pas désavoués." See the Duc Victor de Broglie, *Souvenirs, 1785–1870*, 1:282.

13. Constant also omitted from this Restoration collection *De l'esprit de conquête et de l'usurpation* (1814) and *Principes de politique* (1815) because they were published during the Napoleonic Empire and the Hundred Days.

14. Much later, in his "Souvenirs historiques à l'occasion de l'ouvrage de M. Bignon," p. 111, Constant said that there were two grave defects in the Constitution of 1795—the absence of the veto power in the executive and the lack of the right of dissolution of one of the assemblies. Cf. Madame de Staël's analysis in *Des circonstances actuelles qui peuvent terminer la Révolution et des principes qui doivent fonder la République en France*, p. 118: "Le 18 Fructidor c'est le droit de dissoudre le parlement d'Angleterre violenment exercé parce qu'il n'en existait pas un moyen légal."

15. At his installation as president of the canton of Luzarches on the 23rd brumaire, Constant referred to the 18th fructidor as "the immortal day." The *Discours*

tion to the Council of the Five Hundred, Constant asked for the support of Paul Barras, exclaiming: "Whether in the tribune or whenever it becomes necessary to fight side by side with you, I shall always be what I have tried to be, when on the 18th fructidor you saved the French Republic and the liberty of the world."[16]

In his *Discours* of the 30th fructidor (1797) Constant argued:

> After fourteen years of monarchy, only Republicans
> could successfully maintain a republic. To make liberty
> work it is necessary to be partial to liberty. Only those have
> a right to liberty who believe liberty possible. Those who do
> not believe in the rights of the people should be deprived
> of those rights. Twelve centuries of superstition and feudalism
> have been supplanted by equality and light. On the day of the
> 18th fructidor it was not Cromwell suppressing a rebellious
> parliament, it was the genius of the Republic repressing the
> power of unfaithful representatives. [Moreover,] if on that
> day some individual misfortunes can cause regrets, the day
> itself was not less indispensable. No, it was not the power
> of an assembly which was destroyed . . . it was not armed force
> which has subjugated the delegates of the nation, it was the
> patriotic sentiment, which has disentangled the counter-
> revolution in a faction which controlled the Councils.[17]

---

of the 30th fructidor has been published by Carlo Cordie, *Gli scritti politici givanili di Benjamin Constant, 1796–1797.*

16. Letter of Constant (Germinal an VI, 1798) to Paul Barras, in Barras, *Mémoires de Barras*, 3:chap. 5. Cf. Jacques Mallet du Pan's observation in *Mercure britannique*, 25 Dec. 1798, 51: "C'eut été un assez bel épisode de la Révolution que le manteau de Louis le Débonnaire jet sur les épaules d'un roi constitutionnel, ayant Barras pour son maître du palais, Bonaparte pour son connêtable, Tallein ou Talleyrand pour son chancelier, Benjamin Constant pour son secrétaire privé." See also Mallet du Pan's letter of 27 Sept. 1797 to Johannes von Müller, cited in Nicola Matteucci, *Jacques Mallet du Pan*, p. 332: "Benjamin Constant dirige Barras et le pousse aux extrémités; ils veulent dissoudre le Corps législatif, et établir une dictature militaire."

17. In a letter to his uncle, Samuel de Constant, 1 Aug. 1797, Benjamin said that the memory of revolutionary violence had made nine-tenths of France counter-revolutionary. See Jean H. Menos, *Lettres de Benjamin Constant à sa famille, 1795–1830*, p. 154.

Rather than cite these pertinent passages, Sainte-Beuve concentrated upon a particular section of Constant's *Discours* of 1798: "If some precious rights have been momentarily suspended, if some forms [that is, established procedures] have been violated, if some parts of liberty have been dashed, we accuse royalism, which has pushed us into these straits, where danger seemed to motivate the temporary neglect of law." It is most interesting that Constant employed here the reasoning of Robespierre, who had described the "government of the Revolution" as "the despotism of liberty against tyranny."[18] In that period, of course, Constant was denouncing *raison d'état* in the ancient guise of *Salus populi suprema lex esto* in his *Des réactions politiques* and *Des effets de la terreur* (1797).

By the time Constant got around to writing his *Mémoires sur les Cent Jours* (1819–20), he strongly condemned this coup d'état:

> After the 18th fructidor, it was no longer the enemies
> of the Revolution of 1789 or the imprudent friends of the
> Constitution of 1795 who should be blamed; the trouble was
> with those into whose hands the 18th fructidor brought power.
> This illegal day had the effect that every illegal day must
> have; all confidence was destroyed between the rulers and the
> ruled. . . . But I repeat, the 18th fructidor must have its con-
> sequences; a sad experience should enlighten and punish the
> men who believed that illegality is permitted in order to
> arrest menacing counterrevolution.[19]

In his recollections at the close of his life, Constant claimed that "the Directory fell because it wished to rule against opinion and against law; because it believed that it could preserve itself by coups d'état."[20] He then traced to the 18th fructidor the cause of the 18th brumaire of Napoleon Bonaparte in 1799. Is it any wonder that Constant's contemporaries delighted in raking over all these contradictions, *palinodies*, and *volte-face*?

18. See *Le moniteur universel*, 19 Pluviose l'An II (1794), p. 562.
19. *Mémoires sur les Cent Jours en formes de lettres*, pp. 171–72.
20. "Souvenirs historiques," p. 112.

The end of the Directory finally came with the famous coup d'état of the 18th brumaire (9 November 1799). Like the Abbé Sieyès, Constant would have preferred Joubert or Bernadotte to Napoleon, but he accepted at the time the great augmentation of the executive power in one man in order to save France from the return of the *ancien régime* and foreign invasion. In 1826, however, he wrote that "the Republic fell through the application of military force," but "that he neither contributed to nor applauded its collapse," which put France "at the mercy of one man."[21]

Sainte-Beuve also referred to the second great volte-face of Constant's political career at the time of the two restorations when he was known as the chameleon of the Hundred Days. Constant publicly proclaimed in the *Journal des débats* for 19 March 1815 his loyalty to Louis XVIII, who had already fled to Ghent. Then came his famous rally to Napoleon Bonaparte on 20 March, the day after Napoleon entered Paris, for whom within a month he drafted the Additional Act to the Constitutions of the Empire during the Hundred Days. In that famous article, Constant stated that "on the side of the king is constitutional liberty, security, peace; on the side of Bonaparte," whom he had compared to Attila and Genghis Khan a few days earlier, "servitude, anarchy, and war." Then, in an impassioned outburst, he exclaimed: "I shall not go, a wretched turncoat, crawling from one seat of power to another."

Constant's defense of his action is most interesting: "I have been upbraided because I did not die for the throne which I had defended on the nineteenth of March. But on the twentieth I raised my eyes and saw that the throne had disappeared and that France still remained."[22] In other words, Constant is saying that to attack Napoleon would be to attack France and national independence without which there can be neither government nor liberty.[23]

21. See his apology in *Le constitutionnel* for 22 May 1826. Cf. his "Souvenirs historiques," p. 119, where Constant claimed that he was a "spectator rather than a participant" when "he watched the collapse for fourteen years of representative institutions."

22. *Mémoires sur les Cent Jours*, p. 117.

23. "Mémoire to Louis XVIII of July 21, 1815," published in P. T. Real, *Indiscrétions, 1798–1830*, pp. 154–72. Stendhal said that Constant regarded Napoleon's domination of France simply as a fact. See the *Courrier anglais* 1 (27 Nov. 1822): 55–56.

Constant had argued, however, in the opposite fashion in 1814, when he wrote on 27 March to his old Edinburgh friend, Sir James Mackintosh:

> However averse I am in general to any steps which seem to co-operate with foreign forces against French independence, every consideration must yield in my opinion to the necessity of overturning the most systematical and baneful tyranny that ever weighted with iron weight on mankind. My last publication [*De l'esprit de conquête et de l'usurpation*] has already explained to you, I suppose, what are my notions of modern patriotism. It cannot like that of the ancients be irrevocably confined within the narrow bounds of a particular territory. Liberty, religious feelings, humanity are the general property of our species; and when the government of a nation attempts to rob the world of all that ought to be dear to every inhabitant of the world—when it tramples on every idea, every hope, every virtue—that nation, as long as it consents to be the tool of that government, is no longer composed of fellow citizens but of enemies that must be vanquished or madmen that must be chained.[24]

It was in that "last publication" in 1813 where Constant was most anti-French; he even passionately announced that the "flames of Moscow are the dawn of liberty for the world."[25]

These two episodes—Constant's defense of the 18th fructidor during the Directory and of Napoleon during the Hundred Days—have always cast doubt upon his claim in 1830 that he had "defended for forty years the same principle—liberty in everything, in religion, in philosophy, in literature, in industry, in politics" and upon all those who, since Edouard Laboulaye, have found unity in his political theory.[26] In 1820, however, Constant gave an impor-

---

24. *Memoirs of Sir James Mackintosh*, 2:270–72.
25. See the preface to the first edition of *De l'esprit de conquête et de l'usurpation*, dated 31 December 1813. Cf. *Lettres de Madame de Staël à Benjamin Constant*, pp. 64–65. She wrote on 22 March 1814: "Vous n'êtes pas Français Benjamin . . . mais pouvez-vous vraiment désirer voir les cosaques dans la rue Racine?"
26. *Mélanges de littérature et de politique*, p. vi.

tant, if not completely convincing, defense of his actions from the Directory to the Restoration: "I have always believed, and this belief has been the rule of my conduct, that in matters of government it is necessary to start from the point where one is; that liberty is possible under all forms [of government]; that it is the end and the forms only the means. . . . As a result, it is not against a form [of government] that I have argued; there is none that I require exclusively. The one which exists has the advantage of existing and to substitute what does not exist for what does demands sacrifice that it is always good to avoid"—a very conservative position, similar to that of Edmund Burke.[27]

One final observation of Sainte-Beuve must now be considered. He asserted that Constant's public life is to be explained by his vacillating private life, where, among other things, he seemed to be unduly influenced by strong women, such as Madame de Staël, not to mention Madame de Charrière and Madame Récamier.[28] This opinion raises the controversial question of the relation of biography to the study of ideas. It would appear that what Ernst Cassirer once wrote about Jean-Jacques Rousseau applies equally to Benjamin Constant—that, although Rousseau's "fundamental thought . . . had its immediate origin in his nature and individuality, it was neither circumscribed by nor bound to that individual personality." Otherwise, according to Cassirer, there is danger that "the history of ideas threatens . . . to disappear into biography" or into autobiography, for that matter.[29] The only purpose, then, for linking Constant's personal life with his thought is to understand its psychological, historical, and geographical origins, especially because he lived in a period of rapid revolutionary political and social change.[30] In the end, however, his ideas must stand upon their own feet when one comes to the task of assessing their validity.

27. *Mémoires sur les Cent Jours*, p. 61.
28. Cf. Harriet Taylor's influence on John Stuart Mill, for example.
29. Ernst Cassirer, *Rousseau, Kant, Goethe*, p. 58.
30. "Constant constate que le malaise qu'il éprouve ne lui est particulier, qu'il s'agit non seulement d'un malaise personnel, mais aussi du malaise générale de son époque. . . . Il se rend compte que la solitude morale de l'individu et la décadence de la société sont deux aspects complémentaires du même problème et c'est pour cette raison qu'il ne faut pas séparer ses écrits personnels de ses écrits politiques" (Cecil P. Courtney, "La pensée politique de Benjamin Constant," p. 33). So much for the

Before we leave Constant's detractors to turn to his supporters, it is appropriate to take a look at his autobiographical observations because he was always very frank with himself. Under the influence of Belle de Charrière, he admits that he developed a deep skepticism, especially of dogmatic formulas.[31] He frequently refers to his divided nature: "I am not an entirely real person. There are within me two people, one of whom is the observant of the other."[32] He also speaks of that "strange mania which enables me to see in succession the opposite sides of a thing."[33] He elaborated upon his character further when he asked: "Why . . . should I be accused of having a weak character: This is an accusation to which all well-informed people are exposed because they see the two, or . . . the thousand aspects of things, and, because they are unable to arrive at a decision, they seem to vacillate from one side to the other."[34]

Constant often referred to his "miserable weakness"—his "indecision" and his "hesitation."[35] He also laments: "A peculiarity of my life is always to be considered as the most cold and hard-hearted of men and to have been continually governed and tormented by sentiments independent of all calculation and even destructive of my interests, position, glory, or fortune."[36]

Constant also often reveals his deep pessimism over human destiny that remained during his frustrated and unhappy life, a large

psychological origins of his thought. As for its geographical roots, Constant wrote in "Le cahier rouge" (in *Oeuvres de Benjamin Constant*, ed. Alfred Roulin, p. 164): "Rempli de toute sa [son père] haine contre le gouvernement de Berne . . . je commençai à répéter tous les arguments connus contre les privilèges en politique, contre les droits enlevés au peuple, contre l'autorité héréditaire etc."

31. "Toutes les opinions de Mme de Charrière reposaient sur le mépris de toutes les convenances et de tous les usages" (*Le cahier rouge*," *Oeuvres*, p. 141).

32. *Journaux intimes*, 11 April 1804, p. 76.

33. Letter to Madame de Charrière, 4 April 1794.

34. Letter to his aunt, Madame de Nassau, 23 Jan. 1804. See D. Melegari, *Journal intime de Benjamin Constant et lettres à sa famille et à ses amis*, p. 378.

35. Ibid., p. 383: "L'indécision est le grand supplice de la vie." William James comments in *Varieties of Religious Experience*, p. 259: "He [Constant] can't 'get mad' at any of his alternatives; and the career of a man beset by such an all-around amiability is hopeless."

36. Gustave Rudler, "Lettres de Benjamin Constant à M. et Mme De Gérando," pp. 449–85. See Constant's self-portrait in a letter to Madame de Charrière, 17 Sept. 1792: "Blasé surtout, ennuyé de tout, amer, égoiste, avec une sorte de sensibilité qui ne sert qu'à me tourmenter, mobile au point d'en passer pour sot, sujet à des accès de melancholie qui interrompent tous mes plans et me font agir, pendant qu'ils durent, comme si j'avais renoncé à tout."

part of which he spent in continuous love affairs and compulsive gambling (*vogue la galère*): "I see that morality is vague, that man is wicked, weak, stupid, and base, and I believe that such is his destiny."[37] This was written in 1792. The previous year he was even more gloomy:

> Perhaps it is my misfortune to perceive too well . . .
> that all our pursuits, all our endeavors, all we try to do
> or change, are mere momentary games, which can only lead to
> immediate annihilation. Therefore, we have no more motive
> for gaining fame, for conquering an empire, for writing a good
> book, than we have for taking a walk or playing a game of
> whist. Time flows at a uniform pace independently of us and
> drags us along whether we sleep or wake, whether we are
> active or completely inactive. This trite, but always forgotten
> truth, is constantly on my mind and makes me almost
> insensible to everything.[38]

Constant's feeling of alienation did not prevent but may even have encouraged him to pursue not only an active political career during the Restoration as a deputy representing the Sarthe (1819–22), Paris (1824–27), or Strasbourg (1827–30), but the life of the mind as well, especially in the fields of literature, philosophy, politics, history, political economy, and religion.

Reference should be made to those who, in his own time, looked with favor upon Constant. It is significant that Sir James Mackintosh had a positive as well as a negative estimate of Constant. In 1814, he thought that Benjamin was "an extraordinary man." A year later, he believed that "he is unquestionably the first political writer of the Continent, and apparently the ablest man in France."[39] This is an anticipation of the later judgment of Léon Duguit that

37. Letter to Madame de Charrière, 6 July 1792. Like Lord Acton, Constant was a liberal who thought that human nature was bad rather than good.
38. Letter to Madame de Charrière, 21 May 1791.
39. "On the State of France in 1815," in *The Miscellaneous Works of the Right Honorable Sir James Mackintosh*, 3:199.

Constant possessed "one of the most vigorous and brilliant minds of the first thirty years of the Nineteenth Century."[40]

Chateaubriand, Constant's longtime political rival, said that he was the "man, who, after Voltaire, had the most *esprit*."[41] The great novelist Stendhal thought that Constant was "one of the most remarkable men in France," whereas the poet Alfred de Vigny stated that Constant was a "man with a superior *esprit*."[42] Simonde de Sismondi, who was a member of Madame de Staël's Coppet circle, was in complete agreement when he wrote: "I feel that he remains below what he could be, but he appears to me, at the same time, far above all his contemporaries. ... It is only when compared to himself that one can perceive what is lacking in him."[43]

Moving from Constant's great ability to his intellectual contributions, the testimony of several important French authorities is worth citing. The Marquis de Lafayette wrote: "Endowed with one of the most extensive and varied *esprits* which has ever existed ... the master of all the languages and literatures of Europe, he united to the highest degree sagacity ... and the faculty, especially attributable to the French school, of making clear abstract ideas."[44] Victor Hugo was of a similar persuasion when he observed that Constant was "one of those rare men, who furbish, polish, and sharpen the general ideas of their times."[45]

Constant was, therefore, recognized by many of his contemporaries not just as a facile political journalist, pamphleteer, and politician in the Chamber of Deputies but as a profound political thinker. Sismondi wrote: "In politics Constant created more doctrines than those called Doctrinaires; in philosophy his work on religions contained more new and pure truths than any of the three opposing schools of Lammenais, [Victor] Cousin, and [Antoine

---

40. Léon Duguit, "The Law and the State," p. 105.

41. François Auguste René, Vicomte de Chateaubriand, *Mémoires d'outre tombe*, 4:376.

42. *Courrier anglais*, 3:182, and Alfred Vigny, *Le journal d'un poête*, p. 52.

43. Letter of Sismondi to Mlle Eulalie de Sainte-Aulaire, 13 Dec. 1830, Jean Charles Simonde de Sismondi, *Epistolario*, 3:108–9.

44. *Le mercure de France au XIX siècle*, 15 Dec. 1830, pp. 540–41.

45. Victor Hugo, *Journal d'un révolutionnaire de 1830–1848*, p. 19.

Destutt de] Tracy."[46] Victor de Broglie believed that "it was Benjamin Constant who taught the new nation the principles of representative government," whereas Adolphe Thiers viewed him as "the best informed man of his time in all that concerned the theory of constitutional monarchy."[47]

Constant's lifetime from 1767 to 1830 spans the very important and turbulent period of French history from the end of the *ancien régime* to the Revolution of 1830. It was an age of crisis and transition, much like the period in England from 1649 to 1689, which was always of special interest to Anglophiles in France, including Constant. As Alexis de Tocqueville has observed: "Our history from 1789 to 1830, viewed from a distance and as a whole, affords, as it were, the picture of a struggle to the death between the Ancien Régime and its traditions, memories, hopes, and men, as represented by the aristocracy and the New France led by the Middle Class." The rapid succession of regimes—"the Constitutional Monarchy had succeeded the Ancien Régime; the Republic, the Monarchy; the Empire, the Republic; the Restoration, the Empire and then came the Monarchy of July"—indicated that the people for forty years had "tried everything and settled nothing."[48] The great political instability of this period goes a long way toward explaining Constant's frequent political volte-face as well as those of his contemporaries.

This was the age that shaped the political thought of Constant, the French-Swiss Protestant cosmopolite, whose intellectual heritage was derived from the French philosophes of the Enlightenment, the French Idéologues, the Scottish-English school of thought, and

---

46. Sismondi, *Epistolario*, 3:108–9.
47. Broglie, *Souvenirs*, 1:283, and Adolphe Thiers, *Histoire du consulat et de l'empire*, 19:427.
48. Alexis de Tocqueville, *Recollections*, pp. 2, 73. See also Tocqueville's letter to Reeve, his English translator, dated 22 March 1837, *Oeuvres complètes*, 6:pt.1, 37–38. Cf. Royer-Collard in Prosper de Barante, *La vie politique de Royer-Collard, ses discours et ses écrits*, 2:504: "Il y a ... une grande école d'immoralité ouverte depuis cinquante ans. ... Cette école, ce sont les événements qui se sont accomplis presque sans relâche sous nos yeux. Repassez-les: le 6 octobre, le 10 août, le 21 janvier, le 31 mai, le 18 fructidor, le 18 brumaire; je m'arrête là. Que voyons-nous dans cette suite de révolutions? La victoire de la force sur l'ordre établi, quel qu'il fut, et à l'appui des doctrines pour la légitimer."

German philosophy.[49] His theory of liberalism consisted of a critical reaction to the *ancien régime* in the past and to the French Revolution, Bonapartism, the counterrevolution, and the Restoration in the present.[50]

Constant's political theory was fashioned most, however, by the Great Revolution—its course and consequences—which, as Madame de Staël observed, "is one of the great eras of the social order," affecting everybody and everything.[51] Constant was almost equally influenced, however, by Napoleon's regime, because he saw it as uniting the traditions of the absolute monarchy and the Revolution, especially in its extreme phase of the Terror. Jacobinism and Bonapartism go far, then, toward explaining why Constant believed what he did. Like all great political thinkers, however, Constant spoke in terms that transcended contemporary political phenomena. He is relevant, therefore, not only to his own time, but also to ours in the twentieth century, which has experienced many revolutions patterned on the French and many dictatorships modeled on Bonaparte's.

49. According to Louis Blanc in his *History of Ten Years*, 1:344–45, Constant belonged to "that English and Protestant school of which Mounier was the orator, Necker the financier, and Madame de Staël the heroine."

50. Constant was favorable, by and large, to the ideas of the Girondins and hostile to those of the Jacobins. See his letters to Madame de Charrière published in Gustave Rudler, *La jeunesse de Benjamin Constant, 1767–1794*, pp. 473–88, and in Beatrice W. Jasinski, *L'engagement de Benjamin Constant*, pp. 71–85. In his early *Discours* of 1798, Constant interpreted the Revolution as "made for liberty and equality of all, leaving inviolable the property of each one." It was "carried on against two streams of which the monarchy was composed—arbitrary power and heredity."

51. Germaine de Staël, *Considerations on the Principal Events of the French Revolution*, 1:1.

Chapter II
Conquest, Dictatorship, and Ancient Liberty

WHEN CONSTANT observed that the "usurper who arrives after a revolution made for liberty or in her name has many more means of sustaining himself than any other kind of despot," he shows that he was one of the very first to grasp the real nature of Bonapartism, the first truly modern dictatorship.[1] He saw it as something completely novel and very different from the old despotisms of the past that had rested on a union of throne and altar.[2] The new despotism was based rather on the theory of popular sovereignty, which had been the very foundation of the French Revolution.[3]

Napoleon had made the connection between the new type of rule and the sovereignty of the people even before the coup d'état of the 18th brumaire in 1799. In a letter dated 19 September 1797 to Tal-

1. Constant, "Du parlement anglais sous Cromwell et du tribunat dans la constitution de l'an VIII jusqu' à son épuration," *Mélanges de littérature et de politique*, p. 47.

2. Earlier Edmund Burke had predicted that the French Revolution would end in a military dictatorship in the name of the people that would be more powerful than any previous absolute monarchy.

3. Madame de Staël, speaking of the States General, observed: "Yet there were symptoms of a certain arrogance of power among these sovereigns of a new kind, who considered themselves depositories of a power without limits, the power of the people" (*Considerations on the Principal Events of the French Revolution*, 1:157). Cf. François Guizot's comment that "absolute power cannot belong in France, except to the Revolution and its heirs" (*Mémoires pour servir à l'histoire de mon temps*, 1:34), and Tocqueville's statement: "Until our time it had been supposed that despotism was odious, under whatever form it appeared. But it is a discovery of modern days that there are such things as legitimate tyranny and holy justice, provided that they are exercised in the name of the people" (*Democracy in America*, 1:417).

leyrand, minister of foreign affairs in the Directory, on the subject of constitution making in England and France, Napoleon wrote: "Since the House of Commons is the only body which . . . represents the nation, it is proper that it should have the sole power to impose taxation; it is the only defense they have been able to devise against the insolent tyranny of the Court party. But, why in a government [the French] whose sole authority emanates from the national will, where the sovereign is the people, should be included among the functions of the legislative power things which are foreign to it."[4]

Later, in 1802, when Bonaparte dissolved the Tribunate that dared to oppose him, he defended his action by once again comparing England and France: "Nothing is more natural than the opposition in England, since the king is the enemy of the people but in a country [like France] where the executive power is itself named by the people, it is to oppose the nation to combat its representative."[5] He went on to characterize the opposition to him as "vermin," only "twelve or fifteen metaphysicians" (Idéologues), whom he would not allow to insult him like a king because he was a soldier of the Revolution and of the people.[6]

Napoleon's attitude as first consul was reinforced after he became emperor. Speaking to the Corps Legislatif on 1 January 1814, he exclaimed: "Are you representatives of the people? I am; four times I have been called by the nation and four times I have received the votes of five million citizens; I have a title and you do not;

4. Napoleon Bonaparte, *Letters of Napoleon*, pp. 44–47.

5. Germaine de Staël, "Dix années d'exil," *Oeuvres complètes de Mme la Baronne de Staël*, 15:38–39.

6. See Henri De Ferron, *Théorie du progrès*, 1:285, who links the rationalization of Napoleon's rule with Rousseau: "Il en conclut, d'après la doctrine de Rousseau, que l'autorité illimitée réside dans la société entière, qu'elle est transportée au représentant de cette société. De même que Rousseau avait dit que le corps social ne pouvait nuire à l'ensemble de ses membres ni à chacun d'eux en particulier, Napoléon dit que le dépositaire du pouvoir, l'homme constitué société, ne peut faire de mal à la société, parce que tout le tort qu'il ferait, il l'éprouverait fidèlement, tant il est la société elle-même. De même que Rousseau dit que l'individu ne peut résister à la société, parce qu'il lui a aliéné tous ses droits, sans réserve, Napoléon prétend que l'autorité du depositaire du pouvoir est absolu, parce qu'aucun membre de la société ne peut lutter contre la réunion entière."

you are only the deputies of the departments of the Empire."[7] This is, of course, the classic expression of the theory of plebiscitary democracy.

By the time of the Hundred Days in the spring of 1815, Napoleon, who once again claimed that his power had been delegated to him by the people, became the symbol of liberty against the spirit of counterrevolution. Both the liberal Benjamin Constant and Germaine de Staël and the conservative Chateaubriand attested to this, each in his own way.

Constant wrote briefly, "We are in danger of being attacked because . . . we have for a leader a man who at all times was the representative of all the instincts of the Revolution and who . . . is today . . . the support of all the principles of liberty."[8] Madame de Staël saw it in greater detail:

> Enlightened men could see nothing but a despot in
> Bonaparte; but, by a concourse of very distressing circum-
> stances, this despot was presented to the people as the defender
> of its rights. All the benefits acquired by the Revolution,
> benefits which France will never voluntarily renounce, were
> threatened by the continual imprudence of the party which
> aims at making a conquest of Frenchmen, as if they were
> Gauls; and the part of the nation which most dreaded the
> return of the old government thought they saw in Bonaparte
> the means of preserving themselves from it. The most fatal
> combination that could overwhelm the friends of liberty was
> that a despot should put himself in their ranks, be placed as it
> were, at their head, and the enemies of all liberal ideas should
> have a pretext for confounding popular violence with the evils
> of despotism, thus making tyranny pass as if it were on
> the account of liberty herself.[9]

---

7. P. J. B. Buchez and P. C. Roux, *Histoire parlementaire de la révolution française*, 34:459.

8. "Comparaison de l'ordonnance de réformation de Louis XVIII avec la constitution proposée à la France le 22 avril 1815."

9. *Considerations on the French Revolution*, 2:195–96.

Finally, Chateaubriand explained:

> One may wonder by what magic spell Bonaparte, so aristocratic and so hostile to the mob, came to win the popularity which he enjoyed: for that forger of yokes has certainly remained popular with a nation whose pretension it was to raise altars to liberty and equality: this is the solution to the enigma.
>
> Daily experience shows that the French are instinctively attracted by power; they have no love for liberty; equality alone is their idol. Now equality and tyranny have secret connexions. In these two respects, Napoleon had his fountain-head in the hearts of the French, militarily inclined towards power, democratically enamored of a dead level. Mounting the throne, he seated the common people beside him; a proletarian king, he humiliated the kings and nobles in his ante-chambers; he leveled the ranks of society, not by lowering but by raising them; levelling down would have pleased plebeian envy more; levelling up was more flattering to his pride.
>
> And yet this man, who passed an egalitarian roller over France, was the mortal enemy of equality and the greatest organizer of aristocracy within a democracy.[10]

The true nature of Bonaparte's regime is perceptively delineated by Constant in his most famous political work—*De l'esprit de conquête et de l'usurpation dans leurs rapports avec la civilisation européenne.*[11] This essay is much more than another anti-

---

10. Robert Baldrick, ed., *The Memoirs of Chateaubriand*, p. 297.

11. On the origin of the work see the preface of the first edition dated 1 January 1814, in which Constant observed: "L'ouvrage actuel fait partie d'un Traité de politique terminé depuis longtemps," and the entry for 4 February 1806 of his *Journaux intimes*, p. 279: "Commencé le petit ouvrage que je veux publier bientôt, extrait de mon grand traité de politique." We now know from Constant's *Manuscrits de 1810* that the substance of *De l'esprit de conquête et de l'usurpation*, which was written in two and one-half months at the end of the year 1813, had been composed much earlier. As Olivier Pozzo di Borgo has shown in *Benjamin Constant: Ecrits et discours politiques*, "le grand traité" dates from 1799 and in manuscript is entitled "Fragments d'un ouvrage abandonné sur la possibilité d'une constitution républi-

Napoleonic tract, however.[12] In the first place, Constant, as John Plamenatz has written, "seems to prophesy rather than to describe. . . . To us he often sounds as if he were speaking of Hitler's Germany" rather than of Bonapartist France.[13] In the second, he develops a complete philosophy of history. In the third, he sets forth a very penetrating diagnosis of the ills of modern life that anticipates the pessimistic analyses of Alexis de Tocqueville, Jacob Burckhardt, Sören Kierkegaard, and Friedrich Nietzsche later on in the nineteenth century.

To depict the Napoleonic dictatorship, Constant employed the term "usurpation," which he sharply distinguished from monarchy. He defined the latter as "an institution, modified by time, softened by habit and surrounded by *corps intermédiaires*, like the ancient nobility, which sustain it and at the same time limit it."[14] He viewed the monarch as "an abstract being," not as "an individual," but instead as "a whole line of kings," the "tradition of centuries." In contrast, "usurpation is a force which nothing can modify or soften." Moreover, "it necessarily bears the imprint of the personality of the usurper, who, without the support of the nation, seizes power" or else, invested with "a limited power, destroys the limits imposed upon him."[15]

Monarchy and usurpation or dictatorship are also different in other respects. "There is no element of personal adventure in the

caine dans un grand pays." "L'extrait de 1806" became in 1810 *Principes de politique applicables à tous les gouvernements représentatifs. De l'esprit de conquête* was based on certain chapters in manuscript in *Principes de politique* and *La constitution républicaine*, such as Book 13, "De la guerre," and Book 16, "De l'autorité sociale chez les anciens," of the former and Book 6, "De la monarchie," of the latter.

12. Cf. Germaine de Staël, *Portrait d'Atilla*, and Chateaubriand, *De Bonaparte et des Bourbons et de la nécessité de se rallier à nos princes légitimes pour le bonheur de la France et celui de l'Europe*. See also Bengt Hasselrot, *Lettres à Bernadotte par Benjamin Constant*. Both Constant and Madame de Staël wanted Charles Bernadotte, a former marshal of France and heir to the Swedish throne, to be the successor of Napoleon instead of the Bourbon, Louis XVIII. In fact, Germaine thought Bernadotte "ought to be the William III of France." See *Lettres de Mme de Staël à Benjamin Constant*, pp. 54, 61.

13. John Plamenatz, *Readings from Liberal Writers*, p. 30.

14. The following English translations taken from Helen B. Lippmann, *Prophecy from the Past*, with the exception of the material cited in n. 19.

15. George Washington, William of Nassau, and William of Orange were not usurpers, according to Constant, because they were established by the national will.

action of a king, who ascends the throne of his ancestors." However, "a usurper . . . must justify his rise to power" and "prove by great deeds that he deserves a great position." In fact, Constant quotes Napoleon: "We must give the French people something new every three months."

Constant not only distinguished usurpation from monarchy but also from despotism. In his treatment of this subject, he showed that he owed much to Montesquieu, who said that in a "despotic government . . . a single person directs everything by his own will and caprice" and maintains himself by the principle of fear.[16] Constant portrayed despotism as a "government in which the master's will is the only law; where corporations . . . are but his creatures, where the master considers himself as the sole owner of his empire . . . ; where liberty can be taken from subjects without explanation . . . ; where the courts are subordinated to the caprices of power."[17] Therefore, "the principle of arbitrariness" characterizes both usurpation and despotism.[18] On the other hand, "despotism, which is a legitimate government, only imposes on its subjects at intervals and in times of crisis what is a constant state and daily practice of usurpation."

The real difference, however, between usurpation and despotism lies in the fact that the former is dynamic and the latter is static. Despotism is antiquated, whereas usurpation is new. What makes it novel is its revolutionary and democratic character.

Constant's classic analysis of Napoleonic dictatorship is worth quoting at some length because his description is not only very perceptive but is prophetic of subsequent dictatorships right down

16. Montesquieu, *The Spirit of the Laws*, Book 2, chap. 1, p. 8. J. L. Lerminier, *Philosophie du Droit*, p. 256, ranks Constant with Montesquieu because of *De l'esprit de conquête et de l'usurpation*.

17. Constant referred to how Louis XIV had destroyed the authority of the parlements, the clergy, and all the other *corps intermédiaires*.

18. In a letter to Charles de Villers dated 27 December 1813, Constant noted that his little treatise was originally entitled *De l'esprit de conquête et du despotisme à cette époque de la civilisation européenne*. "Despotisme est-il scabreux? Mettons arbitraire." See Johann and Witmer Isler, *Briefe von Benjamin Constant, Görres, Goethe, etc.*, pp. 25–26. Evidently Constant decided on the word "usurpation" to describe Napoleon's dictatorship rather than either "despotism" or "tyranny."

into the twentieth century.[19] Bonapartism, or usurpation, is seen as quite different from the older forms of despotism.

> Despotism does away with all forms of liberty; usurpation in order to bring about the overthrow of what it seeks to replace, has need of these forms, but in securing them it profanes them. The existence of public sentiment being dangerous to it, and the appearance of public sentiment being necessary to it, it strikes the people with one hand to stifle any real sentiment, and it strikes them again with the other to compel them to the simulacrum of a pretended sentiment.
>
> When a great Sovereign sends one of his ministers in disgrace to the scaffold, the executioner, like the victims, does his part in silence. When a usurper condemns innocence, he orders calumny so that, repeated, it will appear to be the judgment of the nation.
>
> The despot forbids discussion and exacts only obedience; the usurper decrees a ridiculous investigation as the prelude to approval. This counterfeit of liberty combines all the evils of anarchy and slavery. There is no end of slavery which wants to drag forth tokens of consent. Peaceable men are persecuted for indifference, energetic men for being dangerous.
>
> It is usurpation that has invented that pretended sanction of the people, those speeches of adherence, a monotonous tribute that in every age the same men lavish on the most contradictory causes. Who does not feel that the more a government is oppressive the more quickly the terrified citizens will hasten to pay it homage in their enthusiasm for command? Do you not see beside the registers that each signs with a trembling hand the informers and soldiers? Do you not hear the proclamations declaring those whose voting would be negative, seditious or rebellious? What is this questioning of a people, surrounded by dungeons and under the sway of the arbitrary, but an effort to obtain a list from the

19. English translation for this passage taken from Guglielmo Ferrero, *The Principles of Power*, pp. 202–4.

adversaries of the government so as to recognize and strike them at leisure?

Despotism stifles freedom of the press, usurpation parodies it. Now when the freedom of the press is altogether suppressed public opinion may slumber, but nothing leads it astray. On the other hand, when bribed writers take possession of it, they argue, as though it were a question of convincing, they fly into a passion, as though there were any chance of replying. Their absurd defamations presage savage condemnations; their fierce jestings announce illegal condemnations. Their exhibitions would have us to believe that their victims are resisting. . . .

In a word, despotism reigns by silence and allows man the right to remain still. Usurpation condemns him to speak, it pursues him into the sanctuary of his thought, and by forcing him to lie to his conscience, deprives him of the only consolation that remains to the oppressed. When a people have only been enslaved without also having been degraded, there is still the possibility that they may attain a better state of things. If some happy circumstances should reveal it, they show themselves worthy of it. Despotism leaves mankind that chance. The yoke of Philip II and the scaffold of the Duke of Alba did not degrade the noble Dutch. But usurpation debases a people at the time that it oppresses them.[20]

It is interesting to compare Constant's description of Bonapartism with Madame de Staël's more specific characterization of the Napoleonic regime a few years later.

One circumstance, which was singularly favorable to the power of Bonaparte was, that he had nothing but the mass of the nation to manage. All individual existence had been annihilated by the years of tumult (and nothing acts upon a people like military success). Nobody in France could believe

20. Cf. Tocqueville, *Democracy in America*, 1:267: "Despotism debases the oppressed much more than the oppressor; in absolute monarchies the king often has great virtues but the courtiers are invariably servile."

his situation secure; men of all classes, whether ruined or enriched, banished or recompensed, found themselves, if I may say so, one by one, alike in the hands of power. . . . There was not a Frenchman who had not something to ask of the government, and that something was life. . . . A singular occurrence of circumstances placed the laws of the period of terror, and the military force created by republican enthusiasm at the disposal of one man. What an inheritance for an able despot.

The party among the French who sought to resist the continually increasing power of the First Consul, had to invoke liberty in order to struggle against him with success. But at this word the aristocrats and the enemies of the Revolution roared out against Jacobinism, and thus seconded the tyranny, the blame of which they had since wished to throw upon their adversaries.[21]

It is evident that Madame de Staël clearly recognized the new phenomenon of mass society and saw it as a cause for the rise of a novel form of despotism that rested much more on indoctrination and mobilization of consent than on the application of force.

Constant's analysis of the "spirit of conquest" was just as penetrating as his investigation of the "spirit of usurpation." He believed that modern conquest emerged from the French Revolution "more violent than ever" in the form of Jacobinism and Bonapartism. But modern conquest is portrayed as something completely different from the ancient type. In the past, even when a whole nation was conquered, a people's "customs, laws, usages, and gods were left intact." Furthermore, "the primitive conquerors were satisfied with outward submission; they did not inquire into the private lives or local customs of their victims." In contrast to this practice, "the conquerors of today are resolved to gaze over the level surface of their empire . . . and to encounter no deviation from uniformity. . . . The same laws, the same administrative measures, the same rulings, and, if possible, the same language, this is the supreme aim of their

21. *Considerations on the French Revolution*, 2:21.

social organization." Even cities and provinces would be designated by numbers like the legions and the corps of the army. Constant added that he was very much "surprised that the inhabitants have not all been ordered to wear the same costume, so that the master may no longer encounter any irregular variation or any shocking diversity."

Modern conquest, then, is characterized by uniformity and symmetry. It is, to Constant, ironic and "surprising that uniformity should have been so warmly admired by the leaders of a revolution made in the name of the rights of man."[22] In fact, "their systematic minds were at first enraptured by its symmetry. Their love of power soon discovered what a tremendous advantage could be derived from this symmetry." Moreover, "although patriotism exists only by reason of a deep attachment to local interests, customs, and usages, our so-called patriots declared war upon all of these. They dried up the natural springs of patriotism and tried to replace them by a fictitious attachment to an abstract idea . . . stripped of everything that appeals to the imagination, or that speaks to memory." As we shall see, the influence of counterrevolutionary thought upon Constant is pronounced at this point.

Both Napoleon and the French revolutionaries have, to Constant, "adopted the same course. The two extremes have met in this because, fundamentally, they are in agreement on one thing; the will to tyranny," something "which must triumph over any variety." After all, "local interests and traditions contain a germ of resistance, which a centralized authority tolerates unwillingly and attempts to eradicate at the first opportunity. It finds the isolated individual easier to deal with; without effort it crushes him beneath its mighty weight."[23]

As Constant faced uniformity and the leveling process, this liberal opponent of the *ancien régime* sounds like the traditionalist Ultra,

22. Long before the French Revolution and the Empire, the French kings had already centralized their governments by reducing all their subjects to equal and manageable units, thereby achieving uniformity and symmetry. See Tocqueville, *Democracy in America*, 2:295, who thought that "every central power . . . courts and encourages the principle of equality and uniformity."

23. "Those who dread the license of the mob and those who fear absolute power ought alike to desire the gradual development of provincial liberties" (ibid., 1:95).

Louis de Bonald, who was an exponent of communal autonomy, as was Burke. In fact, the very idea of local liberties and differences was of aristocratic and feudal origin.[24] The conservatives before Constant and the liberals after him opposed the generalizing tendencies of modern bureaucracy. For example, the conservative Justus Möser (1720–94) in *The Modern Taste for General Laws and Decrees Is a Danger to Our Common Liberty* (1772) contended that "the gentlemen of the central administration, it seems, would like to see everything reduced to simple principles. If they had their way the state would let itself be ruled according to an academic theory, and every councillor would be able to give his orders to the local officials according to a general plan. . . . That means in fact, a departure from the true plan of Nature, who shows her wealth in variety; it paves the way for despotism by means of a few rules and in doing so loses the wealth of variety."[25] The liberal Tocqueville observed in the nineteenth century that "in olden society everything was different; unity and uniformity were nowhere to be met. In modern society everything threatens to become so much alike that the peculiar characteristics of each individual will soon be entirely lost in the general aspect of the world."[26]

Constant phrased it this way in *De l'esprit de conquête et de l'usurpation*: "Variety is organization, uniformity is mechanism. Variety is life, uniformity is death." He noticed also that because Voltaire and his imitators had loved symmetry, they were naturally shocked by the different and opposing customs that existed in France. But this very diversity of laws was the basis for respect for "the rights of individuals" in Great Britain.[27]

24. See Charles de Rémusat, *Mémoires de ma vie*, 1:383.

25. Quoted in Karl Mannheim, "Conservative Thought," p. 143.

26. *Democracy in America*, 2:328. Constant cited Montesquieu's *L'esprit des lois* (1748) and the Marquis de Mirabeau's *L'ami des hommes* (1756) as opposed to uniformity. See *Spirit of the Laws*, Book 29, chap. 18, pp. 169–70: "There are certain ideas of uniformity . . . the same authorized weights, the same measure in trade, the same laws in the state, the same religion in all parts. . . . And does not a greatness of genius consist rather in distinguishing between those cases in which uniformity is requisite and those in which there is a necessity of differences?"

27. Constant cited Sir William Blackstone for support on this particular point. Cf. Constant in *Le cahier rouge, Oeuvres*, p. 155, where he commented: "L'Angleterre

On the question of the connection between variety, diversity, and liberty, Constant may have been influenced by Wilhelm von Humboldt. The great German liberal had pointed out that "there is . . . another essential—intimately connected with freedom—a variety of situations. Even the most free and self-reliant of men is hindered in his development, when set in a monotonous situation . . . these two conditions, of freedom and variety of situation, may be regarded in a certain sense as one and the same."[28]

For Constant, modern conquest involves something more, however, than uniformity and symmetry. Like usurpation, it "pursues the vanquished into the interior of their existence, it maims them spiritually in order to force them to conform. Formerly, conquerors required that representatives of the vanquished nations appeared on their knees," but "today it is the conscience of man that is being laid prostrate."[29] Constant obviously is aware here of the process of dehumanization of which modern totalitarian dictatorship is capable.

Besides distinguishing between despotism and usurpation, Constant drew a line between an ancient military and a modern commercial society in the same essay. This had been a favorite subject among such English and French political theorists in the eighteenth century as Adam Ferguson, the friend of David Hume and Adam Smith, Montesquieu, and Jean-Jacques Rousseau. The famous Citoyen de Genève had noted that "our philosophy . . . holds contrary to the experience of all centuries that luxury produces the splendor of States. . . . What will become of virtue when one must get rich at any price? Ancient politicians talked about morals and virtue," whereas "those of our time talk only of business and money." Montesquieu, whom Constant quotes on the subject, thought that "the politic Greeks, who lived under a popular government, knew no other support than virtue," whereas "the modern

---

est le pays où, d'un côté, les droits de chacun sont le mieux garantis, et où, de l'autre, les différences de rang sont le plus respectées."

28. Wilhelm von Humboldt, *The Limits of State Action*, p. 16.

29. Cf. Tocqueville, *Democracy in America*, 1:264: "Under the absolute sway of one man the body was attacked in order to subdue the soul; but the soul escaped the blows which were directed against it. . . . Such is not the course adopted by the tyranny in democratic republics; there the body is left free, and the soul enslaved."

inhabitants of that country are entirely taken up with manufacture, commerce, finances, opulence, and luxury."[30]

It was Constant first and then Henri de Saint-Simon who reversed Rousseau, recently labeled "the first great critic of industrial society," by pointing out the superior virtues of modern commercial over ancient military society.[31] Constant contended that war and commerce were only different means of "obtaining what one desires." As civilization advanced, however, commerce replaced war because war was the result of "savagery," whereas commerce was the product of "civilized calculation."[32] Following the lead of Turgot and Condorcet before him, Constant believed that "the unique goal of modern nations is peace, and with peace, comfort, and as the source of comfort, industry." This is, of course, a perfect description of bourgeois society. He then argues that among the ancients war added to public and private wealth, but "among the moderns a successful war inevitably costs more than it is worth." There-

30. Adam Ferguson, *An Essay on the History of Civil Society*, distinguished three types of society—savage, barbarous, and polished or commercial. Montesquieu, *Spirit of the Laws*, Book 3, chap. 3, p. 21, should be compared with Giambattista Vico's differentiation in *The New Science* (1744) between the age of heroes (barbarism) and the age of men (democracy, commerce, and science). Rousseau, *Discourse on the Question . . . Has the Restoration of the Sciences and Arts Tended to Purify Mores*, pp. 49, 50–51. In that first *Discours*, Rousseau said of modern society: "We have physicists, geometers, chemists, astronomers, poets, musicians, painters; we no longer have citizens." Cf. his *Lettres écrites de la montagne*: "Vous [Genevois] n'êtes ni Romains ni Spartiates; vous n'êtes pas même Athéniens . . . vous êtes des marchands, des artisans, des bourgeois, toujours occupés de leurs intérêts privés" (*Oeuvres complètes de Jean-Jacques Rousseau*, 3:881).

31. Henri de Saint-Simon, "L'industrie" (1816). In *Oeuvres*, 19:169. Saint-Simon, who quotes Constant, Ferguson, and Sismondi, presented the difference between military and commercial societies in terms of the contrast between the feudal and industrial systems. See Frank Manuel, *The New World of Henri Saint-Simon*, pp. 237–42. For the characterization of Rousseau see *On the Social Contract with Geneva Manuscript and Political Economy*, p. 143. See also Charles Dunoyer, *Oeuvres*, 3:177: "Je dois dire à la gloire de M. Benjamin Constant qu-il est le premier écrivain . . . qui font fait remarquer le brut d'activité des peuples de nôtre temps."

32. Herbert Spencer, later in the nineteenth century in his *Principles of Sociology*, traced the evolution of society from a militant to an industrial regime. In that connection, José Ortega y Gasset noted that "ever since Spencer's time the spirit of industry has customarily been opposed to the spirit of war and has unhesitatingly been preferred to it. Men of the 19th century were glad to be considered industrialists rather than warriors" (*Invertebrate Spain*, p. 129). To Constant's contemporary, Joseph de Maistre, however, war was a law of the world that would last as long as it did. Cf. Sir Henry Maine, *Ancient Law*, who viewed society as developing from status to contract.

fore, war and conquest, like Napoleon's, are nothing more than an anachronism.[33] Like Immanuel Kant, who was convinced over-optimistically that the spread of republican government would promote peace, Constant was persuaded that the progress of commerce would lead to the same end because "commerce inspires in men an ardent love for individual independence."[34]

The antithesis between ancient military and modern commercial societies is related to the general condition of man in these two states.[35] Constant was very much aware, like Rousseau before him in *Discourse on the Origin and Foundation of Inequality among Men*, of the growing fragmentation and alienation of modern man, which is just as popular a theme in the twentieth century as corruption and luxury were in the eighteenth. Although Constant expressed his concern best in his later work, *De la religion*, he also showed his keen insight into the problem in *De l'esprit de conquête et de l'usurpation*. In the former, he wrote:

> Man looks on a world deprived of protective powers . . .
> all the previous grounds for his exaltation no longer support
> him. . . . He is alone on the earth, which will engulf him. On
> this earth the different generations succeed each other,
> transitory, fortuitous, and isolated . . . what will man do,
> without memory and without hope, placed between an
> abandoned past and a future closed before him? . . . He has

33. According to John U. Nef, *War and Human Progress*, pp. 337–38, Constant seemed unaware of the "dangers inherent in material abundance for future wars and violence among men." William W. Holdheim, however, in *Benjamin Constant*, p. 96, asks whether Constant had a presentiment of an alliance between industrialism and militarism, which would seem to be the correct conclusion.

34. Constant, "De la liberté des anciens comparée à celle des modernes," *Cours de politique*, 2:546. Cf. Charles Dunoyer, who made the same point in *L'industrie et la morale considérée dans leurs rapports avec la liberté*. Earlier, Montesquieu had distinguished peaceful commercial from military democracies and had stressed the connection between England's free government and her commercial society. See Book 20, chap. 7, p. 321, of *Spirit of the Laws*, where he wrote: "They [the English] know better than any other people upon earth how to value, at the same time, these three great advantages—religion, commerce, and liberty."

35. It is interesting to recall in this connection the seventeenth-century "querelle des anciens et des modernes," where the comparative merits of classical and contemporary [modern] literature was the issue.

> spurned the support with which his predecessors encompassed him and is reduced to dependence on his own strength.[36]

In the latter, he stated that without the "support" of such "protective powers" as local customs and loyalties, "individuals, lost in an isolation against nature, strangers to their place of birth, without contact with the past, only live in an ephemeral present, tossed around like atoms on an immense flat plain."[37]

Constant also, like Rousseau, confronted the age-old conflict between egoism and altruism when he revealed that he always had a nostalgic longing for the ideal of the ancient city as a kind of lost paradise where war was heroic and where man had an integral existence or fulfillment in his subjection to the collective whole (*civisme*) and in his devotion to public virtue. In other words, "the ancients experienced complete conviction about everything." Furthermore, "the old elements of a nature anterior to ours, as it were, seem to awaken in us with these memories."[38] This contrast between ancient unity and modern dividedness is also outlined in Wilhelm von Humboldt's *The Limits of State Action*, which may have influenced Constant, as we have already noted.

Rousseau's cure for the dividedness of modern man was political and social. In the *Social Contract*, he expressed the hope of restoring the lost unity by joining together, like the ancients, the individual and society, the private and public sectors; in short, the man and the citizen. But, to Constant, the ancient type of existence and of liberty, which was collective, was an anachronism in the

---

36. Constant, *De la religion considérée dans sa source, ses formes et ses développements*, 1:55–57. Here we are very close to the concept of "the lonely crowd" of David Riesman.

37. "De l'esprit de conquête," *Cours de politique*, 2:173. Cf. Tocqueville, *Democracy in America*, 2:318: "The first thing that strikes the observation is an innumerable multitude of men . . . each of them, living apart, is as a stranger to the fate of all the rest; his children and his private friends constitute to him the whole of mankind. As for the rest of his fellow citizens, he is close to them, but he does not feel them; he exists only in himself and for himself alone; and if his kindred still remain to him, he may be said at any rate to have lost his country." Such a society, Tocqueville feared, could only end in a new form of despotism.

38. "De l'esprit de conquête," *Cours de politique*, 2:173.

modern age of individualism. Therefore, in place of Rousseau's monistic solution, Constant substituted a dualistic one, where the individual and his rights are preserved by the community instead of being assimilated by it; where the political is distinct from the social; and where the man is distinguished from the citizen.[39]

Constant was also pessimistic about modern man because he is devoid of moral vigor and conviction. In fact, "there is hardly anything about which our conviction is not feeble, wavering, and of an incompleteness to which we try in vain to benumb ourselves." He feared that with the progress of material civilization men were in danger of losing the strength, vitality, and simple virtues of their ancestors, who lived in a frugal, austere, simple, poor, military society.[40]

The idea of Helvétius and Bentham that enlightened self-interest could have the same place in modern society as virtue did in ancient society was only another indication of the general corruption of modern man.[41] In fact, "the cult of antiquity," developed by the Jacobins in particular during the French Revolution, can be seen partly as a reaction against the great vogue of the different hedonistic philosophies of enlightened self-interest that prevailed at the end of the eighteenth century.[42] In short, to Constant, utilitarianism was responsible for the decline of civic courage.[43] It is interesting to note here that, like Rousseau before him and Nietzsche after him, Constant appealed to classical antiquity to support his reservations about modernity.

39. Holdheim, *Benjamin Constant*, pp. 88–89.

40. Cf. Adam Ferguson, "Relaxations in the National Spirit Incident to Polished Nations," *Essay on Civil Society*, pp. 280–85.

41. See Antoine Destutt de Tracy, *Commentaire sur l'Esprit des Lois de Montesquieu*, Book 13: "On ne saurait trop le redire, la liberté c'est le bonheur." Cf. Hobbes and Hume, who thought that wealth and not virtue would be the strength of the commonwealth.

42. See Harold Parker, *The Cult of Antiquity and the French Revolutionaries*, p. 62, and Elizabeth Rawson, *The Spartan Tradition in European Thought*, p. 268. The former observed: "Antiquity (that is, early Rome and Sparta) was liberty, equality, and virtue; poverty, austerity, frugality and courage; and a self-sacrificing love of country"; the latter comments: "Sparta's place in the literature of and about the Revolution can only be understood if the history of her reputation in the previous half century be kept in mind."

43. As J. G. A. Pocock has said in "Civic Humanism and Its Role in Anglo-American Thought," p. 179, "The concept of the citizen or patriot was antithetical

The ancients, then, demonstrated a heroism, patriotism, and vitality that we can only envy because they were living in the "youth of the moral life," whereas the moderns are in the stage of "maturity" and "perhaps old age."[44] Constant's very pessimistic philosophy of degeneration founded on a questionable biological analogy strongly indicates that he believed that an advanced bourgeois industrial civilization is rooted in a hedonism it cannot renounce because it cannot recapture its youth.[45] In any event, it is evident that he thought Montesquieu was wrong when he attributed the difference between the ancients and moderns to the distinction between the forms of government—republics and monarchies. Instead, the contrast between the virtue of the ancient cities and the commerce and luxury of modern states was due to the dissimilarity between ancient and modern times. In other words, Constant showed that he did not believe, like Rousseau, who followed Plato, that human regeneration depended as much on the form of government as on moral factors.

Parallel to the antithesis between ancient military and modern commercial society, Constant drew another between ancient and modern liberty. In his judgment, the liberty that was in vogue at the end of the eighteenth century was an anachronism, borrowed from the ancient republics by such political theorists as Jean-Jacques

---

to that of economic man, multiplying his satisfactions." Cf. Leo Strauss, *Natural Right and History*, p. 253: Moderns "lack the public spirit or the patriotism of the ancients. They are more concerned with their private or domestic affairs than with the fatherland. They lack the greatness of soul of the ancients. They are bourgeois rather than citizens." In "De l'esprit de conquête," *Cours de politique*, 2:207, Constant wrote: "L'époque de ce patriotisme (Cicero) est passé car ce que nous aimons dans la patrie, comme dans la liberté, c'est la propriété de nos biens, la sécurité, la possibilité de la repos . . . ce mille genres de bonheur."

44. See Patrice Thompson, "Constant et les vertus révolutionnaires," pp. 49–62.

45. See Sir James Mackintosh, *Memoirs of the Life of the Right Honorable Sir James Mackintosh 1767–1832*, 2:327: "The conversation consisted in a dispute between Constant and myself on a principle advanced by him, that every particular form of civilization, by multiplying the number of enjoyments, which may be attained without reason or virtue, tends to its own destruction; that the mental qualities are destroyed and the mechanical products only remain; that a foreign force is necessary to revive such a civilization, like the invasion of the barbarians, which supplied mental energy, while all the outward results of ancient civilization were preserved to be the instruments of that energy." Is not Constant influenced perhaps by Vico here?

Rousseau and the Abbé de Mably. Ancient or political liberty "consisted more in active participation in the collective power than in the peaceful enjoyment of individual [personal] independence" that characterized modern liberty.[46] Furthermore, "in order to guarantee such participation, it was necessary that the citizens sacrifice this enjoyment in large part," although "in the era which we have reached, it is absurd to require such a sacrifice and impossible to obtain it." Constant therefore concluded that "modern or civil liberty was unknown among most of the ancient peoples." He cited for support of his position Condorcet in his *Mémoire sur l'éducation* and Sismondi in *L'histoire des républiques italiennes du Moyen Age.*[47]

Constant then elaborates in *De l'esprit de conquête* upon his thesis by noting that the Greek democracies, with the exception of Athens, submitted men to an unlimited social jurisdiction. In fact, in republican Rome the citizen was a slave of the city.[48] "The ancients found more enjoyment in their public existence and less in their private existence; as a result when they sacrificed individual liberty to political liberty they sacrificed less to obtain more." In contrast, "almost all the enjoyment of the moderns is in their private existence; the immense majority, forever excluded from power, necessarily take only a very passing interest in their public existence." The connection of this idea with private property should

46. See Hannah Arendt, *The Human Condition*, chap. II, "The Public and the Private Realm," p. 38: "In ancient feeling the private trait of privacy, indicated in the word itself, was all-important; it meant literally a state of being deprived of something. . . . A man who lived only a private life, who like the slave was not permitted to enter the public realm . . . was not fully human. We no longer think primarily of deprivation when we use the word 'privacy' and this is partly due to the enormous enrichment of the private sphere through modern individualism."

47. Condorcet, *Oeuvres*, 8:417: "Des autres anciens . . . connaissent peu des lois de la justice naturelle, les droits des hommes et les principes de l'égalité." Sismondi, "De la liberté des italiens pendant la durée de leurs républiques," *Histoire des républiques italiennes du Moyen Age*, 10:chap. 8.

48. See Isaiah Berlin, *Four Essays on Liberty*, pp. xl–xli: "There is no convincing evidence of any clear formulation of it [individual liberty] in the ancient world." Cf., however, Benedetto Croce, "Constant e Jellinek," pp. 294–301: "So little did the Roman allow the individual to be submerged in the State, that, to him, on the contrary, the entire State . . . appeared to be placed at the service of the individual. Even in the *Digest*, only the definition of civil liberty and not that of political liberty is kept."

be noted. Furthermore, "because our modern means of individual happiness have increased, our sacrifice would be greater." Therefore, "in imitating the ancients the moderns sacrificed more to obtain less." Besides, there is a great difference between the small Greek city states with their direct democracy and the large modern national states with their indirect democracy or representative government. Constant concludes that the choice of a representative is less meaningful than the direct exercise of power. The former is "un plaisir de réflexion," and the latter "un plaisir d'action."

At the end of the eighteenth century, certain "reformers" emerged in France who sought to "regenerate the human race."[49] Constant thought that the two most influential were Jean-Jacques Rousseau and the Abbé de Mably, both of whom were so seduced by the mirage or myth of the ancient city that they sought to imitate it. It has also been suggested that these "reformers" did not distinguish between the abuses of the *ancien régime*, which they wished to correct, and the complete social transformation, which they hoped to realize.[50]

In contrast to his own historical method, Constant refers to the "subtle metaphysic of the *Social Contract* which has furnished arms and pretexts for all kinds of tyranny, whether of the one, or of the many." He views Mably's *De la législation ou principes des lois* as the "code of the most complete despotism that can be imagined."[51] As an austere admirer of Sparta and Egypt, Mably was representative of those "who speak of the sovereign nation, in order that the citizen can be more completely subjected and of the people free in order that each individual be more fully a slave."[52] Both Mably and

49. See Edmund Burke, who first said that the French Revolution was not political but doctrinal. Cf. Tocqueville in *The Old Regime and the French Revolution*, pt. l, chap. 3: "The ideal the French Revolution set before it was not merely a change in the French system but nothing short of a regeneration of the whole human race."

50. Georges De Lauris, *Benjamin Constant et les droits individuels*, p. 63.

51. Constant also thought that Johann Fichte's *Der Geschlossene Handelsstaat* would lead to despotism à la Robespierre. "Ces idées Spartiates recommenceraient Robespierre avec les meilleures intentions du monde" (*Journaux intimes*, 27 May 1804, p. 91).

52. Cf. Thomas Hobbes, *Leviathan*, chap. 21: "The Athenians and Romans were free; that is, free commonwealths; not that any particular men had the liberty to resist their own representative but that their representative had the liberty to resist or invade other people."

Rousseau have "taken authority for liberty." In fact, "Mably in all his works regrets that the law can only affect action and not thoughts" as well.[53]

The abstract idea of law as the expression of the general will and the doctrine of popular sovereignty led these reformers to believe that even the memory of centuries could be erased. In fact, the word "regeneration" leads to the destruction of everything. Such extreme claims could never be made acceptable, even by relying on Rousseau's famous admonition from *The Government of Poland*—"the laws of liberty are a thousand times more austere than the yoke of tyrants."

Among the methods employed to attach ancient liberty to modern times Constant cites the great phrases—"the safety of the people," "the supreme law," "the public interest," and "despotism as indispensable to the foundation of liberty."[54] This last idea had been advanced by Adrien de Lezay in 1797 and been refuted by Constant in that same year.[55] Constant thought that it was especially true of France that tyrannical government had been denounced and then the same type of rule had been erected in its place.[56]

53. According to Constant, Rousseau and Mably wanted to reestablish the ancient censors, and an obscure deputy named Rouget proposed in 1795 to the Convention a plan for reviving the practice of ostracism.

54. Madame de Staël believed that Robespierre's power rested on this maxim: "Je prononce donc hardiment que, dans tout pays où l'on adoptera pour principe que le salut du peuple est la suprème loi, la justice et l'humanité ne seront jamais respectées." In her view, instead of the safety of the people, the supreme law is justice. See *Des circonstances actuelles qui peuvent terminer la révolution et des principes qui doivent fonder la République en France*, pp. 230, 249. Napoleon, of course, sided with Robespierre when the first consul argued: "La première loi, c'est la nécessité; la première justice, c'est la salut public." See Guizot, *Mémoires*, 1:68. To Constant, however, experience has shown the following to be the result of this theory: "A chaque crime politique qu'ils commettaient on les entendit s'écrier: nous avons encore une fois sauvé la patrie" ("De l'esprit de conquête et de l'usurpation," *Cours de politique*, 2:250).

55. See Lezay's "Des causes de la révolution et de ses résultats." Constant's *Des effets de la terreur* was abridged in his *Mélanges* as "Des effets du regime qu'on a nommé révolutionnaire relativement au salut de la liberté en France."

56. Constant cites Stanislas de Clermont-Tonnerre: "Tout ce qui tend à restreindre les droits du roi, disait M. de Clermont-Tonnerre en 1790, est accueilli avec transport, parce qu'on se rappelle les abus de la royauté. Il viendra peut-être un temps où tout ce qui tendra à restreindre les droits du peuple sera accueilli avec la

Constant was convinced that Napoleon's regime was "based on the same principle" as the Jacobin government. "This principle is arbitrariness." In the last analysis, "the only difference is that instead of being exercised in the name of many, it is wielded in the name of one man." But the idea had been advanced that "arbitrary power in the hands of one man is not as dangerous as when it is being fought over by contending factions" because "the interests of one man invested with unlimited power are always the same as those of his people." Constant, however, serious'ʒ questions this supposed identity of interest. He asks: "Is that authority [of one man] not subdivided, not shared with thousands of subordinates? Are the interests of these innumerable officials the same as the interests of those who govern?" Here Constant objects, arguing that "to defend this system . . . it is not enough to prove the identity of interests but to prove the existence of universal disinterestedness." He reminds us that "when despotism is extolled, it is always taken for granted that all dealings would be with the despot; but necessarily there must also be dealings with his subordinates. It is then no longer a question of ascribing superlative intelligence and supreme intelligence to one man, but of assuming that there can be one hundred or two hundred thousand of such godlike creatures."

In 1819, Constant elaborated upon the two categories of liberty in his lecture, "De la liberté des anciens comparée à celle des modernes."[57] In this essay he was more specific in his definition of ancient and modern liberty: "The first consisted in the collective but direct exercise of many privileges of sovereignty, deliberating upon the public welfare, upon war and peace, voting upon laws, pronouncing judgments." The second, at least in England, France, and the United States

> means for every one to be under the dominion of nothing but the law, not to be arrested, detained, or put to death,

même fanatisme, parce que l'on aura non moins fortement senti les dangers de l'anarchie" ("De l'esprit de conquête," *Cours de politique*, 2:217).

57. See Croce, "Constant e Jellinek," pp. 294–301; C. Calogero, "La liberta degli antichi e la liberta dei moderni," pp. 56–73; Norberto Bobbio, "Della liberta dei moderni comparate a quella dei posteri," pp. 160–94; Alberto Signorini, "Constant

nor maltreated in any way as a consequence of the arbitrary will of one or more individuals. It is for every one to have the right to express his opinion, to choose and exercise his occupation, to dispose of his property and even to abuse it, to go and come without having to obtain permission, and without having to give an accounting of his motives or actions. It is the right of each person to associate with other individuals, either to discuss their interests, or to practice the form of worship they prefer, or simply to fill the days and hours in a way which best suits their inclinations and fancies.

This is, of course, a definition of liberty that was characteristic of all nineteenth-century liberals, at least before Thomas Hill Green.

Constant attributed political liberty to the ancients and civil liberty to the moderns. "Individual liberty . . . is the true modern liberty" and "political liberty is the guarantee." "Political liberty among the ancients was itself an enjoyment"; whereas among the moderns it is "only a guarantee of their enjoyments."[58]

Rousseau, whom Constant described as a "great man" of "prodigious talent" and a "sublime genius," was nevertheless blamed for "transporting to our times an extent of social power, of collective sovereignty, which belonged to other centuries." To Constant, this is to forget the entire evolution of society—"la marche des idées" and "la force des choses." In fact, Rousseau is the thinker who is chiefly responsible for the "confusion of these two kinds of liberty" that became "the cause of many evils" during the French Revolution. Constant seems to have a love/hate attitude toward ancient liberty as he did toward Rousseau. He was hostile to it because of his opposition to Jacobinism and the Terror, which he thought had adopted it along with the "cult of antiquity." He admired it,

e la liberta dei moderni," pp. 115–28; and Nicola Matteucci, "La liberta degli antichi e la liberta dei moderni," *Il liberalismo in un mondo in transformazione*, pp. 195–204.

58. Cf. Constant, *Mémoires sur les Cent Jours en formes de lettres*, Introduction, p. xxvi: "Les plus ignorants comme les plus instruits, savent que la liberté civile, c'est-à-dire les jouissances ne sont assurés que par la liberté politique, c'est-à-dire par les garanties."

)wever, as we have already seen, for providing integration and solidarity that are so lacking in modern times that contemporary thinkers of ours, like Hannah Arendt, have viewed the loss of civic spirit as one of the preconditions of the rise of totalitarian regimes today.

Madame de Staël agreed with Constant about the confusion of ancient and modern liberty during the Great Revolution. She phrased it this way:

> Political liberty is to civil liberty as the guarantee is to
> the end for which it stands, security; it is the means and not
> the end and what contributed especially to make the French
> Revolution so disorderly was the displacement of ideas which
> took place in this respect. They wanted political liberty at the
> expense of civil liberty. . . . Political liberty is . . . to exercise the
> duties of citizenship but the fruits of these sacrifices is civil
> liberty. Political liberty is of consequence to ambitious men
> who desire power. Civil liberty interests peaceful men
> who only do not want to be dominated.[59]

For Constant, then, ancient and modern liberty are two distinct historical experiences of liberty just as there are two historical experiences of democracy, the direct democracy of the ancients and the representative democracy of the moderns, with each type having its merits and its risks. "The danger of ancient liberty was that man, anxious to have a share in social power, overlooked individual rights and enjoyments." Furthermore, concentrating as it did on loyalty and sacrifice, it reduced liberty to a capacity to suffer.[60] On the other hand, "the danger of modern liberty is that, absorbed in the enjoyment of our private independence and in the pursuit of our

---

59. Staël, "Reflexions sur la paix intérieure," *Oeuvres complètes*, 2:142–45. Cf. Paul Bastid, *Benjamin Constant et sa doctrine*, 2:737: "En conséquence, le gouvernement constitutionnel s'occupe de la liberté civile et le gouvernement révolutionnaire de la liberté politique."

60. "Les hommes ne sont pas libres en raison de leur puissance de souffrir, mais en raison de leur pouvoir de se satisfaire" ("De M. Dunoyer et de quelques uns de ses ouvrages," *Mélanges*, pp. 153–54).

particular interests, we renounce too easily our right of participating in political power."

Because Constant espoused the concept of historical progress, he was inclined to think that modern liberty was not only different from ancient liberty but better. He always had a nostalgic feeling for ancient liberty and for direct democracy, but he was convinced that we cannot go back to them because they had been discredited by the passage of time. "Far from renouncing any one of these two kinds of liberty, it is necessary to combine them." Moreover, "the institutions must complete the moral education of citizens, while respecting their individual rights, independence, and occupations. They must, however, dedicate the influence of citizens to public things, calling them to contribute with their decisions and votes to the exercise of power."

Constant frequently expressed his dissatisfaction with hedonism. He asks: "Is it so true that happiness, of whatever sort it might be, is the unique end of man? In that case, our road would be quite narrow, and our destination not a very happy one . . . it is not for [individual] happiness alone, it is for self-perfection [human betterment] that destiny calls us."[61] Constant is setting forth here an ethical in place of a hedonistic standard. However, "political liberty is the most powerful, the most energetic means of perfection that heaven has given us." In other words, he saw political liberty as a method of rescuing man from the hedonistic dangers of civil liberty.

Constant contrasts, then, a negative and a positive type of liberty. The one is the negative liberty of guarantism or protection against the state, and the other is the positive liberty of the people to govern itself. According to Guido de Ruggiero, "This is a simple statement of the distinction between Liberalism and Democracy, which would avoid the perplexing questions arising from their confusion."[62] To phrase it another way, limited government and self-government are

61. Cf. Rousseau on freedom in the sense of perfectibility: "The faculty of self-perfection . . . which, with the aid of circumstances, successively develops all the others, and resides among us as much in the species as in the individual" (*Second Discourse*, pt. l, pp. 113–15, pt. 2, p. 168, note j, p. 208).
62. Guido de Ruggiero, *The History of European Liberalism*, p. 370.

) be distinguished.[63] José Ortega y Gasset puts the problem as follows:

> Democracy and Liberalism are two answers to two completely different questions. Democracy answers the question —"Who ought to exercise the public power?" The answer it gives is—"The exercise of public power belongs to the citizens as a body." Liberalism, on the other hand, answers the other question—"Regardless of who exercises the public power, what should its limits be?" The answer it gives is—"Whether the public power is exercised by an autocrat or by the people, it cannot be absolute; the individual has rights which are over and above any interference by the State."[64]

This means that political liberty is to be separated from civil liberty.

Constant's distinction between ancient and modern liberty is the same as Sir Isaiah Berlin's between positive and negative freedom. In his inaugural lecture at Oxford University, *Two Concepts of Liberty*, Berlin wrote that "the answer to the question 'Who governs me' is logically distinct from the question 'How far does government interfere with me?' It is in this difference that the great contrast between the two concepts of negative and positive liberty . . . consists." In Berlin's judgment, "no one saw the conflict between the two types of liberty better, or expressed it more clearly than Benjamin Constant."[65] It has even been suggested that the "distinction between ancient and modern liberty was the key to liberal doctrine."[66] To put it another way, it was the liberals who differentiated between political and civil liberty. This antithesis was

---

63. See George H. Sabine, "The Two Democratic Traditions," pp. 451–74, where the one tradition is traced back to Locke and the other to Rousseau.

64. Ortega y Gasset, *Invertebrate Spain*, pp. 125, 127: "In contrast to the public power and the law of the state, liberalism means private right and privilege. . . . Read Boulainvilliers [*Histoire de l'ancien gouvernement de la France*] or Montlosier [*De la monarchie française depuis son établissement jusqu'à nos jours*]."

65. Berlin, *Essays on Liberty*, p. 163. Liberty *from* has also been contrasted with liberty *to* or *for* and liberty, independence, or autonomy with liberty of participation.

66. Ephraim Harpaz, *L'école libérale sous la Restauration*, p. 32. Cf. Edwin Mims, *The Majority of the People*, p. 167, who said that "the writings of Herbert Spencer" are "the final, complete testament of the liberty of the moderns."

expounded both before and after Constant by several important liberal political theorists, whose ideas will now be examined.

In the eighteenth century, at least four theorists had considered the subject. Jean Louis de Lolme observed:

> Certain writers of the present age, misled by their inconsiderate admiration of the government of ancient times, and perhaps also by their desire of presenting manners of our modern times, have cried up the governments of Sparta and Rome as the only ones fit for us to imitate. . . . But these writers are seemingly in the right: a man who contributes by his vote to the passing of a law, has himself made the law; in obeying it, he obeys himself; he therefore is free. A play on words and nothing more . . . we grant that to give one's suffrage is not liberty itself, but only a means of procuring it.[67]

Joseph Priestley asserted that "political liberty consists in the power, which the members of the state reserve to themselves, of arriving at the public office, or, at least of having votes in the nomination of those who fill them," whereas "civil liberty [is] that power over their own actions, which the members of the state reserve to themselves and which their officers must not infringe." Priestley concluded that "political and civil liberty, though very different, have, however, a very near and manifest connection" because "the former is the chief guard of the latter."[68] At the same time, Adam Ferguson thought that "to the ancient Greek or Roman the individual was nothing; and the public everything," whereas "to the modern . . . the individual is everything and the public nothing."[69]

Two of Constant's friends belonging to the Coppet circle, Madame de Staël and Sismondi, developed the ideas of the contrast

---

67. Jean Louis De Lolme, *The Constitution of England,* pp. 221–26. His distinction was also outlined by Sismondi's teacher, Pierre Prevost, *L'économie des anciens gouvernements comparée à celle des gouvernements modernes,* pp. 39–40.

68. Joseph Priestley, *An Essay on the First Principles of Government and of the Nature of Political, Civil and Religious Liberty,* pp. 12–13, 54.

69. Ferguson, *Essay on Civil Society,* p. 92.

between ancient and modern liberty in terms very similar to his own. Germaine de Staël wrote that "the liberty of the present time is whatever guarantees the independence of the citizens against the power of the government. The liberty of ancient times is whatever assured the citizens the largest share in the exercise of power."[70]

Jean Charles Simonde de Sismondi gives a more detailed analysis. He contends that "until the seventeenth century the liberty of the citizen was always considered as participation in the sovereignty of his country, and it is only the example of the British constitution which taught us to consider liberty as a protection of repose, happiness, and domestic independence." Then, switching from the categories of ancient and modern liberty to civil and political liberty, Sismondi defined civil liberty as "that passive faculty that guarantees against the abuse of power in whatever hands it is lodged and which the moderns claim, whereas one would reserve the name political liberty to that active faculty, to the participation of all in the power exercised, to the association of the free man in the sovereignty." Both kinds of liberty signify what is proper for a citizen, but "one should only be a citizen who enjoys active liberty and who participates in the sovereignty," whereas "every man, without being a citizen, has the right to passive liberty, or to being protected against the abuse of power." In words reminiscent of Montesquieu and Rousseau, Sismondi concludes that "the liberty of the ancients, like their philosophy, had for its objective, virtue," whereas "the liberty of the moderns, like their philosophy, only proposes happiness.[71]

---

70. Staël, *Des circonstances actuelles*, pp. 94–95.

71. Sismondi, "De la liberté des Italiens pendant la durée de leurs républiques," *Histoire des républiques italiennes*, 10:chap. 8, pp. 327–63. According to Jacob L. Talmon, *The Origins of Totalitarian Democracy*, p. 92, "The strongest influence on the fathers of totalitarian democracy was that of antiquity—the image of liberty equated with virtue. Robespierre said 'C'est dans la vertue et dans la souveraineté du peuple qu'il faut chercher un préservatif contre les vices et le despotisme du gouvernement.'" Robespierre had also proclaimed (Report to the Convention, 5 Feb. 1794): "If the basis of popular government in time of peace is virtue, the basis of popular government in time of revolution is virtue and terror; virtue without terror is powerless, terror without virtue is murderous." Cf. Croce, "Constant e Jellinek," pp. 294–301: "In fact, however, despite the guise of the ancient idea, the political movement of Jacobinism took its origin not from ancient times but from the seventeenth and eighteenth centuries and their anti-historical cult of nature and reason."

Edouard Laboulaye, who, as we have already noted, edited some of Constant's political writings in 1861, also published an essay on "La liberté antique et la liberté moderne" in 1863, which shows clearly the influence of Benjamin. As Laboulaye phrased it, "To be free in Athens was to be a member of the sovereign. Liberty is the sovereignty and the people is the king. To proclaim that God has rights is to tear asunder the unity of despotism. There is the germ of revolution which separates the ancient from the modern world."[72] Rousseau understood this. "In his *Social Contract* (Bk IV Ch VIII) he writes: 'Jesus came to establish on earth a spiritual realm; which, separating the theological and political systems caused the State to cease to be one, and brought about divisions which have never stopped agitating Christian peoples.' By 1789 there were ideas of modern liberty from the influence of Montesquieu, the Physiocrats, Lafayette, and the Americans. With the Convention and Rousseau and Mably ancient liberty was introduced. 'It is Robespierre, pupil of Rousseau, who wants a civil religion and state education.' 'The more one is a slave as an individual, the more one is sovereign as a people and as a result the freer one is.' Saint-Just and Robespierre have a phrase of Rousseau's [*The Constitution of Poland*] to silence those who object: 'the laws of liberty are a thousand times more austere than the yoke of tyrants.' "[73]

Saint-Marc Girardin, who quoted Constant with approval, noted that "in ancient society man was above all a citizen," whereas "in modern society man is first a father of a family, adorer of God, a proprietor"; "he is after that a citizen." Therefore, "the state has only what the family and the church leave it."[74]

---

72. Cf. John Emerich Acton, "The History of Freedom in Antiquity," *Essays on Freedom and Power*, p. 57: "But when Christ said: 'Render unto Caesar the things that are Caesar's and unto God the things that are God's' those words . . . gave to the civil power . . . a sacredness it had never enjoyed, and bounds it never acknowledged; and they were the repudiation of absolutism and the inauguration of freedom."

73. Edouard Laboulaye, *L'état et ses limites*, pp. 103–37.

74. François A. Saint-Marc Girardin, *Jean-Jacques Rousseau*, 2:403. Cf. Edouard Laboulaye in his introduction to his 1861 edition of Constant's *Cours de politique*, pp. ix–x: "L'antiquité place au premier rang la souveraineté politique, elle subordonne et sacrifie l'individu à l'état; les modernes mettent au premier rang l'individu; l'état n'est plus qu'une garantie. A Rome le citoyen éclipse l'homme; à Paris et à Londres on est homme d'abord, c'est-à-dire chef de famille, propriétaire, fabricant,

Numa-Denis Fustel de Coulanges (not strictly a liberal), in his classic *La cité antique*, published in 1866, has been the most quoted subsequently on the subject of ancient liberty. Chapter 17 of Book 3 of his essay is entitled "Omnipotence of the State. The Ancients knew nothing of individual liberty." More specifically, "the ancients knew neither liberty in private life, liberty in education, nor religious liberty"; in other words, "individual liberty." Furthermore, "the dangerous maxim that the safety of the state is the supreme law was the work of antiquity."[75]

About the same time in England, Lord Acton observed that "the ancients understood the regulation of power better than the regulation of liberty. They concentrated so many prerogatives in the state as to leave no footing from which a man could escape its jurisdiction or assign bounds to its activity. The vice of the classic state was that it was both Church and State in one. . . . What a slave was in the hands of his master, the citizen was in the hands of the community."[76]

Earlier, in America, Francis Lieber examined the same problem of the difference between ancient and modern liberty:

That which the ancients understood by liberty differed essentially from what we moderns call civil liberty. Man appeared to the ancients in his highest and noblest character when they considered him as a member of the state or as a political being. . . . There was no sacrifice of individuality too great for the ancients. The greatest political philosophers of

---

ouvrier, écrivain, artiste, chrétien, philosphe; et l'on n'est citoyen, c'est-à-dire électeur, juré, garde national que pour maintenir le libre exercice des droits individuels. L'état a perdu l'importance dans la proportion même ou l'individu a grandi."

75. Numa-Denis Fustel de Coulanges, *The Ancient City*, pp. 219–23. In our day, Gustave Glotz, in *The Greek City and Its Institutions*, pp. 4–5, takes issue with Fustel de Coulanges: "The great mistake which Fustel de Coulanges made is, therefore, clear. Conforming to the theory which dominated the liberal school of the Nineteenth Century, he established an absolute antinomy between the omnipotence of the city and individual liberty, whereas, on the contrary, state power and individualism progressed side by side, each supporting the other." Cf., however, Elizabeth Rawson's comment in *Spartan Tradition*, p. 2: "What Sparta in fact was is of less importance to us than what she was thought to be."

76. Acton, "History of Freedom in Antiquity," p. 45.

antiquity unite in holding up Sparta as the best regulated commonwealth. . . . We, on the other hand, acknowledge individual primordial right and seek one of the highest aims of civil liberty in the most efficient protection of the individual action, endeavor, and rights. . . . The ancients had not that which the moderns understand by *jus naturale*, or the law which grows from individual rights of man. . . . On what supreme power rests, what the extent and limitation of supreme power ought to be . . . these questions have never occupied the ancient votaries of political science.

Lieber continued his presentation with the proposition that

Aristotle, Plato, and Cicero do not begin with the question [the scope and limits of power]. Their works are mainly occupied with the discussion of the question, Who shall govern? The safety of the state is their principal problem; the safety of the individual is one of our greatest. No ancient, therefore, doubted the extent of supreme power. If the people possessed it, no one ever hesitated in allowing to them absolute power over everyone and everything. If it passed from the people to a few, or was usurped by one, they considered in many cases the acquisition of power unlawful, but never doubted its unlimited extent. Liberty with the ancients consisted materially in the degree of participation in government "where all are in turn the ruled and the rulers." Liberty with the moderns consists less in the forms of authority, which are with them but means to obtain the protection of the individual and the undisturbed action of society in its minor and larger circles.[77]

It is clear from this account that many liberals did their thinking in the shadow of Constant's differentiation between the liberty of the ancients and the liberty of the moderns.[78] This distinction

---

77. Francis Lieber, *Civil Liberty and Self-Government*, 1:58.
78. One of the most recent is José Ortega y Gasset, who always spoke of himself as "un vieux libéral": "The ancient democracies were absolute powers, more abso-

was criticized, however, as early as 1867 by Henri De Ferron, who quotes Constant, Guizot, and Laboulaye.[79] He contends, first, that in their estimate of ancient liberty they "took the liberty which existed in the time of Aristotle and Cicero for the same liberty which was in effect three centuries earlier." But he was convinced that "Vico has shown that all nations of the past passed through an aristocratic phase, the essence of which is individual independence." Second, Laboulaye was right in making Athens an exception, because Thucydides placed these words in the mouth of Pericles: "We announce freely our opinion of the public interest, but in the particular commerce of life, we do not cast suspicious eye on the actions of others" (Book 2, chap. 37). This proves, according to De Ferron, that at least Athenian democracy did not sacrifice individuals to the state. Therefore, third, what is true in Constant's distinction is that "none of the polities of antiquity rose above the doctrine of the absorption of the individual in the state as an ideal of political science. Plato, Aristotle, and Cicero, for example, were looking for such an ideal as a means of countering the state of disintegration to which the abandonment of ancient beliefs and skepticism had reduced the society of their time."[80]

Modern critics have also had reservations about Constant's differentiation. Guido de Ruggiero comments:

> Like all clear-cut historical oppositions this may be
> shown to be fallacious. The republics of antiquity, especially

---

lute than those of any European monarch of the period called absolutist. Greeks and Romans did not recognize the inspiration of Liberalism. More than that, the idea that the individual might limit the power of the state, that there could be any part of the person which is outside the public jurisdiction, had no place in classic mentalities" (*Invertebrate Spain*, pp. 124, 126).

79. See François Guizot, *Histoire générale de la civilisation en Europe*, 11ᵉ leçon, pp. 3–36: "C'est par les barbares germains, que le sentiment de la personalité a été introduit dans la civilisation européenne; il était inconnu au monde romain, inconnu à presque toutes les civilisations anciennes. Quand vous trouvez dans les civilisations anciennes la liberté, c'est la liberté politique, la liberté du citoyen, ce n'est pas de la liberté personnelle que l'homme est préoccupé. Il appartient à une association, il est dévoué à une association, il est prêt à se sacrifier à une association."

80. De Ferron, *Théorie du progrès*, 1:306–9. Cf. the reservations of Benedetto Croce, *History of Europe in the Nineteenth Century*, pp. 6–7. Croce addresses himself to the "differences in character between the liberty suited to the modern

Athens and Rome, recognized many liberties of the so-called modern type; what they lacked, and in a limited sense this lack justifies Constant's assertion, was any idea of legal and political limitations of the individual's right. But, on the other hand, the moderns have begun to value liberty in the ancient sense of the word, because granted the necessity of political liberty to guarantee the rights of individuals (and Constant certainly does) this implies their participation in government; and the progressive extension of this participation can only result from a complete development of political activities.[81]

Benedetto Croce's critique is much more penetrating:

Their [Constant and Sismondi] judgment [on the difference between ancient and modern liberty] fell into the
error of confusing and mistaking a problem of chronology and
classification for an historical problem. In the classification of
history, that is, in constructing historical periods, it is not only
admissible but indispensable to distinguish between ancient
and modern liberty, and more, by means of subdivision to
distinguish between other periods and other liberties. [More-
over,] we must not believe that the two liberties, thus
distinguished for the purpose of classification, are really
distinguishable. For, if within liberty could be discerned two
liberties, each with its own particular character, it is evident

world and that of the ancient Greeks and Romans and Jacobins of yesterday. . . . But
though the problem has its kernel of reality, it was not presented correctly when a
contrast was made between the ancient and the modern, in which Greece, Rome and
the French Revolution (as following the Graeco-Roman ideals) stood on one side,
and on the other the modern world. . . . In consequence, the investigation that was
based on the supposed contrast ran the risk of being lost in abstractions, separating
state and individual, civil liberty and political liberty; the liberty of one man and that
liberty of all other men which limits his own. It ran the risk of assigning political but
not civil liberty to the ancients, and to the moderns civil but not political liberty. . . .
This error of abstractions always reappears when the attempt is made to define the
idea of liberty by juridical distinctions, which are practical in character and concern
single and transitory institutions rather than the superior and supreme idea that
embraces them all and transcends them all."

81. Ruggiero, *History of European Liberalism*, p. 168.

that either one of them would not be liberty, or both would be superior and the only effectual liberty. And, therefore, the differences that these authors adduce, recognizing among the Greeks and Romans a liberty they called political and among the moderns a liberty they called civil, adding that one corresponded to the concept of Virtue and the other to the concept of Happiness etc., these differences do not support critical examination. The reason for this failure is that there is no political liberty which is not at the same time civil liberty, and there is not a society which can govern itself by means of virtue without well-being or well-being without virtue.[82]

To be fair to Constant, however, he realized, as we have already noted, that a way must be found of combining political and civil liberty.

Croce was pointing out in his critique that "ancient liberty is not so much a different form as an early one of the same consciousness of liberty."[83] Moreover, he is right in calling attention to the fact that the distinction made between ancient and modern liberty is too rigid and simplistic, because it does not take account of the historical evolution of freedom from the beginnings of Christianity to the Middle Ages, the Renaissance, the Reformation, the Industrial Revolution, and the Enlightenment.[84] In other words, he is suggesting that there is a great difference between a logical or conceptual differentiation and a historical or empirical classification. Constant did not always seem to realize this in his analysis of liberty. Moreover, it must be remembered that long before Max Weber, Constant was writing history through the use of ideal

82. Benedetto Croce, *History as the Story of Liberty*, pp. 245–46.
83. Croce, "Constant e Jellinek," pp. 294–301.
84. Relying on George Simmel, Emile Durkheim, and Max Weber, Stephen Taylor Holmes has stressed the difference between the modern social order, which is characterized by structural differentiation, and the ancient social order, where no line was drawn between the state and society. In other words, he suggests that there is a vast difference between the *Gemeinschaft* of the ancient small city state and the *Gesellschaft* of the large modern society. See "Aristippus In and Out of Athens," pp. 113–28.

types—ancient military and modern commercial society and ancient and modern liberty. To be fair, however, Constant relied in general much more upon concrete historical and institutional experience in the development of his political theory than upon metaphysical abstractions and ideal types.

Chapter III
Popular Sovereignty

ACCORDING TO Emile Faguet, "from Jurieu to Robespierre, through Burlamaqui and Rousseau, there is a constant tradition of Jacobinism."[1] Constant sought to refute this Jacobin tradition by reprinting with some additions and alterations a chapter "De la souveraineté du peuple," with which he had begun his *Principes de politique applicables à tous les gouvernements représentatifs*, published during the Hundred Days, when Napoleonic rule based on that concept was the menace to freedom. This revised version—"De la souveraineté des peuples et de ses limites"—was added to the second edition of Constant's *Réflexions sur les constitutions, la distribution des pouvoirs et les garanties dans une monarchie constitutionnelle*, published in 1818.[2] In this essay it is clear that Constant perceived, to use the words of Alexander Passerin D'Entrèves, that "positive liberty [ancient liberty] and popular sovereignty go hand in hand" and that "one is the ideological justification of the other."[3]

Constant begins his essay by explaining in 1818 that four years earlier he had no reason to deal with the subject of popular sovereignty, because at that time liberty was not in jeopardy from that direction. In 1815, however, things were quite different, because Bonaparte, as we have already noted, always had justified his despotic power upon the basis of the sovereignty of the people. Therefore, this theory had to be contested once again during the Hundred Days.

1. Emile Faguet, *Le Libéralisme*, pp. 331–32.
2. I have referred to the following sources for partial English translation of the essays quoted in this chapter: John Plamenatz, *Readings from Liberal Writers*, pp. 199–203, and Walter Simon, *French Liberalism, 1789–1848*, pp. 64–69.
3. Alexander Passerin d'Entrèves, *The Notion of the State*, p. 212.

Constant stated first that he had not been able to find anywhere a "precise and exact definition" of the principle of popular sovereignty, but in his analysis he specifically criticizes Montesquieu, Rousseau, and Thomas Hobbes on this subject.[4] He does not, interestingly enough, cite the well-known delineation of popular or national sovereignty by the Abbé Sieyès, who wrote: "The nation is prior to everything. It is the source of everything. Its will is always legal. The manner in which a nation exercises its will does not matter; the point is that it does exercise it; any procedure is adequate and its will is always the supreme law."[5]

Constant's own thesis was then outlined—"The abstract recognition of popular sovereignty in no way increases the sum of the liberty of individuals."[6] Not only that, but "unlimited sovereignty" is positively dangerous. If true, then, why have party leaders or even the lovers of liberty been so "reluctant to limit sovereignty"?

4. Cf. Joseph de Maistre's refutation of Rousseau in his "Etude sur la souveraineté" and Louis Bonald's in his *Essai analytique sur les lois naturelles de l'ordre social ou du pouvoir, du ministre et du sujet dans la société.* Constant, however, does not connect Rousseau with the French Revolution, as these Ultras did.

5. Joseph Sieyès, *What Is the Third Estate?*, pp. 124, 128. Cf. Antoine Boulay de la Meurthe, *Essai sur les causes qui en 1649 amènerent en Angleterre à l'établissement de la République*, pp. 121, 117, whom Constant answered in *Des suites de la contre-révolution en Angleterre:* "Quand un changement politique est fait dans l'intérêt et avec l'approbation du peuple, il est évident que toutes les mesures nécessaires à son affermissement sont non seulement autorisées, mais commandées par la justice. . . . Nous distinguons tout-à-l'heure dans un gouvernement la chose et la personne; celle-ci n'est pas moins importante que l'autre; car il est constant que de bons gouvernans rendront le peuple plus heureux avec une mauvaise constitution qu'une bonne constitution ne le fera, confie à de mauvais gouvernans; le peuple est bien meilleur juge de ceux-ci que de celle-là . . . en un mot, s'il n'y a ni liberté publique ni liberté particulière, le peuple le voit, le sent très bien; et sa voix est alors la voix de Dieu."

6. See Montesquieu, *The Spirit of the Laws*, Book 11, chap. 2: "In fine, as in democracies the people seem to act almost as they please, this sort of government has been deemed the most free, and the power of the people has been confounded with their liberty." Cf. Chateaubriand, "Essai historique, politique et moral sur les révolutions anciennes et modernes considérées dans leurs rapports avec la révolution française," *Oeuvres complètes* (1870), 4:238: "Le principe de la souveraineté du peuple n'est d'ailleurs d'aucun intérêt pour la liberté." See also Alexis de Tocqueville, *Recollections*, pp. 201–2. This theorist said of Armand Marrast (1801–52), one of the founders of the republican party under the July Monarchy, that "he belonged to the ordinary type of French revolutionaries, who have always understood the liberty of the people to mean despotism exercised in the name of the people." Tocqueville also said, in "Voyages en Sicile et aux Etats Unis," *Oeuvres complètes*, Paris, 1951–V (1): "The people are always right is a republican dogma just as the 'king can do no wrong' is the religion of monarchical states."

It is because they have objected to "this or that kind of govern-ment" or "this or that class of governors"; in short, to the "harmful possessors of power and not to the power itself." In other words, "instead of destroying it they have thought only of replacing it."[7]

In a footnote, Constant noted that Montesquieu seemed to limit popular sovereignty in certain passages of *The Spirit of the Laws*. For example, the baron said that "justice existed before the laws," which is "to imply that the laws and consequently the general will of which the laws are only the expression, must be subordinated to justice."[8] But what happened to Montesquieu's proposition? Namely this: that "often the depositories of power are parties of the principle that justice existed before the laws in order to subject individuals to retroactive laws or to deprive them of the benefit of existing laws."

Constant continued that Montesquieu in his definition of liberty had misunderstood the limits of social authority. The baron had interpreted liberty as "a right of doing whatever the laws permit," which is a statement of the rule of law whereby one may do what-ever the law does not forbid (prohibit).[9] In other words, liberty consists of that sphere within which man is unrestrained by law. But Constant objected that Montesquieu "had confused two things: liberty and its guarantee." "Individual rights, that is liberty; politi-cal rights, that is the guarantee." His famous maxim "that indi-viduals have the right to do whatever the laws permit is a principle of guarantee. I mean that no one has the right to prevent another from doing what the laws do not forbid but it does not explain what the laws have or do not have the right to prohibit."[10] But

---

7. Cf. Montesquieu's comment in *Spirit of the Laws*, Book 29, chap. 27, p. 309: "For whoever is able to dethrone an absolute prince has a power sufficient to become absolute himself." When sovereignty was shifted from the king to the people lèse-nation was put in the place of lèse-majesté.

8. The relevant passage in ibid. is to be found in Book 1, chap. 1, p. 2: "Before laws were made there were relations of possible justice. To say that there is nothing just or unjust but what is commanded or forbidden by positive laws, is the same as saying that before the describing of a circle all the radii were not equal. We must therefore acknowledge relations of justice antecedent to the positive law by which they are established."

9. Ibid., Book 11, chap. 3, p. 150.

10. Cf. Jeremy Bentham, *Deontology or the Science of Morality*, 2:59: "The usual definition of liberty—that is the right to do everything that the law does not forbid—

"there is where liberty resides," because "liberty is nothing more than what individuals have the right to do and what society does not have the right to proscribe."

Now to return to the body of the text. Constant submits that popular sovereignty legitimately means "the supremacy of the general will over all particular wills."[11] To cite the notes again, "the axiom of the sovereignty of the people has been considered as a principle of liberty," whereas instead "it is a principle of guarantee" because it is designed "to prevent one individual from seizing the authority, which only belongs to the entire association."

Constant, however, always denied that "society as a whole exercised unlimited sovereignty over its members," because "there is . . . a part of human life which of necessity remains individual and independent and which, as of right, remains outside the jurisdiction of society.[12] Sovereignty exists only in a limited and relative way. The jurisdiction of this sovereignty stops at the point where the independence of individual life starts. If society crosses this border, it becomes as culpable as the despot whose title rests only on the sword of destruction; society cannot exceed its competence without usurpation; the majority cannot do so without becoming a faction. The consent of the majority by no means suffices in all cases to make its acts legitimate; there are some acts which nothing can make legitimate. When any authority commits acts of this sort, it matters little from what source it claims to derive; it matters little whether it is called an individual or nation, it might be the entire

---

shows with what carelessness words are used in ordinary discourse or composition; for if the laws are bad, what becomes of liberty? and if they are good, where is its value?"

11. See the original chapter 1 of "Principes de politique," *Cours de politique*, 1:8: "En un mot il n'existe au monde que deux pouvoirs l'un illégitime c'est la force, l'autre légitime c'est la volonté générale."

12. Cf. John Stuart Mill, *On Liberty*, chap. 1: "The only part of the conduct of any one, for which he is amenable to society, is that which concerns others. In the part which merely concerns himself, his independence, is, of right, absolute. Over himself, over his own body and mind, the individual is sovereign." Lord Acton agreed that liberty lies in the maintenance of an inner realm immune from the encroachment of state power. Cf. Hannah Arendt's comment that "our philosophical tradition is almost unanimous in holding that freedom begins where men have left the realm of political life . . . , and that it is not experienced in association with others but in intercourse with one's self" ("What Is Freedom," p. 157).

nation with the exception of the citizen whom it oppresses, and the act would still not be legitimate."[13]

By thus equating freedom with independence within a certain sphere, Constant was defining, of course, negative freedom. This places him in what John Stuart Mill called "the newer generation of European liberals . . . who thought the central problem of political theory was the limits of what a government may do." Mill had noted that "the earlier generation saw the central problem in making the ruling power emanate from the periodical choice of the ruled [self-government]."[14] It is instructive to compare Constant's definition of freedom with Tocqueville's. His liberal successor wrote: "According to the modern notion of liberty every man . . . is inherently entitled to be uncontrolled by his fellows in all that only concerns himself and to regulate at his own will his own destiny."[15] In all three—Constant, Tocqueville, and Mill—"there is the same negative definition of liberty as freedom from external control and the same delineation of an area of self-regarding actions, which should be properly left to the individual himself."[16]

Constant's treatment of popular sovereignty in his *Principes de politique* and *Réflexions sur les constitutions* should be compared with his analysis of the same subject later on in his *Commentaire sur l'ouvrage de Filangieri (The Science of Legislation)*: "In the portion of human existence which must rest independent of legislation, resides individual rights, which legislation must not touch, rights over which society has no jurisdiction." Constant adds in summary that "the legitimacy of authority depends on its object as much as on its source. When authority extends over objects, which are beyond its sphere, it becomes illegitimate."[17]

Constant thought that because Gaetano Filangieri, an eighteenth-century Italian philosophe, would have the law fix the rights of each individual, who had only such rights as legislation left to him,

13. In his article "De la competence du gouvernement" in *Le temps* for 1830, Constant cites some examples of usurping laws, such as the laws of the Convention against the nobles, those of the Constituent Assembly imposing oaths on the clergy, and all censure laws.

14. *On Liberty*, chap. 1.

15. "Etat social et politique de la France depuis 1789 or Political and Social Condition of France," pp. 165–66.

16. Jack Lively, *The Social and Political Thought of Alexis de Tocqueville*, p. 12.

17. *Commentaire sur l'ouvrage de Filangieri*, 1:51–52.

his system was just as unlimited in nature as Rousseau's, whose "*Social Contract,* so often invoked on behalf of liberty," was instead "the most terrible auxiliary of all kinds of despotism."[18] But once again Constant repeated in a footnote that he was "far from joining the detractors of Rousseau," who "are numerous in our day. A mob of inferiors, who hope to become successful by calling into question all courageous truths, occupy themselves in an attempt to blemish his glory. That is but one reason the more for being wary of blaming him. He was the first to popularize the feeling for our rights. Generous hearts and independent souls were awakened at the sound of his voice."

Constant was convinced, however, that "what Rousseau felt strongly he did not always define clearly; many chapters of the *Social Contract* are worthy of the scholastic writers of the fifteenth century."[19] Constant adds that "the fomenters of despotism can draw an immense advantage from Rousseau's principles." He then cites one, without naming him. It was Louis-Mathieu Molé, who in his *Essais de morale et de politique* (1806) contended that the power of society's representative was not arbitrary because "it was no longer a man but a people."[20] After such reasoning, how, Constant asks, can Rousseau ever be reproached for his "abstractions?"[21]

18. In his article "De la souveraineté" in *Le temps* for 1830, Constant wrote: "Rousseau devenait le précepteur de la tyrannie comme Bossuet." Cf. the judgment of a contemporary scholar of ours, Sir Isaiah Berlin, who has called Rousseau "the most sinister and most formidable enemy of liberty in the whole history of modern thought" (BBC broadcast 5 Nov. 1952 in the series *Freedom and Its Betrayal*).

19. "Que signifient des droits dont on jouit d'autant plus qu'on les aliène plus complètement: Qu'est-ce qu'une liberté en vertu de laquelle on est d'autant plus libre que chacun fait complètement ce qui contrarie sa volonté?" ("De la souveraineté du peuple et de ses limites").

20. In the manuscripts of 1810 Constant comments: "L'auteur de certains *Essais de morale et de politique* [Molé] a reproduit en faveur de l'autorité absolu tous les raisonnements de Rousseau sur la souveraineté" (F 93). In a chapter, however, of *Principes de politique* in the manuscripts of 1810, entitled "De Hobbes et du Hobbisme," Constant connects Molé with Hobbes rather than with Rousseau: "Un écrivain de nos jours l'auteur des *Essais de morale et de politique* [Molé] a renouvelé le système de Hobbes avec beaucoup moins de profondeur seulement et moins d'esprit et de logique" (F 103). "A ses [Constant's] yeux, Rousseau avec sa doctrine de la souveraineté, fondait, dans l'ordre intellectuelle, l'alliance monstreuse de la démocratie et de la monarchie absolue" as developed by Antoine-François-Claude Ferrand, in particular, in *Le rétablissement de la monarchie*. See Jean Roussel, *Jean-Jacques Rousseau en France après la Révolution, 1795–1830*, p. 502.

21. Madame de Staël has already referred to Rousseau's mathematical method. See her "Lettres sur les écrits et le caractère de Jean-Jacques Rousseau" (1788),

In 1820, Constant observed that "every time laws are proposed against liberty Jean-Jacques Rousseau is quoted for authority. With much love for liberty, Rousseau has always been cited by those who wish to establish despotism. Rousseau has served as a pretext for despotism because he had the feeling for liberty but not for theory."[22] Constant, however, thought it was wrong to apply Rousseau's concepts, which were developed in a period of history when liberty was not yet established, to a later generation of men that is wiser after thirty years of unfortunate experiences, such as the French Revolution (The Terror and Babeuf) and Bonapartism.

In his critique of Rousseau, in "De la souveraineté du peuple et de ses limites," Constant devotes special attention to Chapter 6 of Book I of the *Social Contract* entitled "The Social Pact." He points out that Rousseau defines the "contract entered into by society and its members" as

> the complete alienation without reserve of each individual and all his rights to the community. To reassure us as to the consequences of such an absolute abandonment with respect to all phases of our existence for the benefit of an abstract being, he tells us that the sovereign, that is to say, the social body, cannot do injury either to its members collectively or to any one of them in particular; and each giving himself completely, the conditions are the same for all and, therefore, it is in no one's interest to make the conditions onerous for others.

Oeuvres complètes de Mme la Baronne de Staël, 1:6: "Rousseau emprunte la méthode des géometres, pour l'appliquer à l'enchainement des idées; il soumet au calcul les problèmes politiques."

22. *Discours de M. Benjamin Constant à la Chambre des Députés*, 1:211. Some modern critics have reached a conclusion similar to Constant's. See Peter Gay's introduction to his translation of Ernst Cassirer's *The Question of Jean Jacques Rousseau*, p. 27: "Used as a critical yardstick, Rousseau's political thought has been invaluable to democratic movements; used as a political blue-print, it has had a pernicious effect on libertarian ideas and institutions." Gay said that he owed to Franz Neumann the judgment: "Rousseau is the theorist of democratic movements but not of the democratic state." Cf. Judith N. Shklar, *Men and Citizens*, p. 17, who wrote that Rousseau's *Social Contract* "was not meant to be a plan for any future society, but a standard for judging existing institutions. It was a yardstick, not a program."

Finally, Rousseau contended that "each in giving himself to all, gives himself to no one; and since each acquires over all his associates the same rights that he surrendered to them, he gains the equivalent of everything he loses, with more power to conserve what he has."[23]

In his detailed refutation, Constant argued that Rousseau

> forgets all these preservative attributes, which he confers upon the abstract being called the sovereign and the consequence of its being composed of every individual without exception. But as soon as the sovereign must make use of the power which he possesses, that is to say, as soon as he finds it necessary to proceed to a practical organization of authority, because the sovereign cannot exercise it himself, he delegates it, and all these attributes disappear.[24] Acts done in the name of all, being necessarily in the control of only one person or a few, the result is that in giving one's self to all it is not true that one gives oneself to nobody: on the contrary, one gives one's self to those who act in the name of all. From that follows that in giving one's self completely the conditions are not the same for all, since some profit exclusively from the sacrifice of the rest. It is not true that it is in no one's interest to make the conditions onerous for others. . . . It is not true that all those associated acquire the same rights, which they cede; they do not gain the equivalent of what they lose.

Continuing with his confutation, Constant is very cogent in his analysis.

> As soon as the general will becomes all powerful, the representatives of this general will will become all the more

23. To Isaiah Berlin, *Four Essays on Liberty*, p. 164, "Constant could not see why, even though the sovereign is 'everybody' it should not oppress one of the 'members' of its indivisible self, if it so decided."

24. Constant seems not to have read carefully enough Book 3, chap. 1, "On Government in General" of the *Social Contract*, where Rousseau said that "the executive power cannot belong to the general public in its legislator's or sovereign capacity." Constant is confusing government with sovereignty, something Rousseau never did.

formidable in that they call themselves only docile instruments of this pretended will. . . . What no tyrant would dare do in his own name, they legitimize through the limitless social authority. . . . The most unjust laws, the most oppressive institutions, are obligatory as the expression of the general will, for, as Rousseau says, individuals being entirely dedicated to the benefit of the social body, can have no will other than this general will. In obeying this will, they obey only themselves.

Constant then reminds his readers that "the consequences of this system . . . unfolded themselves to their full extent during . . . the Revolution"; in fact, "the crudest sophistries of the most impetuous apostles of the Terror were merely perfectly appropriate consequences of Rousseau's principles."[25] Constant quickly added, however, that "Rousseau himself was afraid of these consequences." Therefore, he "declared that sovereignty could be neither transferred nor delegated nor represented."[26] To Constant, however, this simply meant that "it could not be exercised"; in fact, "it amounted in practice to destroying the principle he [Rousseau] had just proclaimed."

At this point, Constant makes reference to Hobbes, who "reduced despotism to a system." The great English theorist had argued that sovereignty was unlimited and that "it is clear that the absolute character which Hobbes attributed to the people's sovereignty is the basis of his entire system." In fact, however, Hobbes developed the concept of ruler rather than popular sovereignty.

Continuing his examination of Rousseau, Constant states that "this word 'absolute' makes liberty . . . impossible under any kind

25. See Edwin Mims, *The Majority of the People*, p. 154: "Rousseau was too close to the sources of Jacobinism to have any misapprehension as to what the real Rousseau thought about liberty."

26. "For Sieyès, as for the French Revolution, the full power of the absolute and unlimited sovereignty of the people was attributed to a representative assembly, which, it was assumed, being the embodiment of the people, was not susceptible of any limitations nor of needing any, for the people could not be supposed to be capable of exercising tyranny over itself. The logical consequence of popular or national sovereignty is to identify contrary to fact the people with the government, and the rulers with the ruled" (Alfred Cobban, *A History of Modern France*, 1:162).

of institution," for "when sovereignty is not limited there is no means of protecting individuals from governments.[27] It is in vain that you claim to submit governments to the general will. It is they who dictate this will and all precautions become illusory. Rousseau said we are sovereign in one respect and subject in another. But in practice these two aspects are confounded. It is easy for authority to oppress the people as subject in order to force it to manifest as sovereign the will which it prescribes to it."[28]

What is the remedy for this? Constant replied that "you can try a division of powers in vain; but, if the sum total of powers is unlimited, the divided powers have only to form a coalition for despotism to be installed without remedy." This point was also made by Bentham when he treated the subject of the separation of powers. To Constant, then, "what is important . . . is . . . not that . . . rights may not be violated by one power without the approval of another, but rather that such a violation be forbidden to all powers."

Constant concludes that "no authority on earth is unlimited, neither that of the people nor that of the men who claim to be their representative nor that of the king nor that of the law."[29] The boundaries to authority "are fixed by justice and by the rights of individuals," such as personal liberty, religious liberty, industrial liberty, inviolability of property, liberty of opinion, and "the guar-

27. "Avant moi, il s'est trouvé des hommes célèbres pour s'élever contre la maxime de Rousseau. Beccaria, Condorcet, Franklin, Payne et enfin Sieyès, qui, dans une opinion, émise à la tribune, a déclaré que l'autorité social n'était point illimitée. Mais il ne parait pas que la logique de ces écrivains ait fait impression. L'on parle encore sans cesse d'un pouvoir sans bornes, qui réside dans le peuple ou dans ses chefs, comme une chose hors de doute" (Manuscrits de 1810, F, 93).

28. "Le triomphe de la force tyrannique est de contraindre les esclaves à se proclamer libres; mais en se prêtant à ce simulacre monsonger de liberté, les esclaves devus complices aussi méprisables que leurs maîtres" (*Discours*, 2:60).

29. Cf. a statement Constant made in *De la religion considerée dans sa source, ses formes et ses développements*, 1:75–76, which demonstrates the close connection between his religious and political ideas: "Il en est de la raison infaillible du genre humain comme de la souveraineté illimitée du peuple. Les uns ont cru qu'il devait y avoir quelque part une raison infaillible; ils l'ont placée dans l'autorité. Les autres ont cru qu'il devait y avoir quelque part une souveraineté illimitée; ils l'ont placée dans le peuple." To Constant, however, "il n'y a point de raison infaillible; il n'y a point de souveraineté illimitée." Constant especially denounced legislative omnipotence, referring particularly to the Constituent Assembly in France and the Long Parliament in England, a subject to be considered later.

antee against *tout arbitraire*."[30] Therefore, "not even the will of an entire people can make just what is unjust. The representatives of a nation do not have the right to do what the nation itself has not the right to do. . . . The consent of a people cannot make legitimate what is illegitimate."[31]

Constant was convinced, unlike the Doctrinaires, that the "limitation of power in the abstract is not sufficient." In addition, "we must look for the foundations of political institutions. . . . Limitation of sovereignty is, therefore, . . . possible. . . . It will be safeguarded first by the force of public opinion and second . . . by the distribution and balance of powers."[32]

Having examined Montesquieu's definition of liberty as "the right of doing whatever the laws permit" and Rousseau's that "liberty is obedience to a law which we prescribe to ourselves," Constant concluded that for him freedom was "the triumph of individuality as much over a government which seeks to rule by

30. "Il y a deux dogmas également dangéreux: l'un de droit divin et l'autre la souveraineté illimitée du peuple; l'un et l'autre ont fait beaucoup de mal. Il n'y a de divin que la divinité. Il n'y a souveraineté que la justice" (*Discours*, 1:211). It is interesting to note that in America John Quincy Adams in "Publicola," pp. 70–71, relied upon the same concept of justice and individual rights to refute Thomas Paine's position in *The Rights of Man*, p. 13, that "whatever a nation chooses to do it has the right to do." Adams wrote: "This principle that a whole nation has a right to do whatever it pleases, cannot in any sense whatever be admitted as true. The eternal and immutable laws of justice and morality are paramount to all human legislation. The violation of those laws is certainly within the power, but it is not among the rights of nations. The power of a nation is the collected power of all the individuals which compose it. . . . If, therefore, a majority . . . are bound by no law human or divine, and have no other rule but their sovereign will and pleasure to direct them, what possible security can any citizen of the nation have for the protection of his unalienable rights. The principles of liberty must still be the sport of arbitrary power, and the hideous form of despotism must lay aside the diadem and the scepter, only to assume the party-colored garments of democracy."

31. "Le peuple peut errer en masse comme chaque citoyen en particulier et quand il fait des lois injustes, sa volonté n'est pas plus légitime que celle du tyran" (*De la religion*, 1:76).

32. "L'on peut affirmer que, lorsque de certains principes sont complètement et clairement démontrés, ils se servent en quelque sorte de garantie à eux-mêmes. . . . S'il est reconnu que la souveraineté n'est pas sans bornes, c'est-à-dire, qu'il n'existe sur la terre aucune puissance illimitée, nul, dans aucun temps, n'osera reclamer une sembable puissance. . . . L'on n'attribue plus, par exemple, à la société entière, le droit de vie et de mort sans jugement. Aussi, nul gouvernement ne prétend exercer un pareil droit." In other words, the mere discovery of the truth was optimistically seen as the guarantee of its victory. As for the "distribution and balance of powers," it is interesting to note that Tocqueville believed that mixed government was a chimera (*Democracy in America*, 1:260).

despotic methods as over the masses who seek to render the minority a slave to the majority."[33] "Despotism has no rights," however. "The majority has the right to compel the minority to respect public order, but everything which does not disturb public order, everything which is only private, such as our opinions, everything which, in manifestation of opinion, does no harm to others either by provoking physical violence or opposing contrary opinions, everything which, in industry, allows a rival industry to carry on freely— this is something individual that cannot legitimately be subjected to the social power."[34]

In 1859, John Stuart Mill, many of whose ideas are very similar to Constant's noted, in *On Liberty*, chapter 1, that the ideas that "the nation did not need to be protected against its own will" and that "there was no fear of its tyrannizing over itself" were "common among the last generation of European Liberalism."[35] He also stated that "those who admit any limit to what a government may do . . . stand out as brilliant exceptions among the political thinkers of the Continent." Although he was not named, Constant was just such an exception. He had, however, his liberal predecessors and successors, who attacked the theory of popular sovereignty and its chief exponent, Rousseau, as well.

During the French Revolution, Jean Joseph Mounier had contended in 1792 that occasionally in history civil liberty had existed

33. Constant, *Mélanges de littérature et de politique*, Preface. Cf. Mill, who argued that "the tyranny of the majority is as menacing as any tyrant of old" (*On Liberty*, chap. 1). Constant quotes Thomas Jefferson (First Inaugural Address, 4 March 1801) in the preface written in 1810 (Manuscrits) to his *Principes de politique*: "Though the will of the majority is in all cases to prevail, that will, to be rightful, must be reasonable. The minority possesses their equal rights, which equal laws must protect and to violate them would be oppression."
34. Cf. *Mélanges*, Preface. See Mill's conception of "the appropriate region of human liberty" (*On Liberty*, chap. 1). First, "liberty of conscience in the most comprehensive sense; liberty of thought and feeling; absolute freedom of opinion and sentiment on all subjects practical or speculative, scientific, moral or theological; liberty of expressing and publishing opinions"; second, "liberty of tastes and pursuits; of framing a plan of our life to suit our own character; of doing as we like, subject to such consequences as may follow: without impediment from other creatures, so long as what we do does not harm them, even though they should think our conduct foolish, perverse or wrong"; third, "the liberty, within the same limits, of combinations among individuals."
35. Mill is referring here to Bentham's idea of an omnipotent legislature rather than to Rousseau.

under the absolute power of a king, but never under the absolute power of the people. In fact, he concluded that "the government the least favorable to liberty would be a pure democracy, that is to say, supreme power without limits in the hands of the people, which leads to the majority tyrannizing over the minority."[36] This idea, that all democracies are essentially despotic is, of course, as old as Plato and Kant and as new as Vilfredo Pareto, Gaetano Mosca, and Robert Michels. Moreover, in anticipation of Constant, Mounier had observed in 1789 that "people sustain the despotism of the multitude because they share in it, little realizing that popular despotism often ends in the arbitrary power of one man."[37]

In 1793, the Swiss polemicist Jacques Mallet du Pan suggested that "with the exception of Condorcet, all the revolutionaries of France, beginning with Sieyès and ending with Marat, were the disciples of Rousseau," who "alone innoculated the French with the doctrine of popular sovereignty and with its most extreme consequences."[38] According to Mallet, this theory established the "despotism of the majority, that is, the right of the strongest over the minority." Furthermore, "this unlimited power of the majority can only be based on sheer force unless it is grounded in justice and reason." It was Mallet's conclusion, therefore, that because "Locke and Cicero placed justice and reason above the right of the multitude, they are to be preferred to revolutionaries like Sieyès and Louvet." It is no wonder, then, that the "English, much more advanced than the rest of Europe in public law, have always despised the *Contrat Social.*"

Counterrevolutionary conservatives, such as Burke and Joseph de Maistre, as well as such liberals as Constant and Madame de

---

36. Jean Joseph Mounier, *Recherches sur les causes qui ont empêché les Français de devenir libres et sur les moyens qui leur restent pour acquérir la liberté*, chap. 1, pp. 1–8. Cf. De Lolme, who in the *Constitution de l'Angleterre*, p. 188, stated that the result of popular sovereignty would be the submergence of the individual "in the crowd," which is an interesting anticipation of Tocqueville and Mill.

37. Jean Joseph Mounier, *Considérations sur les gouvernements et principalement sur celui qui convient à la France*, p. 9.

38. Jacques Mallet du Pan, *Considerations on the Nature of the French Revolution and on the Causes which Prolong the Duration*, p. 8; "Du degré d'influence qu'a eu la philosophie française sous la révolution," p. 362; *Correspondance politique pour servir à l'histoire du républicanisme française*, pp. xx–xxi.

Staël, participated at the time in the general denunciation of popular sovereignty.[39] The liberal reaction to the French Revolution, however, is our chief concern. Germaine de Staël depicted in 1795 and again in 1816 the disastrous effect of the French Revolution on civil liberty, yet she always distinguished 1789 from 1792 and the Girondins from the Jacobins. She would have agreed with Charles de Rémusat, who declared later, "Liberal ideas are born in revolutions. It is almost always through revolutions that they are founded and that they prevail."[40]

In the middle of the nineteenth century, Prosper de Barante commented on Rousseau and popular sovereignty in terms that are remarkably similar to those of his friend Benjamin Constant. Barante claims that Rousseau saw no difficulty at all in having each person by contract abdicate his individual rights in favor of the community. He adds that popular sovereignty gives tyranny its most powerful arm. The government that exercises this sovereignty is not an abstract being but instead a man or several men, who are always animated by personal interests and moved by passions and subject to mistakes. Therefore, the doctrine of popular sovereignty results in our not taking sufficient precautions against the abuse of power, which is what makes it so dangerous to liberty. Barante then cites the controversy between Jacques Bossuet and Pierre Jurieu in the seventeenth century. The Catholic bishop accused the Huguenot pastor of asserting a right to do wrong, a right against justice, when

39. See Joseph de Maistre, "Etude sur la souveraineté," Book 2, chap. 6, pp. 385–86. Louis de Bonald presents a more detailed condemnation in "Essai analytique sur les lois naturelles de l'ordre social dans la société" (1800), *Oeuvres complètes de M. de Bonald*, 1:1018: "Après les détails dans lesquels nous venons d'entrer, il en coute à l'homme qui a quelque justesse dans les idées, de discuter l'opinion de la souveraineté du peuple, néant, c'est-à-dire, abstractions sans réalité, système où Dieu n'est pas, où l'homme seul est tout et, même les extrêmes, pouvoir et sujet, faux puis qu'il est impracticable de l'aveu même de ses défenseurs, et où l'on est toujours placé entre une conséquence et un blasphème. En effet, si l'on fait craindre aux apologistes de cette souveraineté que l'ignorance et les passions humaines n'égarent la faculté législative de l'homme ou du peuple ils vous répondent tantôt avec Jurieu. Que le peuple est la seule autorité qui n'avait pas besoin d'avoir raison pour valider ses actes, tantôt que le peuple est juste et bon et qu'il ne saurait failler, et par de là seul ils reconnaissent une justice et une bonté au dessus de peuple, puis qu'il y conforme ses pensées, et une règle antérieure au peuple, dont il ne peut s'écarter dans ses actions; et ils sont ainsi ramenés à la souveraineté de Dieu ... auteur nécessaire de tout ordre."
40. Prosper Duvergier de Hauranne, "M. Charles de Rémusat," p. 335.

Jurieu said that "there needs to be in a society a certain authority which does not need to be right to validate its acts and this authority is only in the people."[41] Barante concludes that there is no right in the people to do wrong, because all authority that does not offer guarantees of justice and reason is usurpation and tyranny.[42]

Saint-Marc Girardin attacked Rousseau as well as the "absolute power of the state and the sovereignty of the people" in his *Cours* given at the Sorbonne in 1848. In his presentation, he argues that "to the end of the seventeenth century the idea of the state was confused with royalty and the expression of Louis XIV 'L'état c'est moi' denoted this theory. With the eighteenth century the idea of the state began to be confused with the idea of the people, and the *Contrat Social* of Rousseau is the strongest expression of this new theory of the state."

Saint-Marc Girardin claims that

> in passing from the hands of royalty to the hands
> of the sovereignty of the people, the theory of the absolute
> state, far from becoming more modest and mild, became more
> haughty and imperious. When the absolute power was only
> the absolute power of the king, the theory had the prince in
> favor of it but it had the subjects against it, for our enemy is
> our master. When it was understood that the state represented
> the people, and that the sovereignty of the state proceeded
> from the people, the vanity of everybody was flattered,
> without thinking that in this theory one is hardly a sovereign
> for a part and a slave for all the rest. Just as the monarchy of

---

41. See my *The Political Theory of the Huguenots of the Dispersion*, pp. 67–68.

42. Prosper de Barante, *Questions constitutionnelles*, chap. 1, "De la souveraineté," pp. 1–17. Cf. Jean-Claude Clausel de Coussergues, *Considérations sur l'origine, la rédaction, la promulgation et l'exécution de la Charte*, pp. lxxviii–lxxix. This conservative argued that the king, in granting the Charte to France, repudiated the pernicious doctrine of popular sovereignty: "La dernière conséquence de cette doctrine est que la justice ne vient pas des lois éternelles établis par Dieu même, mais qu'elle n'est autre chose que la volonté du peuple; de sorte que (comme l'a exprimé formellement Jurieu, disciple de Buchanan, et après Jurieu, Rousseau et les encyclopédistes) le peuple est la seule autorité qui n'ait pas besoin d'avoir raison pour légitimer ses actes; principe monstreux repoussé par tous les philosophes de l'antiquité, et avec tant de force et d'éloquence, par Ciceron, etc."

Louis XIV was the apogee of the theory of the state identified with the monarchy the Convention and the Committee of Public Safety are the apogee of the sovereignty of the state proceeding from the sovereignty of the people. But there was no more individual liberty under the Convention and the Committee of Public Safety than there was under the monarchy of Louis XIV.

In the words of Jean Jacques Chevallier, "l'état c'est moi" of Louis XIV becomes "l'état c'est nous" of Rousseau.[43]

Returning to Rousseau, Saint-Marc Girardin referred to the great Swiss thinker's argument in Book 3, chapter 1, of the *Social Contract* that "the more the state is enlarged the more freedom is diminished." Rousseau wrote: "Suppose the state has for his own share only 1/10,000th part of the sovereign authority." But "if the people is increased to 100,000 men," then the subject's "share of the suffrage is reduced to 1/100,000th." But Saint-Marc Girardin asks, what is it to be only 1/35,000,000th part of the sovereignty in a state of thirty-five million souls?[44]

Francis Lieber in America examined the same problem of popular sovereignty employing his own peculiar terminology: "That which . . . must be pronounced to be Gallican liberty is . . . the idea of the universal sovereignty of the people." In fact, "liberty is believed in France . . . to consist in the absolute rule of the majority." Rousseau in his *Social Contract* "assigns all power to the majority and teaches what might be called a divine right of the majority." Furthermore, the "*Contrat Social* was the bible of the most advanced Convention men. Robespierre read it daily and the influence of that book can be traced throughout the Revolution. Indeed we may say that two books had a peculiar influence in the French Revolution; Rousseau's *Social Contract* and Plutarch's *Lives*."[45]

43. Jean Jacques Chevallier, *Les grandes oeuvres politiques de Machiavel à nos jours*, p. 153.
44. Saint-Marc Girardin, *Jean-Jacques Rousseau*, 2: chap. 15, "Le Contrat Social. Du pouvoir absolu de l'état et de la souveraineté du peuple," pp. 356–411, 358, 360, 364–65.
45. Francis Lieber, *Civil Liberty and Self Government*, 1:301. Lieber defined An-

John Stuart Mill also confronted the question of popular sovereignty, which he refuted in 1859:

> The notion that the people have no need to limit their power over themselves, might seem axiomatic when popular government was a thing only dreamed about and read as having existed at some distant period of the past. . . . In time, however, a democratic republic came to occupy a large portion of the earth's surface . . . it was now perceived that such phrases as "self-government" and the "power of the people over themselves" do not express the true state of the case. The people who exercise the power are not the same people with those over whom it is exercised; and the "self-government" spoken of is not the government of each by himself but of each by all the rest. The will of the most numerous or the most active . . . part of the people; the majority . . . the people consequently may desire to oppress a part of their number; and precautions are as much needed against this as against any other abuse of power. The limitation, therefore, of the power of government over individuals loses none of its import when the holders of power are regularly accountable to the community.[46]

Another English liberal of the nineteenth century, Lord Acton, also treated the theory of popular sovereignty. His method was to contrast what he called the "true and false democratic principles."

---

glican liberty as "the guarantee of those rights which experience has shown to be most exposed to the danger of attack by the strongest power in the state, namely, the executive."

46. Mill, *On Liberty*, chap. 1. Cf. Alexander Hamilton, *The Federalist* No. 84, who asserted that the people did not need to be protected against its own will: "They [bill of rights] have no application to constitutions professedly founded upon the power of the people, and executed by their immediate representatives and servants. . . . 'We, the People of the United States . . . do ordain and establish this Constitution of the United States of America'. Here is a better recognition of popular rights, than the volumes of those aphorisms which . . . sound better in a treatise of ethics than in a constitution of government." See also James Madison, *The Federalist* No. 51, who wrote that "a dependence on the people is, no doubt, the primary control on the government, but experience has taught mankind the necessity of auxiliary precautions."

First, "the true democratic principle that none shall have power over the people is taken to mean that none shall be able to restrain or elude its power." Second, "the true democratic principle that the people shall not be made to do what it does not like is taken to mean that it shall never be required to tolerate what it does not like." Third, "the true democratic principle that every man's will shall be as unfettered as possible is taken to mean that the free will of the collective people shall be fettered in nothing."[47]

In France, Edouard Laboulaye outlined his position in much the same vein as Constant and Mill, but, following his Swiss-French predecessor, he addressed himself to Rousseau, in particular: "The government of the *Contrat Social*, instead of being the government of each by himself as Rousseau believed, is in theory the government of each by all the others; in fact, it is the reign of a majority; the most often the rule of a turbulent and audacious minority. In this system the state is everything and the citizen, king but man, nothing."[48]

One other French liberal who had his doubts about popular sovereignty and Rousseau was Henri De Ferron, who was writing at the same time as Edouard Laboulaye. He claimed that the sovereignty of the people had two meanings—"the sovereignty of humanity, that is, the ensemble of generations past, present, and future or the sovereignty of the present generation" alone. But "the only absolute sovereignty that can be accepted, is that of all humanity." The proponents of popular sovereignty have always confused "material force" with "moral force," with the result, especially in Rousseau's theory, of despotism, both in "logic" and in "fact."[49]

Two of Constant's contemporaries, however, the Doctrinaires Pierre Paul Royer-Collard and François Guizot, developed the most ingenious refutation of the theory of popular sovereignty. They

47. John Emerich Acton, *The History of Freedom and Other Essays*, pp. 93–94.

48. Edouard Laboulaye, *L'état et ses limites*, p. 38. Cf. the conservative thinker, Hippolyte-Adolphe Taine, in *The Ancient Regime*, p. 246: "In the place of the sovereignty of the king the *Contrat Social* substitutes the sovereignty of the people. The latter, however, is much more absolute than the former and in the democratic convent (layman's monastery) which Rousseau constructs on the Spartan and Roman model, the individual is nothing and the State is everything."

49. Henri De Ferron, *Théorie du Progrès*, 1:247–48.

both thought that this concept personified the revolutionary rather than the liberal spirit. In fact, Royer-Collard goes so far as to maintain that "as soon as there is sovereignty, there is despotism, whether vested in king, people, or parliament." It is no wonder that the conclusion has been drawn that "there is no sovereignty is the underlying principle of Royer-Collard's whole political theory."[50]

In a *Discours* on electoral reform (17 May 1820), Royer-Collard contended that the "difference between the sovereignty of the people and the sovereignty of free governments is that in the first there are only persons and wills; in the other there are only rights and interests."[51] In another address on the electoral law, he maintained that "there is nothing more difficult than to be liberated from the sovereignty of the people" because "it rests in the minds of most of those who combat it." In the last analysis, however, "privilege, absolute power, popular sovereignty, they are under different forms ... the empire of force on earth." Therefore, to Royer-Collard, "there are two elements in society: the one material, which is the individual, his force and will; the other moral, which is right resulting from legitimate interests." In developing his argument, Royer-Collard puts this question: "Do you want to make society with the material element?" Then, "the majority of individuals, the majority of wills ... is the sovereign" and "there is popular sovereignty." But, he asks, "Do you want, on the contrary, to make society with the moral element which is rights (law)?" Then, "the sovereign is justice because it is the rule of rights (law). Free constitutions have for their aim the dethronement of force and the reign of justice. Choose then your sovereign. It is force, if your government represents persons; it is justice, if it represents rights and interests."[52]

Royer-Collard thought that as long as the idea of sovereignty is retained, the problem of limiting the power of the state by law becomes insoluble. How those holding power can legitimately impose their wills by force and to what extent they are to be permitted to do so was discussed by him in a famous speech (4 October 1831)

---

50. Emile Faguet, *Politiques et moralistes du dix-neuvième siècle*, p. 260.

51. Prosper de Barante, *La vie politique de Royer-Collard, ses discours et ses écrits*, 2:18. For English translations in part see Léon Duguit, "The Law and the State," pp. 1–185. Quotations below are from Duguit.

52. Barante, *Vie politique de Royer-Collard*, 2:32–33.

on the occasion of the suppression of the heredity of the peerage, which was regarded as inconsistent with the principle of national sovereignty:

> Yes, nations are sovereign in the sense that they are
> not possessed like territories but belong to themselves and
> have in themselves by virtue of their own natural right, the
> means of providing for their own conservation and their own
> salvation. They are sovereign also in the sense that general
> consent is the only true basis of governments, which, therefore,
> exist through nations and for nations. But these incontestable
> truths are rather maxims of morals than principles of gov-
> ernment; they rather express the divine sovereignty of reason
> and justice than this human and practical sovereignty
> that makes laws and administers states.

Continuing to elaborate on his thesis, Royer-Collard then asks: "Is it the majority of individuals, the majority of wills ... that is sovereign?" He replies: "If that be so ... the sovereignty of the people is only a sovereignty of force and the most absolute form of power. Before such a sovereign unguided by rule and unlimited in power, without duty and without conscience, there is no constitu-tion, no law. . . . But force is not destined in this manner to exercise a veritable sovereignty on earth. Force constrains, it does not oblige. To oblige is the attribute of quite another sovereignty."

On what conditions and to what extent can the will of those who govern be imposed on those who are ruled? Royer-Collard's answer is clear: "When such will manifests itself in conformity to law; when it has for its object the protection of the legitimate interests, which have their origin in law." Properly understood, "societies are not numerical assemblies of individuals and wills. They have another element than numbers; they have a stronger bond—law, the privileges of humanity, and the legitimate interests which spring from law. Law does not spring from force, but from justice; societies are formed for the purpose of dethroning force and setting up justice in its place." Furthermore, the division of all "society into rights and interests" instead of "individuals and wills, is ... the reason for and the sanction of representative government."

Royer-Collard thus appealed from "the sovereignty of the people to another sovereignty, the only one which merits the name, a sovereignty superior to people and to kings, immutable and eternal sovereignty like its author ... the sovereignty of reason, the only true legislator of humanity," which takes the form of natural law, known to man because he is a rational being.[53]

Royer-Collard's ideas appear again in a "diffused state in the writings ... of François Guizot," who said that he distinguished two kinds of government.[54] "First, there are those who attribute sovereignty as a right belonging exclusively to individuals, whether one, many, or all those composing a society; and these are, in principle, the founders of despotism. ... The second class of governments is founded on the truth that sovereignty belongs as a right to no individual whatever, since the perfect and continued apprehension, the fixed and inviolable application of justice and reason do not belong to our imperfect nature."

Guizot is particularly concerned with representative government, which he approached as follows:

> The plurality is society; the unity is truth; it is the united force of the laws of justice and reason, which ought to govern society. If society remains in the condition of plurality; if isolated wills do not combine under the guidance of common rules; if they do not all equally recognize justice and reason; if they do not reduce themselves to unity, there is not a society, there is only confusion. And the unity which does not rise from plurality, which has been violently imposed upon it by one or many, whatever be their number, in virtue of a prerogative

53. Ibid., 2:459. Cf. ibid., 1:298, where Royer-Collard speaks of "des principes de la Charte qui sont les principes éternels de la raison et de la justice." Cf. Barante, *Mélanges historiques et littéraires*, 3:20: "Dès qu'une volonté peut prévaloir contre la justice il y a despotisme. ... Rois, sénats, assemblées, peuples, tous sont coupables d'usurpation, dès qu'ils prétendent supérieure à la justice."

54. See Duguit, "The Law and the State," p. 169. It is interesting to note that José Ortega y Gasset in *La révolte des masses*, p. 23, thought that Royer-Collard and Guizot "ont forgé la doctrine politique le plus estimable de tout le siècle."

which they appropriate as their exclusive possession, is a false and arbitrary unity; it is tyranny. The aim of representative government is to oppose a barrier at once to tyranny and to confusion and to bring plurality to unity.[55]

It is obvious that Royer-Collard, Guizot, and Constant were all seeking a point of equilibrium or a *juste milieu* between the evils of autocratic power, on the one hand, and the abuses of the multitude, on the other. All three wished to show that there is no sovereignty without limit. But the Doctrinaires, like Royer-Collard and Guizot, stressed reason and justice, especially when they were delineating the bounds of supreme power. They tried, then, not so much to determine the object of power and the manner of its exercise as to find the rule it must obey. The legislator thus does not create law but discovers it. But, it might be asked, is it easier to secure obedience to a superior law of justice and reason or to a law of competence? To the Doctrinaires, government has an absolute competence as long as it uses it within the confines of the moral law.

It will be recalled that Constant placed first the question of competence: "There are objects over which the legislator does not have the right to make a law." He also spoke of the limits of sovereignty as being "laid out by justice and the rights of individuals." This recognition of rights involves a juridical limitation. The Doctrinaires, however, had no faith in the a priori natural rights of individuals. As Royer-Collard put it, "No will, whether of man over man, of society over the individual, of the individual over society, can be exercised against justice and reason," a formula which implies the legitimacy of every action of society over the individual

55. François Guizot, *History of the Origin of Representative Government in Europe*, 55–64. See also his *Democracy and Its Mission*, p. 39. Cf. his *Du gouvernement de la France depuis la Restauration et du ministère actuel*, p. 201: "Je ne crois ni au droit divin ni a la souveraineté du peuple, comme on les entend presque toujours. Je ne puis voir là que les usurpations de la force. Je crois à la souveraineté de la raison, de la justice, du droit: c'est là le souverain légitime que cherche le monde et qu'il cherchera toujours; car la raison, la vérité, la justice ne résident nulle part complètes et infaillibles. Nul homme, nulle réunion d'hommes ne les possède et ne peut les posséder sans lacune et sans limite. Les meilleures formes de gouvernement sont celles qui nous placent plus sûrement et nous font plus rapidement avancer sous l'empire de leur loi sainte. C'est la vertu du gouvernement représentatif."

conforming to reason. The Doctrinaires were, therefore, "more moral than liberal."[56]

Royer-Collard, earlier than Tocqueville, was not only interested in the theory of popular sovereignty but also in the political and social implications of the destruction of the *ancien régime*.[57] The French Revolution had changed the whole social order from one of hierarchy to one of equality.[58] In fact, to Lord Acton, the abolition of the intermediate powers characterized the Great Revolution even more than the circumscription of government authority.[59] Royer-Collard was one of the first to face the question whether liberty could exist in a society polarized around the individual and the state. In short, he wondered whether liberty could ever be reconciled with a pulverized, atomized society that was no longer sustained by communal values.[60]

Royer-Collard discussed this matter while considering liberty of the press in 1820.

56. M. Berthould, "Deux individualistes," pp. 172–209.

57. See Prosper de Barante, "Réflexions sur les oeuvres politiques de Jean-Jacques Rousseau," p. 301: "Dès les premiers moments de la Révolution, il sembla qu'un vaste et ardente opinion, plus democratique que libérale, désirait et espérait, non pas des libertés et des garanties, mais bien plutôt la formation d'une société nouvelle. Elle voulait avant tout la disparition de l'aristocratie nobiliaire; il lui fallait proclamer que le Tiers Etat, c'était la nation."

58. Barante, *Vie politique de Royer-Collard*, 2:17: "La pairie seul excepté, une société nouvelle est instituée sur la base de l'égalité. La liberté française, toutes nos libertés, même la liberté de conscience, c'est l'égalité."

59. See George H. Sabine, "The Two Democratic Traditions," pp. 451–74, and R. R. Palmer, "Man and Citizen." André de Chénier, during the French Revolution, had asserted: "Unwise and unhappy is the state where there exist various associations—collective bodies whose members on entering into them acquire a different spirit and different interests from the general spirit and the general interest. Happy is the land where there is no form of association but the state, no collective body but the country, no interest but the general good." Note the Loi le Chapelier (14–17 June 1791) abolishing trade guilds and all professional societies. "There are no longer any guilds in the state but only private interests of each individual and the general interest. No one may arouse in the citizen any intermediate interest or separate them from the public welfare by corporate sentiment." Rousseau's dislike of "partial associations" within the state was now translated into legislative action.

60. See Prosper de Barante, *Des communes et de l'aristocratie*, pp. 127–28: "Si les individus d'une nation restent isolés les un; ils seront sans défense contre l'usurpation de leurs droits; mais si par leur consentement implicite ou explicite, il se forme une élite de citoyens éclairés et indépendants en qui se concentrent la force et l'opinion nationale, alors les choses publiques se passent dans le sein de cette nation restreinte et choisie, l'autorité y trouvera résistance contre les abus, protection contre les désordres."

We have seen the old society perish and with it that
crowd of domestic institutions and independent magistrates,
powerful bundles of private rights, true republics in the
monarchy. These institutions, these magistracies did not share
. . . the sovereignty; but they provided [opposed] everywhere
limits to it. Not one survived and none has risen in its [their]
place. The revolution has left standing only individuals. . . .
From pulverized society has arisen centralization. . . . Where
there are only individuals, all the affairs which are not their
own are public affairs, the affairs of state. Where there are no
independent magistrates, there are only delegates of power. It
is thus that we have become a people *d'administrés*, under the
hand of irresponsible functionaries, centralized themselves in
the power of which they are the ministers. The Charte
constituted the government by the division of sovereignty and
the multiplicity of powers. But it is not sufficient, that in order
that a nation be free, that it be governed by several powers,
whatever their nature and origin. The division of sovereignty is
without doubt an important fact . . . but the government
which results, although divided in its elements, is one in its
action; and if it does not meet outside a barrier that it must
respect . . . it is absolute; the nation and its rights are
its property . . . it is the avowed doctrine of despotism and
revolution, since it implies that there are no fundamental
laws or national rights.[61]

What had happened, according to Royer-Collard, was simply
this: "In the place of a single despotism we have a multiple despotism; parliamentary omnipotence after the omnipotence of one.[62]
In the case of the one as in the other, society deprived of institutions, would be without a defense." Therefore, "it was only in
founding the liberty of the press as a public right that the Charte
has truly founded all liberties. . . . It is true that liberty of the press

61. Barante, *Vie politique de Royer-Collard*, 2:131.
62. Cf. Herbert Spencer, *Man versus the State*, p. 183: "The function of Liberalism
in the past was that of putting a limit to the power of kings. The function of true
Liberalism will be that of putting a limit to the powers of Parliament."

has the character and energy of a political institution; it is true that this institution is the only one which has restored to society some rights against the powers which rule it." Elaborating on its importance, Royer-Collard stated that "liberty of the press has this double character of a political institution and a social necessity. Publicity is a kind of resistance to the established powers because it denounces their faults and errors and is capable of causing truth and justice to triumph against them. ... Publicity is an institution; a public liberty; for public liberties are only resistances."[63]

Royer-Collard then observed that "the voice of aristocratic command is no longer heard among us. A little conventional aristocracy, indulgent fiction of the law, but no more true aristocracy. ... Equality of rights (this is the true name of democracy) it is the universal form of society and it is thus that democracy is everywhere."[64] Furthermore, only two guarantees have been given to rights—representative government and freedom of the press. It can be seen at once that Tocqueville was not the first to note that the inevitable tendency was in the direction of democracy, defined as equality of condition.

The most famous and influential opponent of *un nouvel arbitraire*, that is, popular sovereignty, was, of course, Alexis de Tocqueville. In his judgment, "The last generation in France showed how a people might organize a stupendous tyranny in the community at the very time when they were baffling the authority of the nobility and braving the power of kings."[65] In other words, "in the French Revolution there were two impulses in opposite directions, which

63. Barante, *Vie politique de Royer-Collard*, 2:130.
64. Ibid., pp. 137, 133–34. On 22 January 1822, Royer-Collard quoted M. de Serre, who, presenting a law "sur la répression des délits de la presse," said: "La démocratie chez nous ... est partout pleine de sève et d'énergie; elle est dans l'industrie, dans la propriété, dans les lois. ... Le torrent coule à pleins bords dans de faibles digues qui le contiennent à peine." Royer-Collard replied: "A mon tours, prenant, comme je le dois, la démocratie dans une acception purement politique, et comme opposée ou seulement comparée à l'aristocratie, je conviens que la démocratie coule à pleins bords dans la France, telle que les siècles et les événements l'ont faite ... pour moi, je rends grace à la Providence de ce qu'elle a appelé aux bienfaits de la civilisation un plus grand nombre de ses créatures," which is a point to be made by Tocqueville.
65. Tocqueville, *Democracy in America*, 2:314.

must never be confounded; the one was favorable to liberty [constitutionalism], the other to despotism [popular sovereignty]."[66]

Tocqueville was especially concerned with the fact that the "democratic nations are menaced" by a "species of oppression . . . unlike anything that . . . ever before existed in the world and which cannot be described by such old words as 'despotism' and 'tyranny.'" By this he meant in part that "our contemporaries . . . devise a sole, tutelary, and all powerful government but elected by the people. They combine the principle of centralization and that of popular sovereignty; this gives them a respite; they console themselves for being in tutelage by the reflection that they have chosen their own guardians. Every man allows himself to be put in leading strings, because he sees that it is not a person or a class of persons but the people at large who hold the end of the chain."[67] Tocqueville said that he was astonished that "a great many persons at the present day are quite contented with this sort of compromise between administrative despotism and the sovereignty of the people" and "they think that they have done enough for the protection of individual freedom when they have surrendered it to the power of the nation at large. But this does not satisfy me: the nature of him I am to obey signifies less to me than the fact of extorted obedience."[68]

Tocqueville develops this same theme in many different ways. Two more examples are worth citing. First, "When I feel the hand of power lie heavy on my brow, I care but little to know who oppresses me; and I am not the more disposed to pass beneath the yoke, because it is held out to me by the arms of a million men."[69] Second, "Men do not change their characters by uniting with one another. . . . I cannot believe it; the power to do everything, which I would refuse to one of my equals, I will never grant to any number of them." This is because "unlimited power is in itself a bad and dangerous thing. . . . When I see that the right and the means of absolute command are conferred on any power whatever, be it

66. Ibid., 1:96.
67. Ibid., 2:319.
68. Ibid., pp. 319–20.
69. Ibid., p. 12.

called a people or a king, an aristocracy or a democracy, a monarchy or a republic, I say there is the germ of tyranny. And I seek to live elsewhere under other laws."[70]

Like Constant, but unlike the Doctrinaires, Tocqueville recognized the existence of sovereignty. "I am, therefore, of the opinion," he wrote, "that social power superior to all others must be placed somewhere" and "have asserted that all authority originates in the will of the majority."[71] He qualified his statement about sovereignty: "I hold it to be an impious and detestable maxim that politically speaking, the people have a right to do anything. . . . A general law which bears the name of justice, has been made and sanctioned, not only by a majority of this or that people, but by a majority of mankind. The rights of every people are therefore confined within the limits of what is just. . . . " Therefore, "when I refuse to obey an unjust law, I do not contest the right of a majority to command, but I simply appeal from the sovereignty of the people to the sovereignty of mankind."[72] Tocqueville concluded that the "power of the majority itself is not unlimited" because "above it in the moral world are humanity, justice, and reason and in the political world, vested rights."[73]

The striking similarity between the political ideas of Constant and Tocqueville is very pronounced not only in their treatment of popular sovereignty but also of liberty, which rested in both cases on religion as well as law. Tocqueville conceived of liberty as "the joy of being able to speak, to act, and to breathe without restraint under no sovereign but God and the law."[74] He always said that he wanted "a balanced regulated liberty held in check by religion, custom, and law."[75] He thought that this made him "a liberal of a

70. Ibid., 1:259–60 and 227. "Nothing is so irresistible as a tyrannical power commanding in the name of the people."
71. Ibid., p. 259.
72. Ibid. Tocqueville also said that the "maxim that everything is permissible for the interests of society" is "an impious adage which seems to have been invented in an age of freedom to shelter all future tyrants" (ibid., p. 305).
73. Ibid., p. 416.
74. Alexis de Tocqueville, *Oeuvres complètes*, 2:pt. 2, 344.
75. Alexis de Tocqueville, *Recollections*, p. 72.

new kind," and he said that he sought "a liberal but not a revolutionary party."[76]

From Mounier to Tocqueville, then, the liberal political theorists kept trying, especially in France, to find "a medium between sovereignty of all and the absolute power of one man."[77] Constant and Tocqueville both tended, however, to minimize the despotism of the divine right of kings, which looked to the past, in order to concentrate on the new enemy of individual liberty—popular and national sovereignty—which looked to the future. Although both Constant and Tocqueville distinguished between liberty and popular sovereignty, the latter did not try to oppose the two, whereas the former did just that, faced as he was with Jacobinism and the Terror. Instead, Tocqueville thought that, although "liberty is more difficult to found and maintain in democratic societies . . . like our own, than in certain aristocratic societies which had preceded them," still it is not impossible.[78] He realized that aristocratic liberty with privileges for the few had been replaced by democratic liberty with rights for all, just as the inequality of orders and estates had been supplanted by equality of conditions. As we shall see shortly, although Constant was aware of these changes when he evolved his theory of constitutionalism and pluralism, it was left to Tocqueville to formulate a complete theory of liberal democracy in the sense of both a constitutional and a pluralistic regime.

76. Letter to Royer-Collard (25 Sept. 1841) in Léon De Lanzac de Laborie, "L'amitié de Alexis de Tocqueville et Royer-Collard," p. 907.

77. Tocqueville, *Democracy in America*, 1:53.

78. Tocqueville, *Oeuvres complètes*, 9:280, "Correspondance d'Alexis de Tocqueville et d'Arthur de Gobineau."

Chapter IV
Constitutionalism

ON 4 JUNE 1814, a constitution—the Charte—was granted to France by the restored Bourbon king, Louis XVIII, which, to Constant, avoided both "the tyranny of the Revolution and the despotism of Louis XIV."[1] Moreover, according to Chateaubriand in *De Bonaparte et des Bourbons*, a limited monarchy was the only viable alternative for France after her unfortunate experience with a republic and a dictatorship (Bonaparte).

Following the Charte, Restoration France was to have a constitutional (representative) government, but it left unresolved whether it was to have a parliamentary government in which the ministers would be politically responsible to the Chamber of Deputies in the sense that the life of the cabinet depended on majority support. The Charte provided for the irresponsibility of the king and the royal authority to dissolve the Chamber of Deputies. The monarch had the power to choose his ministers, but the question was left undecided whether he was bound to select them from the ranks of the majority. The ministers could be "accused only for acts of treason and peculation."[2] In other words, the responsibility provided for in the Charte was penal rather than political. Furthermore, there was nothing that required ministers in the minority to retire from office.

At the time, a parliamentary regime did not really exist in England either. In the first half of the eighteenth century, the British cabinet was not always composed of members of the majority party,

---

1. "Des élections prochaines," *Cours de politique*, 2:319.
2. Cf. the Acte Additionnel, where it was provided that "any ministers . . . can be accused by the Chamber of Representatives and tried by the Chamber of Peers for having compromised the safety and honor of the nation" (Frank M. Anderson, *The Constitutions and Other Select Documents Illustrative of the History of France, 1789–1901*, p. 477).

and the exact functions of the prime minister did not become clear until the end of the century. In addition, until 1830, the ministry did not always resign because its legislative or even financial measures presented to the House of Commons were rejected. It was necessary to have an express vote of censure of the ministry, and even then the king could dissolve the House of Commons. Lord North, for example, retired in 1782 after a vote of censure in the House. In fact, at the end of the eighteenth and at the beginning of the nineteenth century the responsibility of English ministers was still penal rather than political. Moreover, the Commons could not impose upon the king either the choice or the removal of ministers; the law provided only for their impeachment. Furthermore, the king was still very powerful in matters of policy, and the unreformed House before 1832 was hardly representative of the English people.

The parliamentary system in England had not been noticed by Montesquieu in 1748, by Blackstone in 1765, or by de Lolme in 1771. Although the cabinet system was evolving in the period of Sir Robert Walpole's Whig ascendancy (1721–42), it was not obvious to Montesquieu or to Constant, as we shall see, that the cabinet constituted, in the words of Walter Bagehot, "a hyphen which joins a buckle, which fastens the legislative part of the state to the executive part of the state."[3]

In France, the constitutions of 1791 and 1795 were based on the theory of the separation of powers. Of the revolutionary writers, Mirabeau the younger alone came nearest to comprehending a form of parliamentary government. During the years 1814–48, the idea of mixed government evolved into parliamentary government. As M. J. C. Vile writes, "Royer-Collard and Guizot developed a theory of constitutional monarchy which was suited to the period 1814–1830, whilst Constant went further and formulated a theory closely related to the regime established by the Revolution of 1830."[4] Constant's exposition of the theory is to be found in three principal works—*Réflexions sur les constitutions* (May 1814); *De la responsabilité des ministres* (February 1815), which concerned the

3. Walter Bagehot, *The English Constitution*, p. 15.
4. M. J. C. Vile, *Constitutionalism and the Separation of Powers*, p. 202.

Charte; and *Principes de politique* (May 1815), which involved the Acte Additionnel aux Constitutions de l'Empire, drafted by Constant and, therefore, known as "la Benjamine."[5]

Constant began his analysis by stating that he had identified five powers in a constitutional monarchy, whereas previously only three powers—legislative, executive, and judicial—had been distinguished by such a theorist as Montesquieu. The powers noted by Constant are the royal power, the executive power, the power that represents permanence (that is, the hereditary assembly), the power that represents opinion (that is, the elective assembly), and the judicial power. The principal distinction that Constant drew was between the executive power of the ministers and the royal power of the crown, something he defined as a "neutral power"[6] or as the "judicial power of the other powers."[7] He gave credit to Stanislas de Clermont-Tonnerre, twice president of the Constituent Assembly of 1789, for first making the important differentiation. But Constant said that he also discovered this distinction in the English constitution, in fact, if not in law.[8]

For example, in England laws are made with the consent of the Lords and Commons, executive acts are countersigned by a minister, and judgments are delivered by independent courts of law. "But notice how the English constitution uses the royal power to bring an end to every dangerous struggle and to reestablish harmony among the powers.[9] When the action of the executive power is

5. F. B. Boyer-Fonfrède developed many of the same ideas as Constant about the difference between an absolute and a constitutional monarchy in *Des avantages d'une constitution libérale* (1814). See also the Baron de Vitrolles, *Du ministère dans le gouvernement représentatif* (1815), and Chateaubriand, *De la monarchie selon la Charte* (1816).

6. "Principes de politique," *Cours de politique*, 1:19.

7. "Réflexions sur les constitutions," ibid., p. 179. See also Jean Charles Simonde de Sismondi, "De l'équilibre et de l'harmonie entre les pouvoirs dans la constitution," *Le moniteur*, 8 May 1815, and *Examen de la constitution française*.

8. "Il y a, dit-il, dans le pouvoir monarchique deux pouvoirs distincts, le pouvoir exécutif, investi de prérogatives positives et le pouvoir royal, qui est soutenu par des souvenirs et par des traditions religieuses" ("Réflexions sur les constitutions," p. 176). In his "Souvenirs historiques à l'occasion de l'ouvrage de M. Bignon," p. 120, Constant recalled that "Sieyès a contribué, plus que personne, à poser les bases de la monarchie constitutionnelle. Il a le premier, en France, établi et prouvé que le chef, placé au haut de la hiérarchie politique, devait choisir, mais non gouverner. Son grand-électeur . . . est le type exact et utile d'un roi tel qu'on doit le désirer."

9. "Je dois remarquer que c'est plutôt au fait que de droit que la constitution

dangerous, the king dismisses the ministers. If the action of the elective chamber is menacing, the king uses his veto power or he dissolves the elective chamber. If the action of the judicial power is vexatious, should it apply to individuals general penalties which are too harsh, the king can temper this action by the right of the pardon."[10] Last, if the action of the hereditary chamber is noxious, the king can give a new direction by creating new peers.

Constant states next that the defect of a constitution is not only to be found in the absence of this neutral power but also in the location of all authority in one of the active powers. If one of the three active powers were to exercise the function of stabilization, it would become the superior of the other two. When this authority, for example, is placed in the legislative power, the result is an arbitrary legislature, like the Long Parliament in England or the Convention in France.[11] When this authority is located in the executive, despotism and dictatorship follow, as in Rome. The neutral power belongs then to the crown. It can be seen at once that in many ways Constant's conception is close to the English prerogative, which was defined later in classic terms as "the residue of discretionary or arbitrary authority which at any time is legally left in the hands of the Crown."[12]

The role of a hereditary monarch as an irresponsible but neutral power was understood in America by James Madison and John Adams in 1787. The former asserted that

> the great desideratum in government is such a modification of the sovereignty as will render it sufficiently neutral between the different interests and factions to control one part

anglaise établit la neutralité du pouvoir royal. . . . Aussi y a-t-il dans la constitution quelques prérogatives royales incompatibles avec cette neutralité" ("Réflexions sur les constitutions," p. 177).

10. "Les trois pouvoirs, tels qu'on les a connus jusqu'ici, le pouvoir exécutif, législatif et judiciaire, sont trois ressorts qui doivent coopérer, chacun dans sa partie, au mouvement général, mais quand ces ressorts dérangés se choquent, s'entre-croissent ou s'entravent, il faut une force neutre, en quelque sorte, qui les remettre à leur place" (ibid., p. 176).

11. "Principes de politique," *Cours de politique*, 1:20.

12. Albert V. Dicey, *Introduction to the Study of the Law of the Constitution*, p. 420.

of the society from invading the rights of another and at the same time sufficiently controlled itself, from setting up an interest adverse to that of the whole society. In absolute monarchies the prince is sufficiently neutral toward his subjects but frequently sacrifices their happiness to his ambition or his avarice.

The latter states that "all nations, under all governments, must have parties; the greatest secret is to control them. There are but two ways, either by a monarchy and standing army or by a balance in the constitution."[13] Both Madison and Adams, however, were thinking of absolute monarchies rather than of constitutional or limited ones, where the royal and ministerial powers are distinguished. If these two powers are confused, then Constant thought that the dismissal and the responsibility of the executive power is impossible.

Constant was really thinking of the neutral power of the king in terms of the modern English sovereign, who assumes active responsibility only in times of political or constitutional crisis. According to Vile,

> The work of Constant represents in fact a crucial turning-point in institutional theory, a turning away from the old doctrines of mixed government to a "new modern" theory of constitutional monarchy in which the monarch assumes a new and completely different role from that assigned to him in the "old" balanced constitution. . . . The king was no longer an equal and active branch of the legislature vested with executive power, but a constitutional monarch, above politics, and separated from legislature and executive alike.[14]

Constant also believed that to leave no alternative to ministers except either to continue in power or to go to the scaffold was a

13. James Madison, "Vices of the Political System of the United States," and John Adams, *A Defense of the Constitutions of Government of the United States of America.* See also Carl J. Friedrich, *Constitutional Government and Democracy,* pp. 184 and 619, n. 15.

14. Vile, *Constitutionalism,* pp. 204–5.

vice in any constitution. He shows that "there is between the dismissal of the executive power and its punishment, the same difference as between the dissolution of representative assemblies and the accusation of their members. . . . The representatives after the dissolution of the assembly and the ministers after their dismissal enter into the class of other citizens." The executive, then, can be removed by the king without being persecuted or punished. Changing the government by the dismissal of ministers is compared to the dissolution of parliament. The neutral power then is "preserving and repairing without being hostile to the others."[15]

Constant answered the objection that in England the royal power was not always separated from the ministerial power. The example cited was when the king prevented the emancipation of his Catholic subjects, thereby demonstrating the triumph of his personal will over that of his ministers. But Constant countered that "two things are confused, the right to maintain what exists, a right which belongs to the royal power . . . a neutral and preserving authority, and the right to propose the establishment of something which does not exist, a right which belongs to the ministerial power."[16] Thus in England it was only a question of what existed because the laws against Catholics were already on the books. Constant concluded that because "institutions depend more on the times than on men, the direct action of the monarch is inevitably weakening due to the progress of civilization."[17]

Constant's scheme was very clever. "It took the authoritarian sting out of the monarchial principle, while restoring to it, after the humiliations of the revolution . . . the dignity and self-respect of an institution not only useful but essential to the state."[18] He shows that kings still have great prerogatives, such as the right to pardon, to create peers, to choose ministers, to veto, and to dissolve parliament. Furthermore, Constant saw clearly that the power of dissolution is more efficacious than the power of veto, which had not been exercised in England since the reign of Queen Anne. The dissolution

15. Constant, "Principes de politiques," p. 22.
16. Ibid., p. 26.
17. Ibid., p. 28.
18. Karl Loewenstein, *Political Reconstruction*, pp. 178–80.

of the assemblies is not an attack on the rights of the people, but in a system of free elections it is an "appeal to its rights in favor of its interests." In fact, without this right, the inviolability of representative assemblies cannot be preserved.

William A. Dunning explains, "While the old defenders of the monarchy saw in the distinction between king and ministry or royal and executive power a purpose of reducing the monarchy to a nullity, Constant made it a means of elevating the monarch to a great position in the government."[19] Parliamentary monarchy unites the advantages of a republic and a monarchy.[20] Constant's conception of the monarchy as a neutral power "streamlined the entire institution to fit modern democracy." Moreover, "it fitted modernized monarchy into the concept of the sovereignty of the people."[21]

As we have already noted, however, the tendency of Constant's theory was to put the control of the ministry entirely in the hands of the king, who had complete discretion in its choice. The key question was whether the king was obliged to dismiss ministers who were unacceptable to the Chamber. This, of course, involves the whole problem of ministerial responsibility, about which Constant wrote: "Illegal or arbitrary acts, of which ministers may be guilty, are comprised in responsibility. These acts are private misdemeanors and must be judged by the same tribunals and the same forms as the misdemeanors of other individuals. Responsibility only extends to the bad use of a legal power."

Constant then outlines his conception of the nature of this responsibility: "Thus, an unjust or ill-managed war, a treaty of peace making unnecessary sacrifices, bad financial operations, the introduction of dangerous and defective practices in the administration of justice; indeed every application of power, which, although authorized by the law, would be fatal to the nation or vexatious to the citizen, without being demanded by the public interest, such are the objects to which responsibility extends."

From this enumeration, he thought, "how deceptive will be every

19. William A. Dunning, *A History of Political Theories from Rousseau to Spencer*, pp. 261–62.
20. Even Montesquieu had described England as "a republic, disguised under the form of monarchy" (*The Spirit of the Laws*, Book 5, chap. 19, p. 68).
21. Loewenstein, *Political Reconstruction*, pp. 178–80.

attempt to draw upon the responsibility a precise and definite law" because "there are a thousand methods of undertaking a war unjustly or without necessity, of directing the war, when undertaken with too much rashness or indolence." Turning then to his British model, Constant demonstrates how "the English . . . denote the acts which expose ministers to responsibility, by the very vague terms of high crimes and misdemeanors; words which designate neither the degree nor the nature of the crime." Therefore, "if we preserve in our constitutional charter the authorized terms of malversation and treason, it will indispensable to give them the most enlarged sense. It must be established that a minister betrays the state whenever he exerts his legal authority to its injury."[22]

Continuing to cite England, Constant argues:

> In assuming as an axiom, that the law on responsibility
> cannot be defined like common law, that it is a political law,
> of which the nature and the agency inevitably have something
> discretionary about it, I do not consider myself the upholder of
> arbitrary power, because I have in my favor, as I have said, the
> example of the English; and because for 134 years, not only
> has liberty existed without commotion, but very few of their
> ministers, though exposed to an infinite responsibility, and
> perpetually denounced by the opposition, have undergone
> investigation and none has been punished.[23]

These citations indicate how Constant reacted against Article 56 of the Charte, which reads that "ministers can be accused [impeached] only for acts of treason and peculation." He constantly pointed out the difficulty of specifying in the text ministerial crimes in this way. He enlarged, therefore, penal responsibility into a poli-

---

22. Constant, "On the Responsibility of Ministers," pp. 302–29: "It [the Charte] purports that ministers cannot be accused by the Chamber of Deputies unless for treason or malversation. In fact, treason includes the mismanagement of war, of foreign negotiations, the introduction of a system of judicial forms baneful to the independence of judges or juries and all other public measures inimical to the state; and malversation which implies the abuse of public funds; these are the only two crimes within the scope of responsibility."

23. Ibid.

tical one or, to put it another way, he prepared the ground as a transitional figure for political responsibility.

Turning from the Charte to the Acte Additionnel, Constant reacted to Article 41 of the latter, which provided that any minister could be accused and tried for "having compromised the safety and honor of the nation." He concluded: "Our constitution is, then, eminently wise, when it accords to our representatives the greatest latitude in their accusations, and when it confers a discretionary power on the tribunal [Chamber of Peers], which must pronounce sentence." He repeats what he had said in connection with the Charte:

> There are a thousand ways of undertaking a war unjustly or ineffectually. . . . A minister can do so much wrong without violating the letter of any positive law. If you do not prepare constitutional means to punish this wrong or remove the guilty minister—for it is much more a question of removing the power of the prevaricating ministers than punishing them— then necessity will find these means outside the constitution. The result is that ministers will be denounced often, sometimes accused, condemned rarely, punished almost never.

The objectives of ministerial responsibility are two, according to Constant: "that of taking away the power from the guilty ministers and that of developing in the nation by the vigilance of its representatives, by the publicity of their debates, and the exercise of the freedom of the press applying to the analysis of all ministerial acts, a spirit of examination, an habitual interest in maintaining the constitution of the state" through "an animated sentiment of public life."[24]

It would seem, then, that the penal responsibility of ministers would function in almost the same manner as political responsibility, which is not mentioned in the Acte Additionnel. According to Constant, governing against the will of the nation represented by the Chamber of Deputies, was considered as "compromising the

24. "Principes de politique," p. 83.

safety and honor of the nation." This is, of course, really political responsibility in penal form.

Constant entitled one of the chapters of his essay *On the Responsibility of Ministers*, "On the Declaration that Ministers Are Unworthy of the Public Confidence." There he made the observation that "it was proposed to substitute some proceeding, milder in appearance than a formal accusation, whenever the bad administration of ministers should have endangered the safety of the state, the dignity of the crown, or the liberty of the people, without, however, having directly trespassed on any positive law. It was proposed to lodge a power in the representative assemblies of declaring ministers unworthy of public confidence."[25]

Constant's comments on this proposal are very important. He begins by saying that "this declaration against ministers is virtually understood whenever they lose the majority in those assemblies. When we shall have, what as yet we have not, but which is indispensable to a constitutional monarchy, I mean a confederated ministry, a firm majority, and an opposition unconnected with that majority," then, "no minister can maintain his place without the majority, unless he appeals to the people by a new election."

Constant thought that "these elections will be the criterion of the confidence reposed in the minister." But a "declaration that ministers are unworthy of public confidence is a direct attack on the royal prerogative" because "it denies the king's liberty of selection." However, "it is not the same with accusation. . . . When you accuse ministers, you attack them alone; but when you declare them unworthy of public confidence, either the intentions or the information of the prince are implicated; neither of which should ever occur in a constitutional government. . . . We must never dispute the [king's] right of choosing. The assemblies must not lay claim to the right of exclusion; a right which, if obstinately employed, eventually compromises the right of nomination." Therefore, "it will be better for ministers themselves, if they be sometimes accused, though frivolously perhaps, than if they were constantly exposed to an undefined declaration against which it would be more difficult

25. "On the Responsibility of Ministers," pp. 302–29.

to guard them." Instead of this, "the confidence which a minister enjoys or the suspicion that he excites, is proved by the majority that supports or deserts him." In the last analysis, this is the "legal expedient," the "constitutional sentiment."[26]

It is instructive to compare Constant and Royer-Collard on this point. The famous Doctrinaire thought that "the day the government will only exist by the majority of the Chamber, the day when it will be established in fact that the Chamber can reject the ministers of the king and impose others upon him, who would be its members and not the king's ministers, on that day we will be a republic."[27] The liberals are here defending the prerogative of the king, but at the time of the "Matchless Parliament" it was the opposite. At that moment it was the Ultras or Royalists, in control of the Chamber, who were demanding that the ministers should be responsible not to the king in opposition to them but to the majority in the assembly.

It is obvious that Constant did not understand that ministers should retire after a hostile vote of the Chamber. What he was affirming was not so much the right of the Chamber to obtain the downfall of the government as the necessity for the ministry to govern with the consent of the majority. This meant that if the ministers were in disagreement with the king, then "public opinion is to judge between them."

Constant, therefore, answered in the affirmative the question posed in the title of Chapter 12 of "On the Responsibility of Ministers"—"Should the King's privilege of amnesty be extended to guilty ministers?" "A king may enjoin guilty acts and afterwards pardon his ministers. Any limitation of the king's right would destroy the essence of constitutional monarchy; for, in such a monarchy the king, to borrow the English phrase, should be the fountain of mercy as well as honor." Furthermore, the first principle of constitutional monarchy is inviolability, which "presumes that the king can do no wrong." However, "it is evident that this hypothesis is a legal fiction, which does not exonerate the individual who occupies the throne from the afflictions and frailties of humanity."

26. Ibid.
27. Prosper de Barante, *La vie politique de Royer-Collard, ses discours et ses écrits,* 1:217.

The exponents of constitutionalism, however, have always "felt that this legal fiction was necessary for the interest of order and even of liberty, because, without it, all is confusion and eternal war between the monarch and different factions."[28] In accordance with this principle of constitutional monarchy, Constant contends that "we must only look to ministers for the exercise of power; they are present to answer for it. The monarch is placed apart in a sanctuary: your looks and suspicions must never glance toward him. He has no interests, no frailties, no connivance with ministers, for he is not of mankind, he is a neutral and independent power, who sees the storm roll beneath him[29]. . . . When Charles I was forced by the English to sign Strafford's sentence, the royal power, being once degraded, was soon destroyed."[30]

As late as 1830, Constant was still writing on the subject of ministerial responsibility.

> Ministers whose laws have been rejected cannot govern. Accused ministers can do it even less. Thus the faculty of rejecting laws, of accusing ministers are the means given by the Charte to the Chambers to obtain a new ministry. The king has the right to dissolve [the lower chamber] and to increase the upper chamber by the appointment of peers. The rejection of the budget is not an attack on the prerogative, for the king can retain the ministers and dissolve the chamber. It is to the interest of the king not to keep ministers who do not have the public confidence. Therefore, dismissal of the ministry or

28. Constant defined a political party as a "reunion of men who profess the same political doctrine" ("De la doctrine politique qui peut réunir les partis en France," *Cours de politique*, 2:285).

29. In "On the Responsibility of Ministers," Constant had said that kings shared in the shortcomings and defects of other men.

30. "The advocates of despotism have also said that the king was not a man; but they inferred from it that his will was paramount to law. I say that the constitutional monarchy is above humanity; but it is because his ministers act for him and they can do nothing without law" ("On the Responsibility of Ministers," pp. 302–29). To Constant, as we have seen, the error of Charles I was to cover the ministers with this inviolability. When the ministers are responsible only to the king, the monarch becomes responsible directly, instead of indirectly, to the nation. Constant did not understand that in England usage and custom had done more to restrict the prince to a neutral role than the constitution that gave him prerogatives incompatible with this neutrality.

dissolution of parliament, this is the sole constitutional alternative which the counselors of the crown can recommend without crime.[31]

Once again Constant refers to English experience. Because Charles Fox was alienated from George III by a bill on India, William Pitt replaced him in the ministry. Fox, however, had a large majority in the House of Commons. His successor, vanquished by this majority, dissolved the Chamber. But the majority of the new House was in favor of Pitt. Constant adds that if England had returned a Chamber favorable to Fox, Pitt would have retired from office. In a similar way, the ministries of Walpole, Grafton, and North fell without in any fashion disturbing the public peace or shaking the throne.

From these examples, it can be concluded that Constant exaggerated the arbitral role of the king in harmonizing the executive and legislative powers. This harmony was ultimately to result from the development of the cabinet, which issued from the majority and was responsible to it. As we have already noted, he wanted the king to dismiss ministers or dissolve parliament. If Constant does not expressly say that the ministers should be representatives of the parliamentary majority, he does affirm at least that they are not the simple agents of the king and that this relative independence is the condition of their responsibility, which is itself the condition of royal inviolability. He confounds penal and political responsibility. He claims that a minister cannot maintain himself in power if he does not have a parliamentary majority, but he refuses to the Chambers the right of voting an express declaration of nonconfidence. Instead, he limits himself to asserting that the sole expression of lack of confidence consists in the majority abandoning a minister.

We have already observed Constant's repeated favorable references to English institutions and practices. He definitely preferred Anglican to Gallican liberty, to cite once again the distinction drawn by Lieber. Constant's general approach to politics, like Montesquieu's, was to get away from abstractions and to rely instead on

31. *Le courrier français,* 5 Jan. 1830.

the facts of concrete historical experience. "If I have praised the form of English government, if I have wished that the constitutional monarchy of France should rise from the same foundations, it is because the happy experience of a century and a half has great weight with me. I have not recommended the servile imitation but a profound study of the English constitution and its application among us in all that suits us."[32]

Constant's other contemporaries of the liberal persuasion also highly praised England and its constitution. For example, Madame de Staël wrote: "England is the only great European Empire that has yet attained what, in our present state of political knowledge, appears (to be) the perfection of the social order." In fact, "no people in Europe can be put on a parallel with the English since 1688; there are a hundred and twenty years of social improvement between them and the continent." Besides, the English constitution is "the firmest monument of justice and moral greatness in Europe."[33] Royer-Collard, the Doctrinaire, called the English government "an honor to mankind, one which had raised the nation to the highest degree of liberty in domestic affairs and of glory and power in foreign affairs."[34] Like Jurieu after the revocation of the Edict of Nantes in the seventeenth century and Voltaire, Montesquieu, and de Lolme in the eighteenth century, Constant, Madame de Staël, and Royer-Collard in the nineteenth century saw in En-

32. "De la liberté des brochures," *Cours de politique*, 1:466. See also *Mémoires sur les Cent Jours en formes de lettres*, p. 57: "J'étois fort séduit par l'exemple de la constitution britannique qu'appuyait encore à mes yeux l'autorité de Montesquieu." Recall that Montesquieu speaks of England as the "one nation . . . in the world that has for the direct end of its constitution political liberty" (*Spirit of the Laws*, Book 11, chap. 5, p. 151). Cf. however, Constant in a letter to Madame Recamier in Louise Colet, *Lettres de Benjamin Constant à Madame Recamier*, p. 146: "Il y a plus d'affinité entre le dernier Français le plus exagéré du parti qui proscrit le mien et moi; qu'entre moi et l'Anglais le plus libéral."

33. Germaine de Staël, *Considerations on the Principal Events of the French Revolution*, 1:8 and 2:214.

34. Barante, *Vie politique de Royer-Collard*, 2:219. See also the Duc Victor de Broglie, *Souvenirs, 1785–1870*, 1:376: "J'étudiais passionnement. Le mot n'est pas trop fort, l'histoire, la constitution de l'Angleterre." Charles de Rémusat, *L'Angleterre au XVIIIᵉ siècle*, 1:10–11, declared: "Etudier l'Angleterre et la comparer à la France . . . on peut dire que ce fut pendant trente années le travail de toutes les intelligences ouvertes et consacrées à la politique réalisable." He confessed: "Voici le rêve de ma vie, le gouvernement anglais dans la société française."

gland a model of free government that should be emulated in France in order to condemn its despotism.

It was not the English constitution alone, however, that attracted the liberal political thinkers of the Restoration. In English history they saw parallels to French history. For example, in one of his early political essays during the Directory—*Des suites de la contre-révolution en Angleterre*—Constant had argued against a monarchical restoration in France by citing the crimes of the royalists in England at the time the Stuarts were restored to the throne.[35] In the opinion of Madame de Staël, "the principal points of analogy between the revolutions of England and France are: a king [Charles I and Louis XVI] brought to the scaffold by the spirit of democracy and a military chief [Cromwell and Bonaparte], getting possession of power and the restoration of the old dynasty [Charles II and Louis XVIII]."[36]

On 21 April 1814, Constant had claimed that "the French Revolution of 1814 reunited the advantages of the English Revolution of 1660 and those of the Revolution of 1688." He believed that "before arriving at liberty under monarchy the English had two revolutions, that of 1660 and that of 1688." By the first, the royal power was reestablished; by the second, it was organized. Therefore, "the change which has just taken place today is a happy combination of the two English revolutions of 1660 and 1688, because the Revolution of 1814 reunited the legitimacy of Charles II and the guarantees of William III."[37]

Constant also discussed these historical parallels in 1819:

The English Revolution resembles our own. But fate
has united several years in one and one man in several men.
Bonaparte was at the same time Oliver Cromwell and Richard
Cromwell. Oliver from the 18th Brumaire to his fall in 1814,
Richard after the return from Elba. We have had three reigns

35. This essay was in answer to Antoine Boulay de la Meurthe, who favored the English Restoration. Constant demonstrated his knowledge of the English sources when he cited Edward Hyde, first earl of Clarendon, David Hume, Gilbert Burnet, and Edmund Ludlow.

36. Staël, *Considerations on the French Revolution*, 2:218.

37. *Journal des débats*, 1814.

since the Restoration: Charles II, James II [Charles X was often compared to him], and William III. It was the court which created in 1814 what was similar to Charles II. It was the counterrevolution, which in 1815 believed that the time of Jeffreys and Kirk had come. The 5th of September [the dissolution of the "Matchless Parliament"] in 1816 put an end to the counterrevolution and established the English epoch of 1688 and the reign of William III. The new regime in England was threatened by the counterrevolution. In the reign of Anne divine right was praised. Sachevard [Sacheverell] was put in prison for having recommended submission to authority. Consolidation took place only after a period of thirty years. We are in the same position with more enlightenment experience. It is difficult to pass from slavery to the dignity of a free man.[38]

By the time of the July Monarchy, which Constant lived to witness, Louis Philippe was being compared to William III and the Revolution of 1830 in France with the Glorious Revolution of 1688 in England.

Constant was, as we have noted, preoccupied with the English constitution in many of his political writings, but he gave a special lecture on the subject before the Paris Athenée Royal in 1819.[39] He claimed that there are many things in the English constitution that are inapplicable to France, but they do not include the guarantees or principles of liberty, which apply to all times and places. He then adds that representative government will be the true object of his research and the English constitution a point of comparison, a

38. "De l'état constitutionnel de France," *La renommée*, 15 June 1819. See also "Discours sur la loi des élections" (1820), *Discours de M. Benjamin Constant à la Chambre des Députés*, 1:364: "L'Angleterre elle-même, affranchi sous Guillaume III, aurait, si l'ancienne race des Stuarts n'avait opiniatrement voulu le despotisme, été plus heureuse qu'elle ne le fut durant vingt années qui suivirent la révolution de 1688. Oui, l'Angleterre eut été cent fois plus heureuse, elle eut eu deux guerres civiles de moins, si la pensée d'un pacte rompu d'une succession inverti, n'eut troublé dans beaucoup d'esprits la jouissance de la liberté."

39. See Constant's manuscript from the Archives d'Estournelles de Constant and from the Fonds d'Estournelles de Constant. Note also "Cours sur la constitution anglaise," *Journal du commerce*, 18 Jan. 1819.

means of elucidating the different questions and developing important truths. He thought that the French were closer to true liberty than the English, who have had more years of civil war, anarchy, and reaction than France. This opinion is, of course, the direct opposite of the one he usually sustained.

Historically speaking, however, Constant believed that "liberty was introduced among the English differently from among the French. In England, the nobles and the people have from the very beginning made a common cause for liberty against the kings. In France, the kings and the people have for eight centuries allied against the nobles." Constant hastens to add that he does not "mean that the government of the French kings has not often been despotic and vexatious," but he does "mean that the most habitual oppression, that which has weighed the most constantly on the majority of the inhabitants of French territory, has been that of the nobles over the commons, while in England the oppression of the king, menacing alike the commons and the nobles, has forced them to unite against him."

Continuing his examination of English history, Constant observes: "From the time of Henry I . . . the king stipulated that the concessions he made to his barons should be accorded to their vassals and thus liberty began to be extended to all classes. Likewise the barons and the people united to dictate Magna Carta to King John and this charter abolished the slavery of both lords and vassals." The famous Thirty-ninth Article of the Great Charter is then quoted once again by Constant, who claimed that it included all the clauses of civil liberty, an opinion in great vogue in the nineteenth century, but one that is no longer accepted in the twentieth.[40]

According to Constant, then,

> by a happy combination of circumstances English nobles demanded more rights than privileges from the throne and rights by their very nature benefited all. The French nobles demanded privileges rather than rights and the essence of

---

40. See his early *Opinion sur le projet de loi concernant l'établissement de tribunaux criminels spéciaux 5 pluviôse An IX*, which had condemned such special tribunals by the citation of Article 39 of Magna Carta providing for a legal trial by peers.

privileges is that they only benefit those who enjoy them at the expense of those who do not. Also while the lords made common cause in England with the people and formed with it and for themselves a rampart against the tyranny, the French nobles, while they menaced the throne, oppressed the nation. In 1688 a great part of this nobility agreed to the revolution, which founded constitutional government in England.

Continuing to compare England and France, Constant stated that

in England whatever served liberty, the prerogatives of the nobles, the rights of the communes, the charters of the corporations, the local customs, the hereditary traditions, has been preserved or at least was only modified gradually because with this idea was associated salutary guarantees against the royal power. In France, on the contrary, the first movement of liberty has been to destroy all the partial things [intermediate powers], because the country associated them with the idea of vexations of which it was the victim.

Furthermore, there existed

in England a religious respect for traditions, a singular love for the diversity of local customs, while in France instead of this respect for traditions, there was an insatiable thirst for novelties and instead of this love for local customs, an imperious need for uniformity. This is because in England the vexation originating in the throne was a uniform vexation against which the diversity of customs was a protection, while in France the vexations originating in the nobility were diversified vexations against which we invoked uniformity. It follows that English institutions, founded on traditions, cannot apply to us, whose institutions have no other basis than reason. The English have built their liberty piece by piece, the debris of the past has been their material. Our liberty was established suddenly and in the

past we perceive only obstacles. Struck by the advantages
which the diversity of customs produced for liberty in England,
I formerly believed [*L'esprit de conquête et de l'usurpation*]
that one could apply this system to France. I rose up against
the uniformity to which for twenty-five years our successive
governments tried to submit us. . . . Now I recognized that in
their desire for uniformity there was a basis of justice and an
instinct of reason.

Here, of course, is another most interesting reversal of opinion on
Constant's part from the position he held in 1813–14.

Constant once again discussed England in his *Commentaire sur
l'ouvrage de Filangieri*.[41] "England in spite of absurd commercial
laws and other vices stayed in the first rank.[42] This was because the
political institutions, the parliamentary discussions, the liberty of
the press, which she enjoyed without interruption for 126 years,
counterbalanced the vices of its laws and its government . . . and
England ruled from Sir Robert Walpole to our time by Machiavellian ministers and represented by a corrupt parliament, nevertheless
conserved the language, the habits, and several of the advantages of
liberty."

From Constant's perspective,

England is [was] at bottom a vast, opulent, and vigorous
aristocracy; of large properties united in the same hands,
colossal riches accumulated in the same hands, a numerous
and faithful clientele grouped around each proprietor—lastly,
as a result of this combination, a national representation
composed in part of those salaried by the government and in
part by those chosen by the aristocracy [pocket boroughs];
such has been the organization of England to this day. This
organization, which appears to be imperfect and oppressive in

41. Constant, *Commentaire sur l'ouvrage de Filangieri*, 1:73, 96–99.
42. Constant thought that France was being invited to imitate such vices of the
English constitution as the disproportion of fortunes, the absence of all political
rights for seven-eighths of the proprietors, and septennial parliaments. See "Du
projet de conférer aux chambres le droit de s'épurer," *La minerve française* 8 (Nov.
1819): 193.

theory, was mitigated in practice as much by the good effects of liberty acquired in 1688 as by several circumstances in England, which have not been sufficiently noticed when one wishes to transport elsewhere certain institutions with respect to privileges borrowed from the British constitution.

Constant then admitted that he himself had not been preserved from this error when he discussed the peerage in his *Réflexions sur les constitutions.*

In this treatise Constant faced a very important question in matters of limited government, namely, what is or is not constitutional. "Everything which does not touch the limits and the respective prerogatives of the powers, political rights, and individual rights, is not part of the constitution but can be modified with the consent of the king and the two houses."[43] Much earlier—in 1797—Constant had outlined his idea of the essence of constitutionalism when he wrote: "A constitution is the guarantee of a people's liberty; consequently, everything which has to do with liberty is constitutional and consequently also nothing is constitutional, which is not related to liberty."[44]

Constant observes that this problem of a constitution reminds him of the comparison he is continually making between French history of the past twenty-five years and the constitutional history of England. The English constitution has lasted for a century and a half; none of the French have survived more than three years. He states that he wants to answer those who claim that England is fortunate not to have a constitution because it is not written. Constant replies that England does have a constitution because it has habeas corpus, the Bill of Rights, Magna Carta, national representation, and trial by jury. It does not matter that these things are not written down in a document because they are fundamental laws that cannot be violated. Furthermore, England has what are called precedents but France does not because the Revolution destroyed

43. Réflexions sur les constitutions," p. 263.
44. "Des réactions politiques," *Cours de politique,* 2:123.

what existed and nothing can take its place. In fact, France has had a complete housecleaning every fifty years.

Constant was convinced that constitutions, in general, should never be too detailed and inflexible.[45] Moreover, they are rarely made by the will of man but instead by time, which introduces gradual changes. Here he sounds like Edmund Burke in *Reflections on the Revolution in France* or Joseph de Maistre, in *Essai sur le principe générateur des constitutions politiques et des autres institutions humaines*. This shows once more that Constant's liberalism is traditional and conservative rather than abstract and radical.[46]

Constant often stressed that France was not as fortunate as England.

> We have not yet arrived at the epoch when constitutions
> are sustained by the sole force of habits and independently
> of the energy of those who have a mission to defend them. In
> England, the parliament can be up to a certain point
> *complaisant* about the ministers. Their institutions are firm.
> The rights of citizens, the attributes of the deliberating bodies,
> the prerogatives of the crown have a solidity guaranteed by
> 150 years of experience. The interest of the king, accustomed
> to find his strength in constitutional means, the unshakable
> aristocracy of an ancient peerage, invested from time
> immemorial with immense properties; vigorous activity of the
> commons fortified and modified at the same time by a tradi-
> tion of several centuries, none of these preservatives
> exist among us. Our constitution is not a habit.[47]

45. See Constant's speech of 8 June 1824 on the Septennial Act, *Discours*, 2:246: "Si la constitution d'Angleterre subsiste depuis près d'un siècle et demi, tandis que les nôtres se sont écroulés dans leurs berceaux, c'est qu'il n'y a de constitutionnel en Angleterre que les garanties de l'ordre social et de la liberté publique; nous, au contraire, nous avons, toujours voulu pourvoir par la constitution, à toutes les occurrences tant présentes que futures; nous avons étendu la constitution à tout."

46. But as John Locke has shown, historical arguments can be used for reactionary as well as for liberal purposes. See his *Civil Government*, chap. 8, para. 103: "At least an argument from what has been, to what should of right be, has not great force."

47. Constant, "Des élections prochaines," p. 342.

In fact, in 1814, Constant replied to the objection that there once had existed a constitution in France: "But a constitution forgotten so much that research is necessary to rediscover it and arguments to prove its existence, a constitution which is the subject of disagreement among the publicists and of dispute among the antiquarians, is only the object of erudition."[48]

Continuing with his favorite topic—a political comparison of England and France—Constant demonstrates that it is only when a

> constitution is old, observed for a long time, known, respected, and cherished that it can be suspended for an instant, if a great emergency requires it. But, if a constitution is new and not in practice nor identified with the habit of a people, then every suspension, either partial or temporary, is the end of that constitution. Habeas corpus can be suspended in England because in that country the institutions, the corps, the prerogatives, the rights have a stability guaranteed by 150 years of existence. But none of these preservatives against the dangers of a temporary suspension of the constitution exist in France. There constitutional liberty is completely new. In England the intermediary powers existed before the constitution, which gives them an intrinsic force to defend it. But in France all the intermediate powers have been created by the constitution. Arbitrariness in England finds limits in property consolidated by long possession, in thousands of institutions of ancient origin. In France, in contrast, the revolution wiped out everything, and, therefore, arbitrariness would easily triumph.[49]

As a result of all this, Constant contends that

> the constitutional powers existing only under the constitution cannot suspend it. In the course of our revolution our governments frequently claimed that they had the right to

48. Constant, "Réflexions sur les constitutions," p. 473.
49. Constant, "De la liberté des brochures," p. 471.

violate the constitution in order to save it. It was thus that the
Directory after having commenced with the exceptional law of
the 3rd brumaire was led to the 18th fructidor. It was thus that
Bonaparte after having purged the Tribunate ended with the
Empire. Every time constitutions have been violated it is not
the constitutions that are saved but the governments. The
people might perhaps forget that the government was established through the violation of the rules, which render
it legitimate, but the government would never forget
it.[50]

Constant then interjects the acid comment that "if from the revolution, France has had to be saved by exceptional legislation, certainly
no country has been saved more often."

In spite of his own political activities, which we have already
noted, Constant was convinced that no coup d'état has ever preserved a people or a family from ruin. He cites numerous historical
examples, both ancient and modern.

The adjournment of the legislative body in 1814 is mentioned as the coup d'état of Napoleon; the 18th fructidor
as the coup d'état of the Directory; the parlement of Meaupou
as the coup d'état of the *ancien régime* expiring under
Louis XV; the destruction of the legal government of Sweden
as the coup d'état of Gustave III; the arrest of the five
members of the House of Commons as the coup d'état of
Charles I in England; and Jeffreys and Kirk and the scaffolds
of Essex and Russell were those of Charles II and James II;
the death of the Guises was the coup d'état of Henry III; the
assassination of the Gracchi the coup d'état of the Roman
Senate and from the ashes of the Gracchi Marius was born.
The execution of the accomplices of Catiline without a judgment was the coup d'état of Cicero, who saw the
republic fall which he wanted to save.[51]

50. Constant, "De la suspension et de la violation des constitutions," in "Réflexions sur les constitutions," pp. 372–80.

51. Constant, "Coups d'état," *Le temps*, 1830.

Constant's conclusion is significant: "When it is a question of individuals all that which is not forbidden is permitted. When it is a question of the powers all that which is not permitted is forbidden."[52]

As we have already noticed, Constant as well as Madame de Staël always thought that one of the most dangerous maxims ever coined was that ancient one, *Salus populi suprema lex esto.*

> Demagogues seize upon despotic methods; despots grasp revolutionary means; the pretext of the safety of the people comes to the support of crimes committed in the name of liberty, as it does to the support of crimes committed in the name of maintenance of order and the result is always the same, that is, these means react against those who employ them. Illegalities committed in the name of liberty detach the people from liberty; the illegalities committed in the name of the maintenance of order detach the people from the keeping of order because in the two cases order and liberty seem to be vain words, which are pronounced in order to obliterate them.[53]

Very late in his career, Constant once again expressed his disapproval of illegal methods in connection with Simón Bolívar, whom he saw as a usurper and not a liberator at all, because he had dissolved the parliament when he found that his partisans were in a minority. Furthermore, he had secured dictatorial powers on the ground that his fellow citizens were not enlightened enough to govern themselves. Constant then repeats his previous judgments— "Nothing legitimizes an unlimited power." "Dictatorship is the terrible heritage of oligarchic republics." "When a people is not enlightened enough to be free, it is not to tyranny that it will owe its liberty." He is not at all impressed with the contention that South America would be lost unless Bolívar had unlimited power. He once more asks "whether one man can save a people incapable of saving themselves. Bolívar might use his power temperately but he

52. *Le courrier français*, 21 Jan. 1830.
53. Constant, "Théorie des révolutions," *Mercure de France*, 1817.

could use it otherwise; tyranny is not in usage but in the right that is arrogated to oneself. Besides, is there a single example of a despotism giving to a nation the education necessary for the enjoyment of liberty? Has the dictatorship of Napoleon prepared France for liberty?" In addition, "the pretext for dictatorship in a young republic our common enemies employ to support absolute power in a monarchy they claim is old and decrepit." Finally, "dictators are not only guilty of the wrongs they perpetrate and the crimes they commit in their lifetime, they are responsible for Tiberius and Nero; Cromwell for Jeffreys and Kirk."[54]

Constant concluded that "all the constitutions that have been given to France guaranteed individual liberty, and under the rule of these constitutions individual liberty has been violated without cessation."[55] In fact, individual liberty was suspended in 1815, 1817, and 1820. "This is because," Constant continued, "a simple declaration is not sufficient; positive safeguards are necessary; it is essential to have bodies powerful enough to employ in favor of the oppressed, means of defense, which the written law provided. Our present constitution [Acte Additionnel] is the only one which has created safeguards and the intermediate bodies with enough power. Liberty of the press—ministerial responsibility—lastly, the existence of a numerous and independent representative institution, such are the means by which individual liberty is protected."[56]

Constant then points out that "our ancient laws, the orders [estates], the great bodies of magistrates, the provincial and municipal regime, everything has disappeared [in the Revolution] and there would only be today the throne and slaves, if the legislative power, strong in public opinion, were not placed between the king and his subjects."[57] In addition to a representative body, Constant also relied upon a hereditary peerage to constitute such a further limit to authority as to ensure the preservation of liberty and security.

54. *Le courrier français*, 1, 15, 17 Jan. 1829.
55. Constant, "Des élections prochaines," p. 145, "Principes de politique," p. 322. "Nos lois d'exception sont au nombre de quatre: la suspension de la liberté individuelle, l'arbitraire sur les journaux; la loi sur la presse et la création des cours prévôtales."
56. Constant, "Principes de politique," p. 145.
57. "Histoire de la Chambre des Députés depuis 1816 jusqu'en 1817," *Cours de politique*, p. 270.

Constant castigated the French hereditary nobility in his *Mémoires sur les Cent Jours* and praised it in his *Principes de politique*.[58] In first discussing this institution, Constant follows Guizot's analysis in *Du gouvernement de la France depuis la Restauration et du ministère actuel* (1820) rather than Madame de Staël in *Considérations sur les principaux événements de la révolution française* (1817). The latter outlined *la thèse nobiliaire* by tracing the nobility back to "la nuit de temps" and concluded that "it is of importance to repeat to those who are advocates of rights founded on the past that it is liberty which is ancient and despotism which is modern" because "in all the European states, founded at the commencement of the middle age, the power of the kings was limited by that of the nobles."[59] Acknowledging Guizot, Constant viewed "among the moderns inequality of rank" as having "the most revolting origin of all, conquest" and the "nobles as the descendants of the Franks" [Germans], whereas the Tiers Etats could be traced back to the Gauls.[60]

Constant indicated his reason for forcing a Chamber of Peers on Napoleon during the Hundred Days: "I saw in hereditary magistracy one more barrier against the authority of a man and I was seeking everywhere for barriers."[61] Besides, Constant continued, "I was greatly taken with the example of the British constitution, which, to my way of thinking, was supported by the authority of Montesquieu."[62]

So much for the Hundred Days. In his mature judgment, Constant concluded: "In a hereditary monarchy, the heredity of a class is indispensable. . . . To give additional aid to the monarchy there

58. See his long note in *Mémoires sur les Cent Jours*, pp. 184–89, "De la haine contre la noblesse lors du retour de Bonaparte en 1815."
59. Staël, *Considerations on the French Revolution*, 1:11. Cf. Jean Charles Simonde de Sismondi, *Etudes sur les constitutions des peuples modernes*, pp. 315–16: "Dans le moyen age les rois maintenaient le principe de l'ordre et de l'unité, les nobles celui de la liberté. Tous les vrais progrès de l'independance du caractère, de la garantie des droits, de la limite apportée par la discussion aux caprices et aux vices du pouvoir absolu, furent dus alors à l'aristocratie de naissance, car c'était elle qui fournit l'opposition."
60. Constant, *Mémoires sur les Cent Jours*, p. 185.
61. Ibid., p. 157. See George Kelly, "Liberalism and Aristocracy in the French Restoration," pp. 522–30.
62. Constant, *Mémoires sur les Cent Jours*, p. 156.

must be a *corps intermédiaire*, Montesquieu requires it even in an elective monarchy."[63] For example, "no Englishman would believe for an instant that his monarchy was stable if the House of Lords was abolished."[64] But in England the peerage is not exclusive because the king can create new peers and the younger sons of peers are commoners.

Constant was convinced that the essence of a constitutional system was to be found to a large extent in mixed government à la Aristotle and Montesquieu. This meant the fusion of aristocracy and representative government, defined in terms of a bicameral division of the legislative power.[65] What must be avoided at all cost is an unlimited representative assembly, the vices of which Constant saw particularly, as we have noted earlier, in the Long Parliament in England during the Civil War and in the Convention in France during the Revolution.

When no limits are imposed on the representative authority, the representatives of the people are not the defenders

---

63. *Spirit of the Laws*, Book 2, chap. 4, pp. 15–16: "The intermediate, subordinate, and dependent powers constitute the nature of monarchical government. . . . These fundamental laws necessarily suppose the intermediate channels through which the power flows. . . . The most natural, intermediate and subordinate power is that of the nobility . . . no monarch, no nobility, no nobility, no monarch. . . . Abolish the privileges of the lords, the clergy and cities in a monarchy and you will soon have a popular state, or else a despotic government."

64. Constant, "Principes de politique," pp. 35–36: "Restons fidèles à l'expérience. Nous voyons la pairie héréditaire dans la Grand-Bretagne, compatible avec un haut degré de la liberté civile et politique; tous les citoyens qui se distinguent peuvent y parvenir. Elle n'a pas le seul caractère odieux de l'hérédité, le caractère exclusive. Le lendemain de la nomination d'un simple citoyen à la pairie, il jouit des mêmes privilèges légaux que le plus ancien des pairs. Les branches cadette des premiers maisons d'Angleterre rentrent dans la masse du peuple, elles forment un lien entre la pairie et la nation, comme la pairie forme un lien entre la nation et le trône."

65. Constant condemned unicameralism. Ibid., p. 49, n. 1: "Tous les freins qu'une assemblé unique s'impose à elle-même, les précautions contre l'urgence, la nécessité des deux tiers des voix ou de l'unanimité; tous ces freins, dis-je, sont illusoires. Une chambre unique met en présence une majorité et une minorité avec cette circonstance de plus contre la minorité que le règlement qu'elle invoque est l'ouvrage de la majorité qui a toujours le sentiment de pouvoir défaire de qu'elle fait. La division de deux sections séparées crée au contraire deux corps qui ont l'intérêt à défendre leurs opinions respectives. Il y a majorité contre majorité. Celle du corps le plus nombreux n'étant elle-même qu'une majorité de convention, c'est-à-dire factice, en comparaison de la nation entière, n'ose revoquer en doute la légalité de la majorité moins nombreuse qui lui est opposée."

of liberty but the candidates of tyranny. Moreover, once tyranny is established, it may well be the more frightful for the tyrants being more numerous. . . . An assembly which can neither be curbed nor restrained is, of all possible powers, the blindest in its movements and the most incalculable in its results. . . . It plunges into excesses which, on first sight, seem to be mutually incompatible. An injudicious activity; a multiplicity of laws without limit; the desire to cater to the passionate part of the people by self-abandonment to their impulse . . . the flouting of national sentiment and the stubborn adherence to error; . . . the alternation of temerity and timidity, violence and weakness, favoritism to one and distrust of all; under the sway of purely physical sensations, such as enthusiasm or terror; the absence of all moral responsibility and the certitude of safety in numbers from either the shame of cowardice or the peril of audacity.

Constant concludes that "such are the vices of assemblies when they are not confined within limits which they cannot surmount."[66]

In spite of Constant's defense of hereditary aristocracy, he accepted the results of the French Revolution, which liberated the individual from the hierarchical order of group, corporation, order, guild, and class. The corporations are replaced by individual and personal activities. In the past, the rule of one or despotism came first, then the rule of classes under feudalism, then corporations were formed. "Finally, when industry itself acquired more force, the corporations became useless; everything was individualized. Where there was first a despot, then classes, then associations, there are only individuals because the social state, being perfected, creates for each one of the guarantees which dispense it from being associated with others for self-defense."[67]

Constant was proto-Comtean when he thought that "today industry is upsetting the royal despotism."[68] In fact, he even said that

66. Ibid., pp. 31–32.
67. "Aveux échappées aux ennemis de la loi des élections," *La minerve française* 8 (Nov. 1819):538.
68. "L'aristocratie des guerriers a, jusqu'à un certain point, contre-balancé le pouvoir des prêtres, comme le despotisme des rois a détroné plus tard l'aristocratie

"the general interest is only the reunion, the conciliation of all private interests, which exist simultaneously. If the general interest were anything else, it would be a chimerical abstraction. Society is only the aggregation of private individuals who are members."[69] This is, of course, the position of utilitarians like Helvétius and Bentham, whom Constant criticized.

"The first publicist in France to make an adaptation of Montesquieu's doctrine [of intermediate bodies as a check on power] to the new day of social and political equality and also of industrial group life," according to Paul George, was not Tocqueville but Constant.[70] After the Revolution destroyed the intermediary bodies of the *ancien régime*, Constant, under the new conditions of a pulverized and atomized society, developed the idea of counterweights or countervailing powers to the state, such as juridical forms, local authorities, and religion, before Tocqueville.[71] But Constant did not stress the right of association as did Tocqueville, who regarded it "almost as inalienable in its nature as the right of personal liberty."[72] To Constant, "what protects us from arbitrariness is the

---

guerrière et comme aujourd'hui l'industrie renverse le despotisme des rois" (*De la religion considérée dans sa source, ses formes et ses développements*, 5:175). "L'absence de la civilisation donne à tous les individus une couleur presque pareille. La civilisation, dans ses progrès, développe les différences, mais avec l'excès de la civilisation, ces différences disparaissent de nouveau" (ibid., 3:458). All this is but another facet of Constant's philosophy of history in which he traced the evolution of societies from "l'état sauvage" to "l'état civilisé," from simple to complicated, from small to large, from warlike to pacific, from monarchical to democratic.

69. Constant, "Histoire de la session de 1817 à 1818," *Cours de politique*, pp. 369–70.

70. Paul George, "Montesquieu and De Tocqueville and Corporate Individualism," pp. 10–21.

71. Constant, "Principes de politique," p. 101: "L'on considère à présent le pouvoir locale comme une branche dépendante du pouvoir exécutif; au contraire, il ne doit jamais l'entraver mais il ne doit point en défendre. ... Il faut introduire dans notre administration inférieure beaucoup de fédéralisme, mais un fédéralisme différent de celui qu'on a connu jusqu'ici. L'on a nommé fédéralisme une association de gouvernement qui avaient conservé leur independance mutuelle et ne tenaient ensemble que par des liens politiques extérieures. Cette institution est vicieuse."

72. Alexis de Tocqueville, *Democracy in America*, 1:195–96: "There are no countries in which associations are more needed to prevent the despotism of faction or the arbitrary power of a prince than those which are democratically constituted. In aristocratic nations the body of the nobles and the wealthy are in themselves natural associations which check the abuses of power. In countries where such associations do not exist, if private individuals cannot create an artificial temporary

observance of forms [that is, established procedures]. Forms are the tutelary divinities of human associations. . . . It is to forms alone that the oppressed can appeal. Responsibility of the agents is also a remedy against arbitrariness."[73] He cites the judicial guarantees, such as immovability of judges and the sanctity of juries, as examples of judicial forms.

With the end of the *ancien régime* Constant saw the beginning of a new era, "the epoch of legal conventions." He explains this development in Burkean fashion: "The human mind has too much illumination to let itself be governed for long by force or by craft but it is not enough for it to be governed by reason alone. It is necessary to have something which is at the same time more reasonable than force and less abstract than reason. Hence, the need for legal conventions, a king of common reason, the product of all individual reasons."[74] As an example of such a legal convention, Constant names property, which he views as a form that is a rampart against arbitrariness.

Constant had been concerned with arbitrariness ever since the time of the Directory when he devoted Chapter 9 of *Des réactions politiques* (1797) to an analysis "De l'arbitraire," which he then characterized as "the absence of rules, limits, definitions; in a word, the absence of all that is exact." He then elaborated on the true nature of *l'arbitraire*: "They are the partisans of arbitrariness who reject principles" because "that which is definite . . . must lead to principles." Therefore, "they are supporters of arbitrariness, who say that there is a distance which cannot be bridged between theory and practice." Finally, "they are partisans of arbitrariness who claiming with Burke, that axioms metaphysically true can be politically false, prefer to those axioms considerations, prejudices—all indefinite, undefinable things."

Constant firmly believed that "political institutions are only contracts. The nature of contracts is to pose fixed limits but *l'arbitraire*, being exactly the opposite of what constitutes a contract, under-

---

substitute for them I can see no permanent protection against the most galling tyranny."
73. Constant, "Principes de politique," p. 148.
74. Constant, *Mélanges de littérature et de politique*, pp. 412–13.

mines the basis of every political institution." He illustrates his point. For example, "at the time of the conspiracy of Babeuf, many were irritated over observing *les formes* [established procedures]. It was asked, if the conspirators had triumphed, would they have observed *les formes* against us?" Constant's answer to this contention was sharp: "It is precisely because they would not have observed them that you must" because "that is what distinguishes you from them; it is that which gives you the right to punish them; it is that which makes anarchists of them and of you the friends of order."[75] Constant concluded that the Terror was the worst example of arbitrariness to be encountered in recent history. "Revolutions are *l'arbitraire* employed to destroy," whereas "reactions are *l'arbitraire* used to reestablish."

In spite of Constant's own defense of the 18th fructidor during the Directory and of Napoleon during the Hundred Days, he developed the principle of the rule of law from the beginning of the Directory to the end of the Restoration. "There is no public safety but in justice, no justice but in laws, and no laws without open forms."[76] This was Constant's position from *Des réactions politiques* (1797) to *Eloge de Sir Samuel Romilly* [1757–1818] (1819). "Romilly [the English legal reformer] wanted the security of the citizen to depend on the laws and not on men. He knew that guarantees, which only rested on personal virtues, are precarious and insufficient and that the social order exists precisely in order that men do not put themselves in the place of the laws."[77]

Perhaps the best statement by Constant of his great principle of constitutionalism—"a government of laws and not of men"—is to be found in his assessment of the liberals in France, whom he called Independents, during the Restoration:

> The Independents are those who for thirty years have
> wanted the same things. They are those who have repeated
> the same truths to all governments; who have maintained the

---

75. Constant, "Des réactions politiques," pp. 116–25.
76. Constant, "Principes de politique," p. 72.
77. Constant, *Eloge de Sir Samuel Romilly, prononcé à l'Athenée Royal de Paris le 26 décembre 1818.*

same resistance to all vexatious actions, even when manifested against others than themselves. The independents have adopted no symbol, in order to sacrifice their principles to that symbol. When they have proclaimed the sovereignty of the people, they have said to the people that their sovereignty is limited by the principle of justice. When France passed from the stormy tyranny of popular sovereignty to the symmetrical despotism of a single man [Napoleon], it was the Independents who told that individual that he could maintain his authority only by obeying the laws of the state; that these laws, which he looked upon as obstacles, were in fact safeguards, to subvert which would undermine his throne. . . . The Independents are those who like constitutional monarchy because it is constitutional, who respect hereditary succession because it protects the tranquillity of the people against the strife of factions. The Independents think that the throne exists for the people and to trample upon the rights of citizens is as injurious to kings as it is damaging to the citizens to attempt to subvert the legal powers of the monarchs. The Independents represent that numberless generation which, reared in the midst of our recent troubles, often hurt from youth . . . by the arbitrary actions of successive regimes, detest the arbitrary in government in all its aspects, and discern the falsity of its pretexts. The Independents are those, who, having no wish to detain, despoil, or to banish any person illegally, or to be paid by those who detain, despoil, and banish, want no law which exposes them to being arrested, despoiled, or banished illegally.[78]

If France wished to enjoy completely the benefits of constitutional government, Constant thought that it would have to adopt the direct election of its assemblies and their integral renewal. At the time, the practice of electoral colleges and partial renewal of the Chamber was in operation. He answers the objection that under the proposed change the choice of the people would be bad by

78. Constant, "Des élections prochaines," pp. 330–31.

citing the experience of the House of Commons in England and the authority of Machiavelli and Montesquieu.[79] As a result of this modification, Constant also wanted the Chamber to have the legislative initiative concurrently with the ministry.

Constant did not believe that representatives of the people should be paid, which was the position John Stuart Mill took later in England. They should be recruited from the leisure class because "poverty has its prejudices as well as ignorance." Nonpayment of representatives seemed in Constant's opinion to be the natural consequence of an arrangement by which nonpropertyholders did not possess political rights.

In discussing the suffrage, Constant contended that "no people has considered as members of the state all the inhabitants of its territory. Those that indigence keeps in a state of dependence and condemns to daily labor are no more enlightened than children on public affairs. The suffrage is related to leisure, which is indispensable to the acquisition of enlightenment and rectitude of judgment. Property alone assures this leisure."[80] Constant employs an ancient argument against universal manhood suffrage. Because the aim of those who do not have property is to acquire it, they would, therefore, be expected to use political rights, if they had them, to invade the property rights of others. The representative system in France rests on the mass of proprietors, who have enough to ensure their independence and whose numbers are sufficient to prevent aristocracy. Too poor electors would be the tools of the rich, which is another classic argument against universal suffrage, and too rich electors would tyrannize the poor. In the middle class, therefore, is the enlightenment, the industry, and the interest equal to liberty and good order.[81] This position, advanced in both England and France at the time, is the basis, of course, for the Marxist conclusion that liberalism is nothing more than a class doctrine, directed toward the political domination of the bourgeoisie, who expounded liberal

79. Constant, "Principes de politique," p. 43. "Les hommes, dit le premier quoique sujets à se tromper sur le général, ne se tromper pas sur le particulier. Le peuple est admirable, dit le second, pour choisir ceux à qui il doit confier une partie de son autorité."
80. Ibid., pp. 53–54.
81. *Mercure de France,* Jan. 1817.

ideas against the aristocracy above and conservative ideas against the masses below.

Constant was convinced that "the great benefit of the French Revolution, that which compensates for the evils which that revolution has caused, is the introduction of the middle class into the administration of the affairs of the state."[82] "Political rights are no longer given to a privileged landholding class but to a class whose property is based on industry. This middle class is more impartial than the rich, who see only their own interest, and more enlightened than the poor, who are absorbed with mechanical labor."[83] Therefore, to Constant, tyranny is to be identified with a situation where there are great proprietors and proletarians, but never with a condition where there is a middle class. Because the great majority of the French electors belong to this intermediate or middle class, the French electoral law is superior to the English. Constant defends it against the criticism that it is exclusive. This is not the case because each citizen by his prudence, industry, economy, or competence can become an elector by acquiring property.[84] This means that there is really no aristocracy in France of one hundred thousand voters out of a population of twenty-eight million people because anyone can become an aristocrat by acquiring property and thereby leisure.

According to this scheme of things, "in all France from the beggar, who has no property, to the king on his throne, there is not a citizen, not an individual, not a human being, who does not have rights. They have different rights; some have political rights; others such and such rights; all have the right to be protected and to be sheltered from arbitrariness."[85] In fact, all the French possess individual rights independent of all public or social authority, and these rights include religious liberty, freedom of the press and of industry,

82. Constant, *Mélanges*, p. 416.

83. "Sur le projet de loi relatif à la police de la presse," *Cours de politique*, 2:33.

84. Cf. Guizot's famous statement: "Enrichissez vous par le travail et vous deviendrez les électeurs."

85. Constant, *Discours*, 7 Nov. 1830. See also "Sessions des Chambres de 1818 à 1819," *Cours de politique*, p. 392: "Tous sentent qu'entre les électeurs et qui ne le sont pas encore, faute de payer une contribution suffisante il n'a point de séparation réele. Parents, amis associés, les uns les autres, ils sont de la même classe, ils ont les mêmes intérêts; et les cent mille Françaises qui sont électeurs servent de protecteurs, d'appuis de rempart à ceux qui ne le sont pas."

and the enjoyment of property. Society exists only in order to guarantee these rights. Constant then cites Royer-Collard to the effect that "the right of petition existed everywhere under the despotisms of the Orient as under our Charte. This right is a natural right, which the Charte did not create but the exercise of which it guarantees. Constitutions, as the laws, do not create our rights; they declare them; when they do not declare them, they do not exist less. This principle does not apply, in particular, to the right of petition. It is true for liberty of the press, of conscience, for all faculties which man should enjoy in the social state."[86] Constant always maintained, then, that individuals have rights and that these rights are independent of social authority, which cannot curtail them without being guilty of usurpation.[87]

But it might be asked what should happen if oppressive laws are made contrary to the rights of individuals? In other words, "when authority is abused, what must be done?" "We thus come," said Constant

> to the question of obedience to law, one of the most difficult, which can gain the attention of men. Whatever decision one hazards on this matter, one is exposed to insoluble difficulties. Shall we say that we should only obey laws insofar as they are just? Then, resistance would be authorized in the most senseless cases or in those most worthy of punishment; anarchy will be found everywhere. Or shall we admit that we must obey the law so far as it is the law independently of its content and source? If so, we shall be condemning ourselves to obey the most atrocious decrees and the most illegal authorities.[88]

Constant rejects the authority of Blaise Pascal and Francis Bacon, who wanted complete obedience to law without examination. He

---

86. Constant, "Sessions des Chambres de 1818 à 1819," p. 366.
87. See Constant, "Observations sur le discours," *Cours de politique* 1:489: "Montesquieu a dit la justice existait avant les lois ce qui implique, si je ne me trompe, que les droits existent avant les formes destinées à les garantir."
88. Constant, "Réflexions sur les constitutions," p. 349.

shows first that we cannot obey every act called law without absurd results.

> Should naming a thing a law always suffice to obligate
> a man to obedience? But if a number of men or even a single
> man without authority (whether the Committee of Public
> Safety or Robespierre) . . . entitles the expression of their
> particular will with the name of law, are the other members of
> society obliged to conform to it? The affirmation is absurd; but
> the opposite implies that the mere title of law does not of itself
> impose the duty of obedience and that such an obligation
> supposes a previous examination of the source whence it
> issues. Shall we permit such examination, knowing that it will
> raise a question of ascertaining whether what is presented to us
> as a law proceeds from a legitimate authority, but that once so
> enlightened, the examination should not be allowed as to the
> very content of the law? . . . It will then be necessary, in all
> systems, to concede that the individuals may make use of their
> reason, not only to determine the character of the authorities
> but for the purpose of judging their acts. Therefrom results the
> necessity of examining the content as well as the source of the
> law. Note that those very people, who declare implicit
> obedience to laws, whatever those laws may be, is their
> absolute and strict duty, always except from this rule the thing
> which interests them. Pascal excepted religion; he did not
> submit to the authority of the civil law in a religious
> matter.

In this delicate matter of obedience, Constant thought that it is better to oppose the law with passive resistance. "Obedience to law," he argues,

> is a duty but like all duties it is not absolute; it is relative;
> it rests on the supposition that the law issues from a legitimate
> source and is confined within just limits. This duty does not
> cease when the law only differs in certain respects from this
> rule. We should sacrifice much for public peace; we should find

ourselves guilty in the eyes of morality, if by too inflexible attachment of our rights we should disturb tranquillity as soon as it seemed to us that our rights were being attacked in the name of the law. But no duty binds us to laws like those passed, for example, in 1793 or even later whose corrupting influence menaces the most noble parts of our existence.[89] No duty would bind us to laws which would not only restrain our legitimate liberties and . . . such of our actions as there is no right to prohibit, but which would also command us to act contrary to the eternal principles of justice and of compassion, which man cannot refrain from observing without denying his own nature.[90]

In developing his argument, Constant adds that "the doctrine of unlimited obedience to law has caused, through tyranny and the storms of revolution, more evils perhaps than all the other errors, which have misled man. The most execrable passions have entrenched themselves behind this form under an impassive and impartial appearance, in order to give oneself up to all kinds of excesses."

Constant enumerates the ways by which we may recognize a law that is contrary to right:

Retroactivity is the first of these characteristics. Men
have consented to legal impediments only for the purpose
of attaching to their actions certain consequences, thereby
being able to direct matters themselves and to choose lines of
conduct which they wished to follow. Retroactivity deprives
them of this advantage. It dissolves the conditions of the social
pact. It removes the price of the sacrifice which it has imposed.
A second characteristic of illegality in laws is the compelling of
actions contrary to morals. Any law which commands
informing, denunciation, is not law. . . . Any law which divides

---

89. Ibid. For example, "the laws against the nobles, the priests . . . against the parents of the émigrés were not laws."
90. Ibid., p. 352. Constant quotes Bentham here: "Il faut examiner si les maux probables de l'obéissance sont moindres que les maux probables de la désobéissance."

the citizens into classes, which punishes them for what has not happened on their account, which makes them responsible for acts not done by them—any such regulation is not law.

Finally, Constant claims that we should be cautious about disobedience to the law, which is contrary to right. It is better to resort in that case to passive resistance.

> I do not pretend to recommend disobedience in any way whatsoever. Let it be forbidden, not through deference for the authority which usurps, but through regard for the citizen whom inconsiderate struggles would deprive of the advantages of the social state. As long as a law, even though bad, does not tend to deprave us; as long as authority only requires of us sacrifices which render us neither vile nor ferocious, we can consent to it. We compromise only for our own good. But should the law prescribe . . . that we trample our affection and devotion beneath our feet . . . anathema and disobedience to the drawing up of such enactments of injustices and crimes thus dignified with the name of law.[91]

Closely connected with the problem of obedience to law is the subject of rights. The natural rights theory of property had been incorporated into the Declaration of the Rights of Man and the Citizen in 1789. Constant, however, viewed property as a creation of society.[92] He distinguished the rights of property from other rights of individuals. "Some have represented property as something anterior to society and independent of it. They are wrong. Property is not anterior to society, for without the association which

91. In "De la competence du gouvernement," *Le temps*, 1830, Constant asks: "Who would dare condemn without reserve active resistance which appears natural? The overthrow of the Committee of Public Safety was only an act of resistance. But in resisting actively it is wrong to involve others. Passive resistance would not have this danger."

92. This shows that, unlike Locke's, Constant's individualism is not "possessive" in the sense that it "owes nothing to society." See C. B. Macpherson, *The Political Theory of Possessive Individualism*, p. 255. For theories of property in the eighteenth and nineteenth centuries see Richard Schlatter, *Private Property*, chapters 8 and 9.

gives it a guarantee, it would only be the right of the first occupant; in other words, the right of force, and, therefore, a right which is not a right. Property is not independent of society, for the social state can be conceived without property but one cannot imagine property without a social state. Property is nothing more than a social convention."

Does not this argument justify communism? Constant denies any such implication. "Property is under the competence and jurisdiction of society. Society possesses over it rights which it does not have over liberty, life, and opinion of its members. But property is intimately bound up with other parts of human existence of which some are not at all subject to collective jurisdiction and others are only subject to this jurisdiction in a limited manner. Arbitrariness over property is soon followed by arbitrariness over persons."[93] Having thus established that property is only a social convention and subject to social legislation, Constant concludes, however, that it is as inalienable as such natural rights as personal freedom, freedom of religion, and freedom of opinion.

One of the liberties mentioned in the Charte but very frequently violated during the Restoration was freedom of the press. Constant believed that of all liberties, freedom of the press is the one that is indispensable and can never be suspended because it is the guarantee of all the others. Even if habeas corpus is suspended, as in England, and liberty of the press is retained, any abuses arising from this suspension can be checked by this freedom. In short, all the civil, political, and judicial barriers become illusory without freedom of the press because their guarantee depends on publicity. "It is not the forms of constitutions which preserve them; there is

93. Constant, "Principes de politique," pp. 112–14. Cf. "De l'esprit de conquête et de l'usurpation," ibid., p. 225: "Je ne sais quel écrivain a déjà remarqué que M. de Montesquieu qui défend avec force les droits de la propriété particulière contre l'intérêt même de l'état, traite avec beaucoup moins de chaleur la question de la liberté des individus comme si les personnes étaient moins sacrées que les biens. L'homme auquel on enlève sa liberté est désarmé par ce fait même, au lieu que l'homme qu'on dépouille de sa propriété conserve sa liberté pour la réclamer. Ainsi la liberté n'est jamais défendu que par les amis de l'opprimé; le propriété l'est par l'opprimé lui-même."

no long duration for a constitution without public opinion and there is no public opinion without freedom of the press."[94]

Treating the subject in more depth, Constant said: "Most well-informed men seem agreed that works of some size and extent ought to be published free from any previous censure and control. . . . But pamphlets, essays, and periodical publications . . . may be thought more dangerous in their general effect." However, "I hope, on the contrary, to be able to prove that it is safer even for the interest of government to suffer even writings of that description to be freely published without being previously submitted to the control of the censor." For example, "in England every political question is argued in pamphlets, which follow it through every stage in its progress in Parliament." Thereby, "the Government and the Representatives of the People see at once the question before them in all its bearings and all that can be said for and against it. They are informed not only of the whole truth, they know what the majority of writers or speakers think of the law they are going to pass or the measures they are about to adopt." Public journals alone can create public opinion. "Even in England where everything is more settled . . . the public papers raise and keep alive public opinion."[95]

Constant was trying to show that "the freedom of journals would give France a new existence; it would unite it with its constitution, its government and its political interest. It would create a confidence which has at no time yet existed. It would form just such a communication of ideas, reflections, as makes Manchester, York, Liverpool, Derby, Birmingham repositories of political knowledge as well as of industry."[96]

But, continued Constant,

in all that has been said, I have only considered what was best for the interest of the government: but what could

94. "Observations sur le discours," p. 490.
95. "For this I appeal to De Lolme." Bentham is also quoted on the evils of censorship. See "The Liberty of the Press," *Pamphleteer* 6 (1815): 206–38.
96. "I have quoted England because I know no country that could afford such useful lessons" (ibid.).

I not say, if I touched on the interests of liberty, of individual safety? The only pledge citizens can have against arbitrary power is notoriety; which is most easily and most regularly preserved by the public journals. Illegal arrests, illegal banishments, may take place under the best established constitutions, and even contrary to the intention of the Sovereign. How can they be ascertained, if the press is not free?[97]

Furthermore, "arbitrary power which would allow the control of thought, might equally suppress the most important truths as the most fatal errors. Any opinion may be prohibited or punished." "You give, therefore," concluded Constant, "to authority the power of acting wrongly whenever it happens to reason absurdly."[98] It must be conceded that Constant's discussion of liberty of thought cannot compare in profundity with Mill's classic analysis in *On Liberty*.

Finally, in Constant's judgment, "it is not the liberty of the press that hurried on the confusion and madness of a fatal revolution [in France]. It was by having lived so long without it, that the mass of the people was ignorant and credulous and for that very reason, restless and often savage. In what are called the crimes of liberty, I can only see the offsprings of arbitrary power."[99] Besides, unanimity is always suspect, because it cannot exist when it comes to important and complicated questions. Thomas Jefferson, added Constant, was wrongly quoted against freedom of the press because of his indignation against calumny and defamation, both of which are prohibited by law.[100] Furthermore, "in all questions of morality and of a complicated nature, trial by jury is indispensable. Liberty of the press, for instance, can never exist without trial by jury. Juries alone can determine if such a book in such circumstances be criminal or not. Written law cannot distinguish all the shades of responsibility. The common sense of mankind must decide them. But juries are the

97. Ibid.
98. Constant, "Réflexions sur les constitutions," p. 257.
99. Ibid., p. 250.
100. *Archives parlementaires 1787–1860*, 5 March 1827.

representatives of popular opinion. ... To common sense we still must appeal and juries are its only interpreters."[101] Such are the main outlines of Constant's theory of constitutional monarchy. Between it and a republic the "difference is in the form," but "between constitutional monarchy and absolute monarchy the difference is in the foundation."[102] This is true because "the end of human associations is liberty, order, and the happiness of the people, whereas political organizations are only the means." In 1830, Constant, forgetting his earlier support of a republic during the Directory, said: "I have always thought that a republic was impossible in the state of knowledge, in the industrial, mercantile, military, and geographic state of France. Constitutional monarchy under Louis Philippe is our last ark of safety."[103] Although in the same year Constant contended that "liberty is possible under both a monarchy and a republic," he concluded that "there is no peaceful replacement in a republic; it is either usurpation or overturn."[104] Here Constant anticipated Tocqueville, who wrote that he "considered the Republic an ill-balanced form of government, which always promised more, but gave less liberty than the constitutional monarchy."[105]

101. Ibid.
102. Preface to the 1819 edition of "Des réactions politiques," p. 70.
103. *Discours*, 7 Nov. 1830.
104. *Le temps*, 1830.
105. Alexis de Tocqueville, *Recollections*, p. 238.

Chapter V
Religion and Political Economy

C O N S T A N T ' S political and religious liberalism cannot be separated. In fact, Croce has said that Constant's contribution was ✓ to have identified the religious nature of liberalism before Alexis de Tocqueville and Lord Acton.

Constant worked on and off all his life on a monumental study of religion.[1] The huge project dates from 1785, when he was only eighteen years old. The first volume of *De la religion considérée dans sa source, ses formes et ses développements* appeared forty years later in 1824, the second the following year, the third in 1827, and the fourth and fifth posthumously in 1831.[2]

In the *Cahier rouge* (1811), Constant recalls the genesis of his work on religion: "Having been nurtured on the principles of eighteenth-century philosophy and above all on the work of Helvétius, I had no other thought than to contribute my share toward the destruction of what I called prejudices."[3] He then confessed that he

1. For the evolution of this work see Helen H. S. Hogue, *Of Changes in Benjamin Constant's Books on Religions*; Pierre Deguise, *Benjamin Constant méconnu*; Henri Gouhier, *Benjamin Constant*; and Patrice Thompson, *Deux chapitres inédits de l'esprit des religions, 1803–1804.*

2. This opus was reviewed in the United States in the *Christian Examiner*, Sept. 1834, pp. 63–77, by Orestes Brownson, who used it for the purpose of attacking religious institutionalism. See William Girard, "Du transcendantalisme considérée essentiellement dans sa définition et ses origines françaises," pp. 351–498. It is important to note that Constant was in correspondence with William Clarke Somerville in America, whose *Letters from Paris on the Causes and Consequences of the French Revolution* refer repeatedly to Benjamin and his ideas. See R. L. Hawkins, *Newly Discovered French Letters of the Seventeenth, Eighteenth, and Nineteenth Centuries*, pp. 127–30.

3. "Le cahier rouge," *Oeuvres de Benjamin Constant*, p. 129. Cf. *Cecile*, p. 96: "J'avais été très irréligieux dans ma jeunesse par imitation des principes philosophiques plus encore que par inclination personnelle." Also a letter dated 6 July 1792 to Madame de Charrière: "Je ne suis du reste ni crédule ni incrédule, ni moral ni immoral. Je ne vois aucun preuve, aucune probabilité qu'il y ait un Dieu."

"seized upon an assertion by the author of *De l'esprit* [Helvétius], which claimed that pagan religion was much to be preferred to Christianity."[4] Constant's magnum opus on religion began, then, as a history of polytheism, written in the spirit of the philosophes.[5] Constant referred to another aspect of his intellectual heritage in a letter to Belle de la Charrière: "Ah, Madame, disciple of Suard, of the weighty Marmontel, of the pungent Condorcet, of the affected La Harpe, my pen must tell the effects of the education I have received."[6] Then, after going to school to the Idéologues, such as Antoine Destutt de Tracy, Pierre Cabanis, and Pierre Danou, at the time of the Consulate, Constant observed: "God knows that I do not like what is called religion nor what people call kings."[7] In other words, he was revolting in familiar eighteenth-century terms against both throne and altar, which had reinforced each other, and their abuses according to many a philosophe, who was convinced that political liberalism was synonymous with irreligion.

After about 1808, if not before, the irreligious emphasis of *De la religion* began to evolve gradually in the direction of the "religious impulse."[8] Constant wrote to his friend Prosper de Barante on 21 October 1808 about modifying certain "petites phrases" written in the eighteenth century under the influence of the Encyclopedists.[9]

---

4. As Ernst Cassirer in *The Philosophy of the Enlightenment*, pp. 25–27, 319, has shown, "Helvétius' book *On the Mind* (1759) was one of the most read and most often quoted works of the second half of the century" simply because "in this weak and unoriginal work there is a methodology characteristic of and decisive for the entire Eighteenth Century," namely, "that the foundation of knowledge lies in sense or simple sense perception."

5. See *Du polythéisme romain considérée dans ses rapports avec la philosophie grèque et la religion chrétienne*, which was finally published in 1833 after many revisions.

6. See Eusebe H. Gaullier, "Benjamin Constant et Madame de Charrière ou la jeunesse de Benjamin Constant racontée par lui-même," pp. 193–264.

7. *Journaux intimes*, 7 July 1804, p. 107.

8. On 19 February 1805, Constant had written (ibid., p. 208): "Il y a dans irreligion quelque chose de grossier et d'usé qui me repugne. D'ailleurs j'ai mon coin de religion. Mais il est tout en sentiments vagues; il ne peut se réduire en système." Unlike Charles Du Bos in *Grandeur et Misère de Benjamin Constant*, Pierre Deguise has shown conclusively in *Benjamin Constant méconnu* that Constant was not suddenly converted to religion.

9. See George Dierolf, "Lettres de Benjamin Constant à Prosper de Barante, 1805–1830," pp. 242–72, 528–87. In a letter to Barante, 25 Feb. 1808, Constant wrote: "J'ai eu le malheur hier de dire en pareille société (celle des 'gens qu'on appelle philosophes') que les *Discours de Bossuet sur l'Histoire universelle* me paraissait

On 11 October 1811, Constant wrote to Claude Hochet that he had revised three-quarters of the chapters of his history of polytheism.[10] He continues: "My work is a singular proof of what Bacon said" in his essay on *Atheism*: "'It is true that a little philosophy inclineth man's mind to atheism, but depth in philosophy bringeth man's mind about to religion.'"[11]

On 21 November 1804, Constant made an interesting observation: "How strange eighteenth-century philosophy is, making fun of itself and other people, taking upon itself the task of discrediting not only accepted prejudices and comforting ideas, which would have been separated from these prejudices, but mocks its own principles and takes pleasure in leaving nothing which is free from ridicule, in degrading and disparaging everything." Pierre Deguise has held, however, that this is not a considered general estimate of the philosophes but an irritated reaction to a certain Claude Mercier, compiler and editor of antireligious books.[12]

Then in a letter to Barante on 2 December 1811, Constant speaks of a new influence on his thought:

> German philosophy is of considerable service to me, although it is not progressing in a direction exactly analogous to my own. It follows a way from which I have deviated but which is nevertheless a parallel path. . . . It is a somewhat vague philosophy, but it respects everything which is religious, finding in religion everything that is good and becoming agitated only in its attempts to generalize its ideas and

---

plus un ouvrage historique que *l'Essai sur les moeurs et l'Esprit des Nations* (Voltaire) et j'ai excité un scandal universel."

10. Jean Mistler, *Lettres à un ami*, p. 194. Cf. Constant, 19 Nov. 1804, in his *Journaux intimes*, p. 166: "Le sentiment religieux est très compatible avec le doute," and in his *De la religion considérée dans sa source, ses formes et ses développements*, 5:172: "Le doute n'exclut point le sentiment religieux."

11. In the same letter Constant remarked: "Un professeur d'ici homme d'esprit, avec lequel j'en ai souvent causé, me disait que ce n'était pas moi qui faisais mon livre, mais que mon livre me faisait. C'est parfaitement vrai" (Mistler, *Lettres à un ami*, p. 229).

12. *Journaux intimes*, p. 166. Deguise warns us that this statement should be put in the context of the entry for that day when Constant said that he had read Comparé Mathieu.

locate the divine in everything in order to attain a
more seductive result by its apparent universality.[13]

As early as 1794, Constant had written: "But for philosophy and
history I find the Germans infinitely superior to the French and
English."[14] Moreover, he thought that the philosophy of German
idealism was not "that narrow and cynical philosophy, which in
Voltaire has us born between urine and fecal matter; which in
Helvétius does not distinguish us from horses except for our hands;
which in Diderot wishes to strangle the last priest with the entrails
of the last king and in Cabanis defines thought as a secretion of the
skull."[15]

"Forty years have passed away since the triumph of an infidel
philosophy at the epoch of the French Revolution. Where are we
now?" asks Constant. His answer—"A mysterious agitation, a
desire for religious faith, a longing for religious hope, are everywhere manifested," which is not limited to Lammenais and Maistre,
whom Constant attacks.[16] But Constant sharply differentiated between the religious feeling that is innate in man and religious forms,
that is, established religions, which he divides into sacerdotal and
nonsacerdotal types. Only such a distinction, he thought, could
avoid "two false positions"; first, that "religion is the natural ally

13. Dierolf, "Lettres de Constant à Barante." Cf. Charles Augustin Sainte-Beuve,
who wrote that Constant "appartenait à la descendance de Jean-Jacques croisée de
germanisme." See D. Melegari, *Journal intime de Benjamin Constant et lettres à sa
famille et ses amis*, p. lxvi.

14. Letter of Constant to Madame de Charrière, 6 June 1794. Cf. Constant's
observation in the chapter entitled "De la religion considérée comme utile" of the
manuscript copy of the *Principes de politique*: "Nous sommes de tout les peuples
celui dont les écrivains ont presque toujours envisagé la religion de la manière la plus
imparfaite et la plus étroite." But Constant excepted Bossuet, Fenelon, Necker, and
Chateaubriand.

15. "It is unjust to sum up the thought of Diderot in two verses from Eleuthe
romanes." See Roland Mortier, "Benjamin Constant et les lumières," pp. 144–56.

16. *De la religion*, 5:170. Constant's critique of Félicité Robert de Lammenais,
Essai sur l'indifférence en matière de religion, is to be found in ibid., 1: chap. 3. See
also *Christian Examiner* 10 (July 1831): 273–74: "The most important work from
which we have quoted, written by one of the most able men in politics and literature
of whom France can boast, [Constant] is in itself a proof of the revival of religious
ideas. That such a work, which is built on the reality of a spiritual religion and
disinterested morality, and which assumes the truth of the Christian system as a
philosophical fact, should proceed from the pen of a statesman and scholar, would
have been pronounced incredible at the close of the last century."

of despotism," and second, that "the absence of the religious sentiment is favorable to liberty."[17] At this point it is interesting to note that John Stuart Mill adhered later to these "false positions," viewing religion as "the engine of moral repression" and the source of persecution and bigotry.

Madame de Staël also suggested that the French Revolution had caused much confusion of thought concerning the connection between religion, despotism, and liberty:

> The secret had been found of exhibiting the friends of liberty as the enemies of religion; there are two pretexts for the singular injustice which would exclude from this earth the noblest of sentiments, alliance with Heaven. The first is the Revolution as it was effected in the name of philosophy; an inference has thence been drawn, that to love liberty it is necessary to be an atheist. Assuredly, it is because the French did not unite religion to liberty that their revolution deviated so often from its primitive direction. . . . It is by confusion of thought . . . that endeavors have been made to represent the privileges of the nobility and the absolute power of the throne as doctrines of religion.[18]

As Tocqueville put it later, "The religionists are the enemies of liberty and the friends of liberty attack religion," with the result that "the spirit of religion and the spirit of freedom [were] marching in opposite directions" in France.[19]

According to Philippe Stapfer, Constant's *De la religion* was designed "to fill the gap which for too long a time has separated in France philosophy and belief, religion and liberty. He [you] contributed to putting an end to a separation which is against nature."[20] Constant, therefore, made the point first, before Tocqueville ob-

17. Constant, *De la religion*, 1:86.
18. Germaine de Staël, *Considerations on the Principal Events of the French Revolution*, 2:335.
19. Alexis de Tocqueville, *Democracy in America*, 1:13, 308.
20. Letter to Constant, 26 May 1824. See Gustave Rudler, "Benjamin Constant et Philippe Stapfer," pp. 326–27.

served that he saw in France "ranged on the one side men who value morality, religion, and order and upon the other those who love liberty and the equality of men before the law," which is deplorable because "all the things thus separated are indissolubly united in the light of God as holy things."[21]

For Constant, the religious sentiment in itself contains "no principle, no element of slavery. Liberty, equality, justice, which is only equality, are its favorite doctrines." Furthermore, in studying all the "epochs when the religious sentiment triumphed, it can be seen that everywhere liberty was its companion. In the pagan Roman Empire the first Christians resuscitated the noble doctrine of equality and fraternity among men.[22] Protestantism preserved Germany under Charles V from universal monarchy, whereas to it England owes its constitution and France its liberty."[23]

If the presence of religious sentiment supports liberty, its absence favors tyranny.[24] When the religious feeling disappears, then slavery is near. "Religious people can be slaves, but no irreligious people ever remained free."[25] This same conclusion was reached later by Tocqueville and Acton. The former wrote that "nations that have not the self-governing force of religion within them are unprepared for freedom. . . . Despotism may govern without faith but liberty

21. Letter to Eugene Stoffels, 24 July 1836, in *Oeuvres et correspondance inédites*, 1:432.

22. *De la religion*, 1:86. Cf. Staël, *Considerations on the French Revolution*, 2:335: "Christianity has in truth brought liberty upon earth, justice toward the oppressed . . . equality before God, of which equality in the eyes of the law is only an imperfect image." See also Chateaubriand, "Le génie du Christianisme," *Oeuvres complètes*, 2:5: "La religion chrétienne est . . . la plus favorable à la liberté." Finally, Edouard Laboulaye, "La liberté antique et la liberté moderne," p. 115: "Les palais des Papes ont remplacé les palais des Césars, la vaticane parle de puissance de l'église, mais aux dessous de cet édifice splendide il y a des catacombes, qui parlent de liberté."

23. Constant remembered his Huguenot ancestry when he said: "Les religionnaires apportent en France toutes les idées de liberté. De tout temps le protestantisme conduisent à ces idées." See *Le moniteur universel*, 26 Aug. 1796.

24. On 11 October 1811, in a letter to Barante, Constant wrote: "S'il fallait choisir un peuple athée ou d'un peuple superstitieux il n'y aurait pas à hésiter pour ce dernier." This is a reversal, of course, of Pierre Bayle's famous paradox that was repeated in Denis Diderot's *Pensées philosophiques*, no. 12.

25. Constant, *De la religion*, 1:89, and *Du polythéisme romain*, 2:91–92. Cf. Tocqueville, *Democracy in America*, 1:307: "Democracy may govern without religion, but liberty cannot."

cannot."[26] The latter asserted that "liberty apart from belief is liberty with a good deal of the substance taken out of it."[27]

For Constant, then, "liberty can only be established or maintained by disinterestedness, and all morality separated from the religious sentiment can only be founded on calculation. To defend liberty there must be immolation of self." Therefore, as Constant saw it, "all systems can be reduced to two. The one assigns self-interest as guide and well-being for the goal. The other proposes for the end self-perfection and for a guide the intimate feeling [that is, religion], self-abnegation, and the faculty of sacrifice."[28] He is rejecting, of course, the ethic of "l'intérêt bien entendu" based on Lockean sensationalism and substituting in its place an innate moral sense based on "le sentiment religieux."

But, asks Constant, "What have we seen in all Europe for twenty years? Enlightened self-interest reigning without rival, a system founded principally by Helvétius, which teaches egoism and derides the whole idea of self-abnegation." Such a theory can, in Constant's judgment, only lead to the isolation of men and to the encouragement of the stronger to master the weaker, all of which makes the doctrine of enlightened self-interest the ally of despotism instead of liberty.[29] "When it is egoism which overthrows tyranny, then

26. Tocqueville, *Democracy in America*, 1:44: "Liberty regards religion as its companion in all its battles and triumphs. . . . It considers religion as the safeguard of morality and as the best security of law and the surest pledge of the duration of freedom."

27. John Emerich Acton, *Lectures on the French Revolution*, p. 6. Cf. Tocqueville, *Democracy in America*, 1:12: "Liberty cannot be established without morality and morality without faith."

28. Constant, *De la religion*, 1:89. Cf. Staël, *Considerations on the French Revolution*, 2:338: "It is in the soul, not in the calculation of self-interest, that the principles of liberty are founded."

29. In a letter to Madame de Charrière, 16 Dec. 1795, Constant wrote: "Ainsi la morale fondée sur le bonheur n'a aucune base fixe. Le devoir ou le bien moral doit être absolument étranger aux circonstances et aux calculs." According to Basil Munteano, "Episodes kantiens en Suisse et en France sous le Directoire," p. 445, "Benjamin Constant adopte entièrement la doctrine kantienne du devoir. Mieux même à l'entendre justifier cette doctrine et réfuter celle du bonheur empirique, on dirait qu'il a lu les *Fondements de la Metaphysique des Moeurs* et la *Critique de la Raison pratique*, ou au moins qu'il en a connue et compris les principes directeurs." Constant and Kant quarreled over the question whether it is always a duty to tell the truth regardless of the consequences. See Constant's "Des réactions politiques," *Cours de politique*, 2:113, and Kant's "On a Supposed Right to Lie from Altruistic Motives," pp. 346–50.

it is only a matter of sharing or dividing the spoils of tyranny."
But when "Christians appeared, they placed their point of support
beyond egoism. Liberty is nourished by sacrifices. Liberty wishes
always for citizens, sometimes for heroes. Religious convictions
give men strength to become martyrs."[30] In other words, only
religions can supply the moral basis for the opposition to tyranny.
From all this it is clear that the optimistic hedonism of the century
before 1789 no longer suited an age that had experienced the
Revolution and Bonaparte.

With such an outlook, it is not surprising that Constant was not
only opposed to Helvétius's theory of enlightened self-interest but
also to Jeremy Bentham's doctrine of utility. To Constant, "the
principle of utility awakens in men the hope of profit and not the
feeling of duty. Actions cannot be more or less just, but they can be
more or less useful." The concept of utility, therefore, is more vague
than the theory of natural rights. "Right is a principle, utility is only
a result; right is a cause, utility only an effect." Therefore, "to desire
to subordinate right to utility is like wishing to place the eternal
rules of arithmetic in submission to our daily interests. That which
is not just is never useful."[31]

Even more disturbing to Constant than Helvetius or Bentham
was the Baron Paul Henri d'Holbach. In his *Système de la nature*,
the Baron portrayed atheism as the sole system that can lead men to
liberty, happiness, and virtue.[32] Reacting strongly against atheism,
Constant showed that he was just as opposed to irreligious as to
religious dogmatism.

"We detest an intolerant power but we fear the philosophic
power. The persecutions of Louis XIV have caused much evil. The
so-called enlightenment of Joseph II has brought about as much;

30. Constant, *De la religion*, 1:Preface, p. xxxix. Cf. Alexis de Tocqueville, *The
Old Regime and the French Revolution*, p. 154: "Trained in the hard school of
successive revolutions, all the various classes of the French nation have gradually
regained that feeling of respect for religious faith which once seemed lost forever."

31. "Montesquieu a dit la justice existait avant les formes destinées à les garantir"
("Observations sur le discours," *Cours de politique*, 1:489).

32. Thomas Paine, in Constant's mind, only reproduced in trivial style the superficial metaphysics of the Baron Holbach. William Godwin, however, was more
profound to Constant than Thomas Paine, but he also viewed religion as the enemy
of liberty.

the unwise decrees of the Constituent Assembly have not done less." The consequences, then, of irreligious intolerance are no less terrible than the results of religious intolerance, in the place of which Constant would substitute tolerance or the "liberty of all cults present and future." For him, "error or truth, the thought of man is his most sacred property. Error or truth, tyrants are equally culpable when they attack it. He who proscribes in the name of philosophy speculative superstition, he who in the name of God proscribes independent reason, merit equally the execration of men of good will."[33]

Constant denounced persecution and intolerance, whether religious or civil.[34] Moreover, he felt that a political, secular, or civil religion like the one Rousseau outlined in Book 4, chapter 8, of the *Social Contract* to put an end to the Gelasian dualism would be the very worst kind. "What does it matter if spiritual pretensions have given way to political authority, if this authority makes religion an instrument and thus acts against liberty with a double force?"[35] In this connection, he observed that Rousseau had often been cited in support of civil intolerance. Once again Constant repeated his judgment that Rousseau "cherished all the theories of liberty" and yet he "furnished the pretexts for all the pretensions of tyranny."[36] Constant concluded: "I do not know any system of servitude which has consecrated more horrible errors than the eternal metaphysic of the *Social Contract*."[37]

33. Constant, "Principes de politique," *Cours de politique*, 1:142–43. Cf. Constant's letter of 4 June 1790 to Madame de Charrière in which he seems to reject both first-century Christian folly and eighteenth-century philosophic madness.
34. Constant cited Lammenais, *Essai sur l'indifférence en matière de religion*, and Stanislas de Clermont-Tonnerre, "Réflexions sur le fanatisme," *Oeuvres complètes*, vol. 1.
35. Constant, *Commentaire sur l'ouvrage de Filangieri*, 1:27.
36. "Mais Rousseau, s'agitant au milieu de mille pensées contraires, a rassemblé sur la religion, non moins que sur la politique, de discordantes et confuses hypothèses. Le plus affirmatif des hommes et le plus impatient de l'affirmation des autres, il a tout ébranlé non qu'il voulut, comme on l'a dit, tout détruire, mais parce que rien ne lui semblait à sa place. Il a, dans sa force prodigieuse, arraché de leurs fondements antiques les colonnes sur lesquelles reposait, tant bien que mal, l'existence humaine; mais architecte aveugle, il n'a pu, de ces matériaux épars, construire un nouvel édifice. Il n'est résulté de ses efforts que des destructions, de ces destructions qu'un chaos où il a laissé sa puissante empreinte." (*De la religion*, 1:116). Cf. Fonds d'Estournelles de Constant Manuscrits, Lausanne, Co 3259.
37. See also the reservations of two other contemporary liberals about Book 4,

To Constant, when the French Revolution reached its Jacobin phase to be followed later by the Empire, a new political fanaticism in the form of an irreligious sectarianism developed that was far worse than any clerical sectarianism.[38] Atheism abolished moral values and encouraged thereby relativism, nihilism, cynicism, and Machiavellian politics and, ultimately, as a result, despotism. Constant asserts that the destruction of the spiritual power of the church is often extolled, but he said that he prefers "the religious yoke to political despotism." The reason is that "under the first, there is at least conviction among the slaves that the tyrants alone are corrupted." However, "when oppression is separated from every religious idea, the slaves are as depraved and as abject as their masters."[39]

Constant believed that the Christian religion was not only the foundation of liberty but also of human progress.[40] This idea is, of course, the opposite of Condorcet's theory of progress and perfectibility, which nonetheless greatly influenced Constant's own earlier conception. "Among the different systems . . . one alone seems to explain the enigma of our individual and social existence. That system is the perfectibility of human kind."[41] For this theory Cons-

chap. 8 ("The Civil Religion") of Rousseau's *Social Contract*, which Constant quotes in part in "Principes de politique," pp. 128–29. Pierre Daunou, "De la religion publique ou réflexions sur un chapitre du Contrat Social de Jean Jacques Rousseau," 1:456 and 2:98; and Jean de Lanjuinais, *Examen du huitième chapitre du Contrat Social de Jean-Jacques Rousseau.* Later Tocqueville referred to "a new kind of religion . . . without God, without worship, without another life"; in other words, a political religion of secular salvation (*Oeuvres complètes*, 2, pt. 1: 87–90).

38. See Madame de Staël's observation: "L'exaltation de ce qu'on appelle la philosophie est une superstition comme le culte des préjugés" ("De l'influence des passions sur le bonheur des individus et des nations" [1796], chap. 8, "De l'esprit du parti," *Oeuvres complètes*, 3:153, 176).

39. "De la religion sous l'arbitraire," in "De l'esprit de conquête et de l'usurpation," *Cours de politique*, 2:237.

40. "Le Christianisme est un progrès, le plus important, le plus décisif des progrès que l'espèce humaine ait fait jusqu'à ce jour" (*De la religion*, 4:203, n.1). Cf. Anne Robert Jacques Turgot, who had reconciled progress with Christianity earlier: *Discours sur les avantages que l'établissement de Christianisme a procurés aux genre humain.*

41. Constant, "De la perfectibilité de l'espèce humaine," *Mélanges de littérature et de politique*, p. 387. Cf. Mme de Staël, who wrote: "Le système de la perfectibilité de l'espèce humain a été celui de tous les philosophes éclairés depuis cinquante ans." She names Ferguson, Kant, Turgot, and Condorcet, who lived under different types

tant was indebted to Condorcet but to Johann Gottfried von Herder as well.[42]

In his very first published work—*De la force du gouvernement actuel de la France et de la nécessité de s'y rallier* (1796)—which was answered by Joseph de Maistre in his *Considérations sur la France* (1797), after quoting Condorcet on progress, Constant stated that "the race is advancing toward equality" with "caste, slavery, and feudalism everywhere disappearing."[43] When Constant attacked the royalist Comte Antoine-François-Claude Ferrand, he asserted that "it was a question of deciding between superstition and enlightenment, between the return of the eleventh and the expectation of the nineteenth century."[44]

In *Des réactions politiques* (1797) Constant, contrary to his later position, opposed religious liberty on the ground that it would result in the reestablishment of religious prejudice. He cited the case of the philosophe, Jean-François de La Harpe, who had forsaken philosophy for Catholicism. Constant commented bitterly: "Thereby is reconstructed the triple edifice of monarchy, nobility, and priesthood." In spite of such an unfortunate occurrence, however, Constant believed that "slavery, feudalism, superstition in the religious guise are all on the defensive. The passions are in retreat, conquered by truth. It is necessary that the light extend and the human race equalize."[45]

To Constant, "the human race has no principle more dear and precious to defend than human perfectibility."[46] If we do not believe

---

of government and yet still believed in progress. See *De la littérature considérée dans ses rapports avec les institutions sociales*, Preface. Constant cites Godwin, Priestley, Price, Condorcet, and Turgot. See "Fragments d'un essai sur la perfectibilité de l'espèce humain," *Benjamin Constant. De la Justice Politique. Traduction inédite de l'ouvrage de William Godwin, Enquiry concerning Political Justice*, p. 363.

42. See *Journaux intimes*, 10 Jan. 1805, p. 190: "De la perfectibilité de l'espèce humaine comme une introduction à l'extrait des *Idées sur la philosophie de l'histoire de Herder*." Herder was not translated into French until 1827 by Edgar Quinet. See Henri Tronchon, *La fortune intellectuelle de Herder en France*, pp. 310–60.

43. *De la force du gouvernement actuel de la France et de la nécessité de s'y rallier*, p. 96.

44. *Le républicain français*, 24 July 1795.

45. Constant, "Des réactions politiques," pp. 89, 127–28.

46. Constant, *De la religion*, 5:202–7, 2:212. "Mais le but de l'homme est le perfectionnement."

in the perfectibility of man, then "we ought to close our books, renounce our speculations, release ourselves from vain sacrifices, and confine ourselves entirely to useful or agreeable acts, which would render less insipid a life without hope and adorn momentarily the present time without a future."[47] It "alone has established assured communications between the generations." But he did not accept individual perfectibility. In his conception, there is an interior and an exterior perfectibility. The former concerns morality, such as the abolition of slavery. The latter includes scientific discoveries, such as those of Galileo, Copernicus, and Newton, as well as technological advances, like gunpowder, printing, the compass, and steam power. There is progress, not retrogression, even though Constant had provided for decadence in his comparison of ancient and modern societies, as we have already noted. Although progress is often interrupted by periods of decline, Constant, like Machiavelli and Montesquieu before him, combined degeneration or decadence in the present with a hopeful expectation of regeneration in the future. Like Rousseau, he also made a distinction between the long-range pessimism of the ancients and the short-range optimism of the moderns.[48]

Here are some of Constant's illustrations. Even though the French Revolution had corrupted individuals, morality had advanced. We cannot say that the Athenians were freer than we; therefore, the human race is losing its liberty. After all, they were but a small part of the inhabitants of Greece; Greece a small part of Europe; the rest of the world was barbarous, and the great majority of the inhabitants of Greece were slaves. Today, however, Europe is free of slavery, three-quarters of this part of the globe is free of feudalism, and one-half is free of the privileges of the nobility. No one any longer has the right of life and death over another, and tolerance instead of intolerance prevails.

Continuing his discussion of progress, Constant thought that

47. *De la perfectibilité de l'espèce humaine*, p. 42. The Greeks did not accept the perfectibility of man and yet they never "renounced speculations."

48. See Jean-Jacques Rousseau, *On the Social Contract with Geneva Manuscript and Political Economy*, Introduction, p. 37. Most of the time, however, Constant adhered to the conception of a unilinear progressive evolution toward a millennial end.

there had been four great revolutions—the destruction of theocracy, of slavery, of feudalism, and of the nobility as a privileged class. He believed that history shows us that the establishment of Christianity and the barbarian invasions from the North were the cause of the destruction of slavery; the Crusades were the source of the annihilation of the privileges of the nobility. These events, however, were only the occasion and not the real origin of this destruction. It so happened that human beings were ripe for deliverance. It is the eternal force of things that guides revolutions on their paths. In fact, the four revolutions were so many steps toward the reestablishment of natural equality. In short, "the perfectibility of human kind is nothing more than the tendency toward equality."[49] Inequality is what alone constitutes injustice. Finally, Constant argues that opinions and institutions (because institutions are in their origin nothing more than opinions put into practice) which we consider today as abuses could have had in their time utility, necessity, and relative perfection. Therefore, what we now regard as indispensable can become in a few centuries an abuse.

If Constant is influenced by the theorists of progress such as Condorcet and Herder, he is also indebted to counterrevolutionary theorists such as Burke and Maistre.[50] The eighteenth-century ideal of progress is, of course, contrary to the nineteenth-century liberal glorification of the past through an appeal to historical precedent. In fact, "the adoption of history by liberals . . . was one of the turning points in the development of Liberalism" because "from the time of Burke and Chateaubriand liberals have grown accustomed to conceding history to the conservatives." In fact, "this new generation of Liberals to which Constant belonged, resorted to the antirevolutionary arguments of historically minded Conservatives."[51]

49. Constant, "De la perfectibilité de l'espèce humaine," *Mélanges*, p. 407. Cf. "De la doctrine politique qui peut réunir les partis en France," *Cours de politique*, 2:299, where Constant wrote that "the spirit of the century and even more that of France is equality." See also "De Madame de Staël et ses ouvrages," *Mélanges*, p. 196, where he observed that "liberty appears to many who seek and desire it as less precious than equality," an interesting anticipation of Tocqueville's main theme.

50. Cf. Constant's earlier hostility toward Burke in a letter to Madame de Charrière in December 1790: "I am currently busy reading and refuting Burke's book against the French Levellers. This famous book contains as many absurdities as it does lies. . . . He defends nobility, the exclusion of the sectaires, the establishment of a dominant religion, and other things of this nature."

51. François Guizot, *Historical Essays and Lectures*, pp. xxiv, xxxii.

In Constant's judgment, "one of the most common and grievous errors of our revolution was the persuasion that institutions are created by will."[52] He boldly asserted: "I have much veneration for the past . . . I say it to the great scandal of our modern reformers, who call themselves Lycurguses or Charlemagnes. If I saw a people to whom was offered the most perfect institutions, metaphysically speaking, and who refused them in order to remain faithful to those of their fathers, I would esteem this people and I would believe it happier . . . under these defective institutions, than it would be under the proposed perfections." Constant added, however, that he excepted from his respect for the past whatever is unjust, because "time can never sanction an injustice like slavery."[53]

To Constant, then, progress being gradual, every violent innovation is dangerous. In more than one work he clearly showed his opposition to revolutions in words very similar to those of Maistre.[54] He quoted Rousseau [*Discourse on Political Economy*] to the effect that no revolution is worth the life of an innocent man. Furthermore, "in reversing in the name of liberty, the existing authority, revolutions give to the authority, which replaces it, specious pretexts against liberty," a point he had made earlier.[55] It is interesting to note that Tocqueville was of the same persuasion as Constant when he said: "I think that there is no one in France less revolutionary than myself or any one who has a deeper hatred for what is called the revolutionary spirit (which spirit, in passing, combines very easily with a love of absolute government)."[56]

With such an antirevolutionary attitude, it is natural for Constant to be convinced that "almost all old governments are mild because

52. "Des aveux échappés aux ennemis de la loi des élections," *La minerve française* 8(Nov. 1819): 529–43.

53. Constant, "De l'esprit de conquête," pp. 171–72.

54. See his *Discours* 1:364, 381: "Toute révolution est terrible; tout nouveau gouvernement est dur et vexatoire; l'expérience le dit, les peuples le savent. Mais j'ai l'horreur des révolutions; elles immolent les individus; elles dénaturent les caractères, elles corrompent la morale, elles mettent des devoirs factices à la place des devoirs réels, elles substituent une force aveugle à la force de la raison et à celle de la loi; elles pervertissent la justice, elles attentent aux droits de chacun."

55. Constant, "Madame de Staël et ses ouvrages," pp. 195–96: "D'ordinaire elles [les révolutions] manquent leur but en le dépassant."

56. Letter to Eugene Stoffels, 5 Oct. 1836, *Oeuvres et correspondance inédites*, 1:436: "I knew that, if one great revolution is able to establish liberty in a country, a number of succeeding revolutions make regular liberty impossible for very many years."

they are old and all new governments are harsh because they are new."[57] For example, he refers to the government of William III in England as vexatious. Liberty began with Queen Anne. The advantages of liberty, therefore, cannot really be appreciated until it is already old, that is, with the passage of time, a position Tocqueville also held.

As Constant once phrased it, "It is not with liberty as with a battle. A battle, being the affair of one day, can be won by the talent of a general; but liberty to exist must have its base in the nation itself and not in the virtue or character of a leader." He thought that it was a "strange doctrine that because men are corrupt, it is necessary to give to some of them more power. Instead they should be given less, that is, to place in institutions wisely combined, counterweights against their vices and weaknesses."[58] In the last analysis, liberty rests on the principles of justice and is not solely political but instead the "triumph of individuality."[59]

As Constant once summarized, "Philosophy could declare the principles of liberty; heroic courage could defend it; but it is to commerce and industry, to these two forces, so independent that they only demand of authority not to interfere with them, . . . to found liberty by their slow, gradual action that nothing can prevent."[60] Looking at it historically,

> the dominant need of the fifteenth and sixteenth centuries was for free examination. The chief demand of our epoch is not only for freedom of belief and opinion but independence of material existence as well, without which intelligence is menaced to fall into slavery. . . . Formerly governments were

57. Constant, "Le cahier rouge," p. 164.
58. Constant, "Lettre sur Julie," *Mélanges*, pp. 60–61.
59. Constant, *Mélanges*, Preface, p. vi. Cf. "Fragments d'un essai sur la perfectibilité humaine": "Par le mot d'idées ou de sentiments de liberté politique, je n'entends pas ce qu'on appelle liberté politique mais l'instinct plus ou moins développé de l'indépendance individuelle, des droits de tous les hommes en société, de l'égalité, en un mot, de la dignité humaine."
60. Constant, "Des élections prochaines," *Cours de politique*, 2:314. Cf. Alexis de Tocqueville, *Sur la Démocratie en Amérique* (Fragments inédits) quoted in Melvin Richter, "The Uses of Theory," p. 100: "Commercial institutions produce not only skill in making use of liberty; but also a real taste for it. Without commerce, such a taste for political liberty would amount to no more than childish desires or youthful fears."

considered as the dispensers of riches. The Revolution destroyed this system [mercantilism]. The Restoration completed the victory of the industrial system. Industry is today the chief thought, perhaps the only thought of the century . . . and it needs liberty and peace and it maintains peace and strengthens liberty.[61]

Constant predicted the nature of the social conditions toward which humanity was moving:

> In political economy there will be so far as property is concerned respect and protection, because property is a legal convention, necessary in our time . . . the liberty to preserve, to alienate, to divide, to alter property is, in our social state, the inherent right, the essential need of all those who possess it. Industrial property will be placed higher than landed property because landed property is the value of a thing, industrial property the value of the man.[62] There will be, relative to industry, liberty, absence of every intervention of authority, whether to preserve individuals from their own errors (experience will enlighten them) or to assure the public better articles of consumption (experience will guide its choice), and every monopoly privilege, every corporation protected to the detriment of the activity of individual enterprise, will disappear never to return.[63]

In an essay in 1822, Constant addressed himself particularly to the subject of political economy. He then published a *Commentaire*

61. "Coup d'oeil sur la tendance général des esprits dans le XIXe siècle," *Revue Encyclopédique*, 1825. Cf. Henri de Saint-Simon, *L'industrie*, who makes the same point, showing the influence of Constant, whom he quotes. See also Montesquieu, who said that "peace is the natural effect of trade" (*The Spirit of the Laws*, Book 20, chap. 2, p. 316).

62. Constant, *Mélanges*, Preface, p. x: "J'ai été d'avis dans mes *Principes de Politiques* (1815) de n'accorder les droits qu'aux propriétaires fonciers, et l'expérience m'a éclairé. J'ai vu que dans notre siècle la propriété industrielle était une propriété plus réelle encore et surtout plus puissante que celle du sol, et, reconnaissant mon erreur, j'ai corrigé mon ouvrage."

63. Ibid.

sur l'ouvrage de Filangieri, an eighteenth-century Neopolitan lawyer and economist, who had written *La scienza della legislazione* (1780) in the spirit of a philosophe, arguing for the realization of liberty through the reforms of enlightened despotism.[64] Constant seems to use Filangieri as a point of departure for the statement of his own ideas rather than as a subject for a detailed analysis and critique.

Constant begins his essay by claiming that he was not so much opposed to Gaetano Filangieri's objective as to the means recommended to achieve it. Like the philosophes, Filangieri would use government to realize reform in agriculture, industry, and commerce without understanding that nature is much stronger than authority. Therefore, Constant thought that Filangieri had made a very common error. Since authority can do much harm, he concluded that it could likewise do much good. Filangieri could rise up against the encroachments of authority and at the same time confer on the legislator what Rousseau gave to society, an unlimited empire over human existence. Writers, therefore, distrust government when looking at it as it is, but when considering it as it ought to be, they present it as an abstraction endowed with virtue. For example, the Abbé de Mably wrote six volumes tracing the history of France in terms of the misery of the people and the crimes of power. But the authority Mably found to be so evil in practice is now seen in theory as beneficial and enlightened. In fact, he even goes so far as to argue that government should control thought as well as actions, a point Constant had made earlier.

Constant then points out that to claim, with Rousseau, Mably, and Filangieri, that the law extends to all subjects is to set up tyranny. Legislation like government has only two purposes: first, to prevent internal disorders and, second, to withstand foreign invasion. This is, of course, the common description of the negative or nightwatchman state from Wilhelm von Humboldt's *The Limits*

---

64. In his "Observations sur le discours," p. 483, Constant had said that "les ouvrages de Montesquieu, de Filangieri, de Blackstone sont les dépots des lumières," but in his *Commentaire sur l'ouvrage de Filangieri*, pt. 1, pp. 1–7, he wrote that "Filangieri n'a ni la profondeur de Montesquieu, ni la perspicacité de Smith, ni l'originalité de Bentham."

of State Action (1792) to Herbert Spencer's *Man versus the State* (1884).

Constant continues to develop his position by stating that it is necessary to distinguish two kinds of crime—actions bad in themselves and actions that are harmful only as violations of contracts. The jurisdiction of the law is absolute over the first and relative over the second, depending on the nature of the contract. Moreover, the law should never fix riches in a state or distribute them with equity. Riches are distributed and divided by themselves in a perfect equilibrium when the division of property has not been restrained and the exercise of industry is not fettered. The law should be neutral and silent. Constant believed, therefore, that the functions of government are purely negative. Most of the time it is not laws that should be made but laws that should be abrogated. These are, of course, well-known arguments of economic liberals, from the physiocrats to Adam Smith, with whom Constant was very familiar.

But of all liberals, it was Constant alone who singled out for express and detailed refutation Rousseau's notion that laws are the expression of the general will. Instead, they are the declaration of the relations of men with each other, which is what Montesquieu had in mind when he wrote that "laws, in their most general signification, are the necessary relations arising from the nature of things."[65] At the moment when society exists there are established certain relations among men. Laws are nothing more than these relations observed and expressed; they are not the cause of these relations, which, on the contrary, are anterior to them. They create nothing but the forms for guaranteeing what existed before their institution. It follows, therefore, that no man, no faction of society, not even the whole society, can attribute to itself the right to make laws. Laws being only the expression of relations that exist among men and these relations preceding the laws, a new law is nothing more than a declaration that has not yet been made of what existed previously. The legislator is for the moral universe what the physical is for the material universe. Newton himself could only observe and declare the laws he had discovered. He was not the creator of these

65. *Spirit of the Laws*, Book 1, chap. 1, p. 1.

laws. Such a theory is very much like the position of the physiocratic thinker Pierre-Samuel Dupont de Nemours in his *De l'origine et des progrès d'une science nouvelle*, published in 1768.

Constant believed that the functions of government were simply to repress evil and let good operate by itself. He suggested that Montesquieu was right when he said that a man condemned to death by laws to which he consented is freer than one who lives tranquilly under laws that have been instituted without his consent. In the same way, one can say that the adoption of an error by ourselves, because it appears to us to be the truth, is an operation more favorable to the perfection of the species than the adoption of a truth on the word of some authority. Constant continued that it was in this sense that he had once declared that free error is worth more than imposed truth. He stated that William Godwin wrote in *An Enquiry Concerning Political Justice* that "a miracle operating to show the truth does produce conviction in the spectators but in the process their judgment deteriorates. It is to submit to force rather than to evidence."

Constant also referred with approval to a distinction the Marquis de Mirabeau drew in his *L'ami des hommes* (1756) between positive and speculative laws.[66] When the government punishes a harmful action or the violation of a contract, it performs a positive function. When it hampers the disposition of property or the exercise of industry or seeks to dominate opinion or education, it is arrogating to itself a speculative function. When the government defends the frontiers of a country from attack there is a positive law, but when it makes war on all peoples suspected of planning an attack, that is an example of a speculative law. Constant concluded, therefore, that if the legislator cannot distinguish better than individuals what is advantageous and harmful, then why extend his power? "The words *comprimer, extirper, diriger* should be removed from the vocabulary of power. For thought, education, and industry the device of governments should be *laissez-faire, laissez-passer,* and *laissez-aller.*"

---

66. Cf. Spencer's differentiation between a government's being negatively and positively regulative. See his essay on "Specialized Administration," Herbert Spencer, *The Man versus the State*, pp. 273–311.

"Turgot, Mirabeau, Condorcet in France; Dohm [Christian Wilhelm von] and Mauvillon [Friedrich Wilhelm von] in Germany; Thomas Paine and Bentham in England; Franklin in America—all these believed in freedom rather than in protection."[67] Constant noted, however, that *laissez-faire*, *laissez-passer*, and *laissez-aller* were treated by economists as applying only to prohibitions and not to encouragements as well, which is the way it should be in order to be consistent.[68]

Constant disagreed with William Godwin when he wrote in his *An Enquiry Concerning Political Justice* that government is a necessary evil. On the contrary, government has a sphere that is proper to it. When it leaves this sphere it becomes an evil, but it is not as a government but as a usurpation that it is an evil. If one says that a government cannot reach the guilty without hurting the innocent sometimes, this inconvenience should not be associated with government but with the nature of man. Government can be mistaken. In order to avoid this, it institutes forms, and if they are good and if they are respected, government is far from being an evil but is a good. According to Godwin, because government is a necessary evil, there should be as little as possible of it. This is a mistake. "Government beyond its proper sphere ought not to have any power; within its sphere it cannot have enough of it."[69]

With such economic views, it is not surprising that Constant reacted strongly against the philosophy of Saint-Simon. In commenting on Charles Dunoyer's works, Constant observed:

> One of the greatest merits of M. Dunoyer was to have separated himself from a new sect—which preaches the enslavement of authority at a time when power is weakening in the face of reason. This sect wished to found an industrial papism, which is deprived of heavenly intervention like Rome. It takes for its foundation the pretensions of some men who

67. Constant, *Commentaire sur l'ouvrage de Filangieri*, 1:14.
68. Constant was influenced by such economists as Germain Garnier, Adam Smith, Jean Baptiste Say, Charles Dunoyer, Charles Comte, and Simonde de Sismondi.
69. Constant, *Mélanges*, p. 218. Cf. Tocqueville's comment: "What I want is a central government energetic in its sphere of action" (Letter to Eugene Stoffels, 5 Oct. 1836, *Oeuvres et correspondance inédites*, 1:436–37).

have proclaimed themselves the guides of all. . . . There is the same desire for unity as in Lammenais and Maistre. The ideas of liberty, say this sect, have little to do today because we are entering into an epoch when it is more urgent to coordinate than to dissolve, when the positive theory must take the place of critical theories. This will lead to a coordination of doctrines and opinions, which means the organization of tyranny, and in doing that this sect is more inexcusable than Lammenais and Maistre, who at least claim divine inspiration for their system.[70]

In fact, Constant calls the positivists "priests of Thebes and Memphis, who are introducing despotism under the guise of that deadly ancient liberty."

It is interesting to compare Constant's reactions to Saint-Simon with Mill's estimate of Comte. Comte was described by John Stuart Mill as aiming at "establishing . . . a despotism of society over the individual, surpassing anything contemplated in the political ideal of the most rigid disciplinarians among the ancient philosophers."[71] In fact, to Mill, almost all the plans of the social reformers of his day, especially Comte's, involved "liberticide."

Both politically and chronologically Constant marked the change between the eighteenth and nineteenth centuries. "We are a generation of passage, of transition, born under arbitrary government, we are sowing the seed of liberty."[72] Here is Constant the optimist speaking. The pessimist remained with him to the end, however. "To take a few steps in the direction of legal liberty and to see oneself pushed back upon despotism, is this," he asks, like Tocqueville, who lived to experience the Second Empire, "the eternal fate of France?"[73]

---

70. Constant, *Mélanges*, pp. 157–61. Saint-Simon and Comte both praised what the latter referred to as "the retrograde school." This "immortal group under the leadership of Maistre will long deserve the gratitude of Positivists" (Auguste Comte, *Système de politique positive*, 3:605).

71. John Stuart Mill, *On Liberty*, chap. 1.

72. *Le constitutionnel*, 21 May 1827.

73. Constant, *Discours*, 1:188.

Chapter VI
Conclusion

BENJAMIN CONSTANT, after his great English contemporary, Jeremy Bentham, was the most widely read liberal thinker of his time. Constant in France and John Stuart Mill in England outlined in classic fashion the liberal defense of a certain area of individual freedom and privacy that should never be infringed.[1] This notion that a line should be drawn between the private and public spheres of life is the key conception in the last analysis of liberalism, but it remains one of the most controversial in the history of political philosophy from Socrates and Plato to Lenin and Mao Tse-tung, because, among other things, it stresses the rights as distinguished from the duties of man.[2]

Constant should not be classified, along with Bentham and Mill, in the utilitarian current of liberalism. In spite of certain similarities between Constant and Mill, Constant belongs instead to the liberal tradition begun by Locke and Montesquieu and continued by Tocqueville and Acton. His liberalism was not abstract and rationalist but institutional and historical.[3] The liberty envisaged by Constant was not "egoist" but the "absence of the arbitrary."[4]

1. Sir Isaiah Berlin describes Constant as "the most eloquent of all defenders of freedom and privacy" (*Four Essays on Liberty*, p. 126).
2. See Mao Tse-tung, "Combat Liberalism," pp. 32–33, where it is argued that liberalism "stems from petty-bourgeois selfishness" because "it places personal interests first and the interests of the revolution second." In contrast, a communist must subordinate "his personal interests to those of the revolution," and he should "be more concerned about the Party and masses than about any private person and more concerned about others than about himself." See Steven Lukes, *Individualism*.
3. Henri Michel was wrong when he wrote in *L'idée de l'état*, p. 300, that the historic spirit is absent from Constant's political philosophy.
4. Emile Faguet, *Politiques et moralistes du dix-neuvième siècle*, p. 230, is incorrect, and Cecil P. Courtney is right, "Témoin et interprète de son Temps," p. 133. "Mes *Principes de politique* étaient une perpetuelle protestation contre les abus de

For Constant, "liberalism meant the rule of law and the constitutional state," an idea he always emphasized far more than the economic theory of laissez-faire.[5]

In developing his constitutionalism, Constant used England for his model and selected Montesquieu for his teacher of free government, although he was never hailed as a second Montesquieu, as Tocqueville was by John Stuart Mill. Following Montesquieu, however, Constant's liberalism was aristocratic because the Terror and Bonapartism resulted in an antidemocratic liberalism that was antagonistic to the egalitarian ideas of Rousseau. Moreover, like Tocqueville's and Acton's, Constant's liberalism was firmly grounded in religion as well as in law and institutions.

In his own time, Constant's philosophy of liberalism presented a real alternative to the political theory of legitimists, like Maistre and Bonald, on the one hand, and Jacobins, like Robespierre and Louis de Saint-Just, on the other. It is no wonder that he was regarded as revolutionary by the former and reactionary by the followers of the latter. He was looking for a *juste milieu*[6] between the *ancien régime* and the Revolution or, to put it another way, between royal despotism (Maistre) and popular despotism (Rousseau), which has been called the "vulgarization of absolutism." He wished to avoid the excess of revolution and the dangers of a revolutionary Right in the form of Bonapartism, but he did not live, as did Tocqueville, to witness after 1848 the potential of a revolutionary Left in the shape of socialism and communism, although he did denounce the Saint-Simonians. From the liberal perspective, both a revolutionary Right and Left were menacing to liberty be-

---

pouvoir" (*Principes de politique*, Preface). In his very first book, *De la force du gouvernement actuel de la France et de la nécessité de s'y rallier*, p. 83, Constant had said: "Aux abus de la liberté, j'aurais opposé les abus de la puissance. La puissance est plus enyvrante que la liberté."

5. See Giovanni Sartori, *Democratic Theory*, p. 362. Cf. Maurice Duverger, *Droit constitutionnel et institutions politiques*, p. 3, who observed that "Constant's *Treatise on Constitutional Politics* could just as well be entitled a *Treatise on Liberal Politics*, because constitutional regimes are Liberal regimes." It is really unfair to view Constant in Marxist terms as just another apologist of the political domination of the bourgeoisie, as does Jacques Droz, *Histoire des doctrines politiques en France*, pp. 69–73. In stressing the invasion of liberty by government, however, Constant neglected its restriction by economic subjection in a period of rising industrialism.

6. See Vincent Starzinger, *Middlingness*.

cause both stressed equality at the expense of freedom. It was left to John Stuart Mill, however, to warn in *On Liberty* of the danger to individual liberty from the "tyranny of the prevailing opinion and feeling" and to Lord Acton to label in his essay on *Nationality* the "theory of nationality . . . a retrograde step in history" because it threatened the rights of minorities.

From the vantage point of the twentieth century, "it is the timeliness of Constant, his modernity, which is his most striking characteristic."[7] As we observe the authoritarian or totalitarian democracies of our age, it can be seen at once that it was Constant who first understood that "the idea of popular sovereignty is the taproot of totalitarianism."[8] His critique of that concept is as relevant to Hitler as it was to Napoleon, because no matter what changes the advance of technology has made in the development of the techniques of arbitrary power, modern plebiscitary democracies, whether fascist or communist, have all sought legitimacy in the sovereignty of the people, whose consent has been obtained even more by indoctrination than by force. It should be added that Constant was also the first to perceive that the transplantation of ancient liberty into modern society ultimately resulted in the justification of despotism in the name of freedom.

If Constant is not always fair to Rousseau and his theory of popular sovereignty, which the famous *citoyen de Genève* at least never attributed to a representative assembly, it must be remembered that these two Swiss-French thinkers were separated in time by the French Revolution and Napoleon. The application of Rousseau's concept of the sovereignty of the people and of a civil religion alarmed Constant. He traced the roots of the latter back to the atheism of a philosophe, like Holbach, whose ideas spawned an irreligious fanaticism, even more dangerous in Constant's mind than the religious dogmatism of the past. Both Constant and Madame de Staël were, therefore, aware of the perilous implications of a political religion of secular salvation and of political messianism as well.

Although, contrary to Rousseau, Constant hailed the evolution of society from a military to a commercial-industrial (bourgeois)

7. William W. Holdheim, *Benjamin Constant*, p. 111.
8. Alfred Cobban, *In Search of Humanity*, p. 193.

state, he had his reservations about the philosophical underpinnings of a material civilization, such as utilitarianism, hedonism, and enlightened self-interest, as presented by Helvétius and Bentham. To Constant, modern society and liberty are based on commerce and industry, and yet he seems to be keenly conscious of the loss of vitality that attends the progress of material civilization. He is nostalgic, like Rousseau and Montesquieu, about ancient society and liberty, where instead of hedonism and dividedness in an open society there was virtue and unity in a closed society. In his mind, only self-perfectioning and religion could do for modern society and liberty what virtue had done for ancient society and liberty.

Before Tocqueville and Mill, Constant presented a penetrating diagnosis of some of the ills of modern life. He noted that the trend toward uniformity and symmetry was detrimental to the variety and diversity that were essential to liberty in his mind. He anticipated Tocqueville in thinking that the "spirit of the century" was equality, which would be regarded as more precious than freedom. Finally, he was very much concerned about the problem of the alienation of man in modern society—his estrangement and fragmentation after the passing of the *ancien régime* with its hierarchy of orders and estates to which all the subjects of the monarchy "belonged."[9]

In the new bourgeois society, Constant, earlier than Tocqueville, transformed the ancient pluralistic doctrine of intermediate bodies into the modern theory of countervailing powers[10] because he feared that without intermediary groups the individual would not be shielded against the political power of the state. In other words, Constant was quite aware of the dangers of a liberalism based on "egoism," which is often his word for "individualism."[11]

9. Cf. Alexis de Tocqueville, *The Old Regime and the French Revolution*, Book 2, chap. 20: "Our fathers did not have the word 'individualism' which we coined for our own use, because in their time there was indeed no individual who did not belong to a group and who could be considered as absolutely alone."

10. See David Truman, *The Governmental Process*. Cf., however, David Riesman, *Individualism Reconsidered*, pp. 26–27: "We must give every encouragement to people to develop their private selves—to escape from groupism—while realizing that, in many cases, they will use their freedom in unattractive or idle ways." But a century earlier Mill distrusted pluralistic groups because he thought they interfered with liberty.

11. Constant, *De la religion considérée dans sa source, ses formes et ses dé-*

But he never squared his defense of individual autonomy with his advocacy of pluralism.[12] Constant, no more than Tocqueville, ever understood that, although new pluralistic groups may help to prevent despotism, the ancient political problem of how to achieve communal integration still remained.

The old ideas of mixed government and the separation of powers were developed by Constant into a modern theory of constitutional monarchy that was not just representative but parliamentary. As a constitutionalist, he defined the authority of government and the liberty of the individual as opposites, existing in a state of continuous tension. This theory of negative freedom, with which the separation of powers has always been associated, has been criticized as too concerned with freedom, seen as the absence of government restraint, rather than with a more positive idea of liberty, viewed as the power of government to act for the public good. In other words, Constant's theory of liberty is regarded as deficient in that sense of community which Thomas Hill Green contributed later to liberalism and which conservatives ever since Edmund Burke have always found lacking in that philosophy.[13]

---

veloppements, 1:Preface, xxxvii: "Or, quand chacun est son propre centre, tous sont isolés. Quand tous sont isolés, il n'y a que de la poussière. Quand l'orage arrive, la poussière est de la fange." Cf. Tocqueville, *Old Regime*, Foreword, p. xiii: "For in a community in which the ties of family, of caste, of class, and craft fraternities no longer exist people are far too much disposed to think exclusively of their own interests, to become self-seekers practicing a narrow individualism caring nothing for the public good. Far from trying to counteract such tendencies despotism encourages them." See also Tocqueville, *Democracy in America*, 2:98: "Individualism is a mature calm feeling, which disposes each member of the community to sever himself from the mass of his fellows and to draw apart with his family and his friends, so that after he has thus formed a little circle of his own, he willingly leaves society at large to itself... individualism, at first only saps the virtues of public life; but in the long run it attacks and destroys all others and is at length absorbed in down right selfishness."

12. In "De l'esprit de conquête et de l'usurpation," *Cours de politique*, 2:151, Constant seems to follow Rousseau in objecting to partial associations in the state: "Un esprit de corps exclusif et hostile s'empare toujours des associations qui ont un autre but que le reste des hommes. Malgré la douceur et la pureté du Christianisme, souvent, les Confedérations de ses Prêtres ont formé dans l'Etat des Etats à part. Partout, les hommes réunis en corps d'armée se séparent de la nation." But, as Arthur Lovejoy has said, there are contradictions in every great writer.

13. In "Liberal Legislation and Freedom of Contract," Green wrote: "But when we thus speak of freedom, we should consider carefully what we mean by it. We do not mean merely freedom from restraint or compulsion," that is, negative freedom,

It has been said that the "old distinction between the liberty of the ancients and the liberty of the moderns" is one "over which Liberals and Democrats have barrenly fought even to this day."[14] This judgment could be taken to imply that Constant's political philosophy is dated. Of course, since his time, liberal regimes were democratized and democratic regimes liberalized in the nineteenth century. Therefore, the differentiation between constitutional-pluralistic and authoritarian-totalitarian democracies is a classification more suited to our age. With all these changes, Constant has not lost his contemporary relevance, however, because the distinction he made between ancient and modern liberty really included the difference between positive and negative freedom and political and civil liberty, which are questions still very much with us today.

It has been suggested that there is both "a majority and a minority rights reading of Liberalism."[15] The term, according to this critique, has been limited to such thinkers as Constant, Tocqueville, and Mill, who concentrated on the tyranny of the majority. But, it has been asked, why should not the term be applied to such theorists as Milton, Locke, and Bentham, who stressed the menace of an arbitrary minority or individual ruler? Constant's approach to liberalism included both in view of his definition of liberty.

Finally, it has been asked recently whether this whole theory of a self-regulating individual liberty does not jeopardize the health of the human personality.[16] Do we not require traditional social controls in order to avoid what Emile Durkheim called *anomie*?[17] Constant did not really face such a question, although the "early" Mill did. In any event, Tocqueville and the "later" Mill perceived that with the development of equality, the growth of conformity could be just as burdensome as the action of government. Furthermore, they connected conformity with the isolation of the individual. Therefore, it was Tocqueville and Mill, rather

---

but "freedom in the positive sense . . . the liberation of the powers of all men equally for contributions to a common good." See John R. Rodman, ed., *The Political Theory of T. H. Green, Selected Writings*, pp. 51–53.

14. Nicola Matteucci, *Il liberalismo in un Mondo in transformazione.*
15. Edwin Mims, *The Majority of the People*, p. 174.
16. See Robert P. Wolff, "Beyond Tolerance," pp. 33–35.
17. See his classic *Suicide.*

than Constant, who became the prophets of mass democracy, so menacing to individual autonomy.[18] It can be concluded that Constant's philosophy of liberalism cannot correctly be reduced to mere legality any more than Tocqueville's or Acton's, who also defended constitutionalism, based on pluralism. It is instead moral and ethical because, like theirs, his political thought is deeply rooted in religion.[19] The impact of natural rights (Locke), utilitarianism (Bentham and Mill), evolution (Spencer), and idealism (Green) upon liberalism has been noted.[20] It is time to point out the influence of constitutionalism and religion upon this philosophy.[21] It is here that Constant made his mark before either Tocqueville or Acton.

As John Hallowell has observed: "If we now live . . . in a postliberal age, the question is: how can we salvage the achievements of liberalism," such as constitutionalism with its emphasis on freedom of thought and conscience and other civil liberties, "from the shallowness of its ideology?"[22] By that standard, we can easily overlook Constant's occasional "shallowness" in view of his great "achievements"[23] that should at long last be recognized.

18. See Herbert Marcuse, *One Dimensional Man*, and David Riesman, *The Lonely Crowd*, who present the case for regaining individual autonomy in our contemporary bureaucratized and large-scale industrial societies.

19. "Benjamin Constant est essentiellement un moraliste en quête de valeurs authentiques" (Cecil P. Courtney, "La pensée politique de Benjamin Constant," p. 33).

20. George H. Sabine, *A History of Political Theory*, chaps. 32–33.

21. Constant did not see that the rule of law can result in the preservation of the status quo or "the containment of social change," to use the language of Herbert Marcuse, a powerful critic of liberalism in all its aspects in *One Dimensional Man* and in "Repressive Tolerance."

22. John H. Hallowell, "Liberalism and the Open Society," p. 130.

23. Note, for example, Constant's naive optimism when he could write: "Je défie le pouvoir absolu d'un seul de subsister dix années dans tout pays éclairé," *Mélanges de littérature et de politique*, p. 199.

Bibliography

Primary Sources

MANUSCRIPTS

France

Paris
  Bibliothèque Nationale.
    Constant, Benjamin. Oeuvres Manuscrits de 1810.
    Fonds Davray. Nouvelles acquisitions françaises.
    Principes de politique applicables à tous les gouvernements.
    Fragments d'un ouvrage abandonné sur la possibilité d'une
      constitution républicaine dans un grand pays.
    Fragments d'un essai sur la littérature du XVIII siècle dans ses
      rapports avec la liberté.
    De la perfectibilité de l'espèce humaine.
    Fragments d'un essai sur la perfectibilité de l'espèce humaine.
    De la justice politique de Godwin.
    De Godwin, de ses principes et de son ouvrage sur la justice
      politique.
Clermont-Créans
  Chateau de Créans, Archives d'Estournelles de Constant.
    Cours sur la constitution anglaise.
    Première lecture à l'Athenée Royal de Paris.

Switzerland

Lausanne
  Bibliothèque Cantonale et Universitaire.
    Fonds d'Estournelles de Constant.
    Nouveau Fonds d'Estournelles de Constant.
      Du moment actuel et de la destinée de l'espèce humaine ou histoire
        abrégée de l'égalité.

PRINTED WORKS BY BENJAMIN CONSTANT

"Trois lettres à un député à la Convention." *Nouvelles politiques nationales et étrangères*, 24, 25, 26 June 1795. Published in Beatrice W. Jasinski, *L'engagement de Benjamin Constant*, pp. 110–25. Paris, 1971.

A *Charles His, rédacteur du Républicain français*, 24 July 1795. Published in ibid., pp. 134–41.

"De la restitution des droits politiques aux descendants des religionnaires français." *Le moniteur universel*, 26 Aug. 1796.

De la force du gouvernement actuel de la France et de la nécessité de s'y rallier. 1796.

Aux citoyens représentants du peuple composant le conseil Cinq-Cent. 1796.

Des réactions politiques. 1797.

Des effets de la terreur. 1797.

Discours prononcé au cercle constitutionnel pour la plantation de l'arbre de la liberté le 30 fructidor an V. 1797. Published in Carlo Cordie, *Gli scritti politici givanili di Benjamin Constant, 1796–1797.* Como, 1944.

Discours prononcé au cercle constitutionnel le 9 ventôse an VI. 1798.

A *ses collègues de l'assemblé électoral du départment de Seine-et-Oise le germinal an VI.* 1798.

Des suites de la contre-révolution en Angleterre. 1799. Republished in 1818–19 under the title *Essai sur la contre-révolution d'Angleterre*.

Discours prononcé sur le projet concernant la formation de la loi, Tribunat, séance du 15 nivôse an VII. 1799.

Opinion sur le projet de loi qui met à la disposition du gouvernement les citoyens qui ont atteint leur vingtième année au premier vendémiaire an VIII, Tribunat, séance du 15 ventôse an VIII. 1800.

Opinion sur le projet de loi relatif aux rentes foncières, Tribunat, séance du 27 ventôse an VIII. 1800.

Discours sur les victoires de l'armée d'Italie, Tribunat, séance du 3 messidor an VIII. 1800.

Opinion sur le projet de loi concernant l'établissement de tribunaux criminels spéciaux, séance du 5 pluviôse an IX. 1801.

Opinion sur le projet de loi concernant la réduction des justices de paix, Tribunat, séance du 2 pluviôse an IX. 1801.

Mémoires sur les communications à établir avec l'intérieur de la France, le 18 novembre, 1813. In Bengt Hasselrot, ed., *Benjamin Constant: Lettres à Bernadotte*, pp. 3–6. Geneva, 1952.

Commentaire sur la réponse faite par Buonaparte à la députation du Sénat le 14 novembre, 1813.

De l'esprit de conquête et de l'usurpation dans leurs rapports avec la civilisation européenne. Hanover, 1814. Partial translation by Helen B. Lippmann, *Prophecy from the Past: Benjamin Constant on Conquest and Usurpation.* New York, 1941.

Réflexions sur les constitutions, la distribution des pouvoirs et les garanties dans une monarchie constitutionnelle. 1814.

Des révolutions de 1660 et de 1688 en Angleterre et de celle de 1814 en France. Journal des débats, 21 April 1814.

De la liberté des brochures, des pamphlets et des journaux considérées sous le rapport de l'intérêt du gouvernement. 1814. English translation in *Pamphleteer* 6 (London, 1815): 206–38.

Observations sur le discours prononcé par S. E. le ministre de l'intérieur en faveur du projet de loi sur la liberté de la presse. 1814.

"Observations sur une déclaration du Congrès de Vienne." *Journal de Paris,* 24 April 1815.

"Comparaison de l'ordonnance de réformation de Louis XVIII avec la constitution proposée à la France le 22 avril 1815." *Journal des débats,* 1 May 1815.

De la responsabilité des ministres. 1815. English translation, "On the Responsibility of Ministers," in *Pamphleteer* 5 (London, 1815): 302–29.

Principes de politique applicables à tous les gouvernements représentatifs. 1815.

De la doctrine politique qui peut réunir les partis en France. 1815.

Adolphe. London, 1816.

Considérations sur le projet de loi relatif aux élections, adopté par la Chambre des Députés. 1817.

Questions sur la législation actuelle de la presse en France et sur la doctrine du ministre public relativement à la saisie des écrits et à la responsabilité des auteurs et imprimeurs. 1817.

Des élections prochaines. 1817.

Note sur quelques articles de journaux. 1817.

Entretien d'un électeur avec lui-mème. 1817.

Histoire de la session de la Chambre des Députés depuis 1816 jusqu'en 1819.

Annales de la session de 1817 à 1818.

Annales de la session de 1818 à 1819.

Lettre à M. Charles Durand, avocat, en réponse aux questions contenus dans la troisième partie de son ouvrage intitulé Marseilles, Nîmes et ses environs en 1815. 1818.

De l'appel en calomnie de M. le marquis Blosserville contre Wilfrid-Regnault. 1818.

Des élections de 1818. 1818.

Lettre de M. Benjamin Constant à M. Odillon-Barrot sur le procès M. Lainé, serrurier, entrainé au crime de fausse monnais par un agent de la gendarmerie et condamné à mort. 1818.

A MM les électeurs de Paris le 23 octobre 1818.

A MM les électeurs de Paris le 29 octobre 1818.

Collection complète des ouvrages publiés sur le gouvernement représentatif et la constitution actuelle de la France, formant une espèce de politique constitutionnel. 4 vols. Paris, 1818–20. See also the J. P. Pagès edition of the *Cours de politique constitutionnelle* (Brussels, 1837); and the Edouard Laboulaye editions of 1861 and 1872 published in Paris in 2 volumes. Note also Charles Louandre, *Oeuvres politiques de Benjamin Constant* (Paris, 1874); and finally Olivier Pozzo di Borgo, *Benjamin Constant: Ecrits et discours politiques* (Paris, 1964), and his *Benjamin Constant: Choix de textes politiques* (Paris, 1965).

Eloge de Sir Samuel Romilly, prononcé à l'Athenée Royal de Paris le 26 décembre 1818. 1819.

Lettre à MM les habitants de département de la Sarthe. 1819.

De l'état de la France et des bruits qui circulent. 1819.

De la liberté des anciens comparée à celle des modernes. 1819.

Mémoires sur les Cent Jours en formes de lettres. 1820. Published first in *La minerve française* (Paris, 1818–20). See also Olivier Pozzo di Borgo, *Mémoires sur les Cent Jours par Benjamin Constant* (Paris, 1961).

Des motifs qui ont dicté le nouveau projet de loi sur les élections. 1820.

De la dissolution de la Chambre de Députés. 1820. English translation in *Pamphleteer* 18 (London, 1821).

Troisième lettre à MM les habitants du département de la Sarthe (21 March 1820).

Lettre à M. le marquis de Latour-Mauborg, ministre de la guerre sur ce qui s'est passé à Saumur les 7 et 8 octobre 1820.

Pièces relatives à la saisie de lettres et papiers dans le domicile de MM Goyet et Pasquier. 1820.

Du triomphe inévitable et prochain des principes constitutionnels en Prusse d'après un ouvrage imprimé traduit de l'allemand de M. Koreff, conseiller intime de régence par M. avec un avant-propos et des notes de M. Benjamin Constant, député de la Sarthe. 1821.

Lettre à M. le Procureur général de la cour royal de Poitiers. 1822.

Note sur la plainte en défamation adressé à MM les conseillers, membres de la cour de cassation contre M. Mangin. 1822.

Commentaire sur l'ouvrage de Filangieri. 2 vols. 1822.

Appel aux nations chrétiennes en faveur des Grecs. 1825.

"Coup d'oeil sur la tendance générale des esprits dans le XIX siècle, extrait du discours prononcé dans le séance d'ouverture de l'Athenée royal de Paris, le 3 décembre 1825." *Revue encyclopédique*, 1825.

"Christianisme." *Encyclopédie moderne* 7 (1825): 30–52. Also published in Charles-François Dupuis, *Abrégé de l'origine de tous les cultes* (Paris, 1895).

"Religion." *Encyclopédie progressive ou collection des traités sur l'histoire, l'état actuel et les progrès des connaissances humaines.* 1826.

Discours de M. Benjamin Constant à la Chambre des Députés. 2 vols. Paris, 1827–28. For the complete discourses of Benjamin Constant, especially from 1827–30, see *Archives parlementaires 1789–1860: Receuil complète des débats des chambres françaises* (Paris, 1862–).

Mélanges de littérature et de politique. Paris, 1829.

"Souvenirs historiques à l'occasion de l'ouvrage de M. Bignon." *Revue de Paris* 9 (1830): 115–25; 16 (1830): 102–12, 221–33.

De la religion considérée dans sa source, ses formes et ses développements. 5 vols. Paris, 1824–31. Note Pierre Deguise, *Benjamin Constant De la religion Livre I* (Lausanne, 1971); and Patrice Thompson, *Deux chapitres inédits de l'Esprit des religions, 1803–1804* (Geneva, 1970).

Du polythéisme romain considérée dans ses rapports avec la philosophie grecque et la religion chrétienne. 2 vols. Ouvrage posthume, 1833.

Le cahier rouge. Paris, 1907.

Journaux intimes. Edited by Alfred Roulin and Charles Roth. Paris, 1952.

Cécile. Edited by Norman Cameron. London, 1952.

CORRESPONDENCE

Baldensperger, Ferdinand. "Lettres de Constant à Bottiger, 1804–1815." *Revue politique et littéraire* 9 (1908): 481–86.

Berthoud, Dorette. "Belle et Benjamin. Lettres inédites de Benjamin Constant." *Revue de Paris* 7–12 (Oct. 1964): 65–75.

Colet, Louise. *Lettres de Benjamin Constant à Madame Récamier.* Paris, 1864.

Constant de Rebecque, Adrien de. "Lettres de Benjamin Constant à sa famille." *Revue internationale* 14 (1887): 25–53, 200–32, 355–76, 584–605.

Crepet, Eugène. "Benjamin Constant d'après une correspondance de famille complètement inédite." *Revue nationale et étrangère* 27 (1867): 161–89, 415–60.

De Lauris, Georges. "Lettres inédites de Benjamin Constant." *La revue* (1904): 1–18, 151–59.

Dierolf, George. "Lettres de Benjamin Constant à Prosper de Barante,

1805–1830." *Revue de deux mondes* 34 (1906): 241–72, 528–67.

———. "Lettres inédites de Benjamin Constant." *Gaulois du Dimanche,* Jan. 1906.

Gaullieur, Eusèbe H. "Benjamin Constant et Madame de Charrière ou la jeunesse de Benjamin Constant racontée par lui-même. Lettres inédites, communiquées et annotées." *Revue des deux mondes* 15 (1844): 193–264.

———. "Benjamin Constant pendant la Révolution d'après de nouvelles lettres inédites à Madame de Charrière." *Bibliothèque universelle de Genève* 6 (1847): 236–67, 344–75; 7 (1848): 50–84, 271–95.

Glachant, Paul et Victor. "Lettres de Benjamin Constant à Fauriel." *La nouvelle revue,* Jan. 1902, pp. 63–68.

———. "Lettres de Benjamin Constant à Fauriel." *Revue politique et littéraire* 5 (Jan. 1906): 36–41.

———. "Lettres inédites de Benjamin Constant à Rosalie de Constant." *La nouvelle revue* Oct. 1903, pp. 289–95.

Harpaz, Ephraim. *Benjamin Constant et Goyet de la Sarthe correspondance, 1818–1822.* Geneva, 1973.

———. *Benjamin Constant. Lettres à Mme Récamier 1807–1830.* Paris, 1977.

Hasselrot, Bengt. *Lettres à Bernadotte par Benjamin Constant. Sources et origines de l'esprit de conquête et de l'usurpation.* Geneva, 1952.

Isler, Johann and Witmer. *Briefe von Constant, Görres, Goethe . . . und vielen Anderen. Auswahl aus dem Landschaftlichen Nachlasse des Charles de Villers,* pp. 5–59. Hamburg, 1879.

Lenormant, A. *Lettres de Benjamin Constant à Madame Récamier, 1807–1830.* Paris, 1882.

Ley, Francis. *Bernardin de Sainte-Pierre, Madame de Staël, Chateaubriand, Benjamin Constant et Madame de Krudener.* Aubier, 1967.

L'inconnue d'Adolphe. Correspondance de Benjamin Constant à d'Anna Lindsay. Paris, 1930.

Melegari, D. "Benjamin Constant à Saumur." *Nouvelle revue retrospective,* 1901, pp. 1–36.

———. *Journal intime de Benjamin Constant et lettres à sa famille et à ses amis.* Paris, 1895.

———. "Lettres de Benjamin Constant à Madame de Charrière, 1792–1795." *Revue de Paris* 5 (1894): 673–718.

Menos, Jean H. *Lettres de Benjamin Constant à sa famille, 1795–1830.* Paris, 1888.

———. "Lettres inédites à la Comtesse de Nassau." *Revue internationale* 21 (1889): 9–31, 149–76, 302–34.

Mistler, Jean. "Benjamin Constant et Madame Récamier." *Revue des deux mondes* 5 (1950): 81–95.

_____. *Lettres à un ami: Cent onze lettres inédites de Benjamin Constant et de Madame de Staël à Claude Hochet*. Neuchâtel, 1949.

Pellegrini, Carlo. "Lettere inédite di Benjamin Constant al Sismondi." *Pegaso* 4 (1932): 641–60.

Roulin, Alfred and Suzanne. *Benjamin et Rosalie Constant: Correspondance, 1786–1830*. Paris, 1955.

Rudler, Gustave. "Une correspondance inédite. Benjamin Constant et Louvet." *Bibliothèque universelle et revue suisse* 67 (1912): 225–47.

_____. "Lettres à Philippe Stapfer." *Mélanges de philologie, d'histoire et de littérature offerts à Jospeh Vianey*, pp. 321–33. Paris, 1934.

_____. "Lettres de Benjamin Constant à M. et Mme De Gérando." *Bibliothèque universelle et revue suisse* 69 (1913): 449–85.

Seznec, J. "Deux lettres de Benjamin Constant sur Adolphe et les Cent Jours." *The French Mind: Studies in Honour of Gustave Rudler*, pp. 208–19. Oxford, 1952.

Thomas, L. "Lettres à Anna Lindsay." *Revue des deux mondes* 60 (Nov.–Dec. 1930): 781–818; and 61 (Jan.–Feb. 1931): 62–97, 373–404.

_____. "Lettres inédites de Benjamin Constant." *Revue politique et littéraire* 21–22 (1914): 481–86, 519–24.

"Trois lettres inédites de Benjamin Constant à Madame de Krudener." *Journal de Genève*, March 1908.

Vauthier, Gabriel. "Une lettre inédite de Benjamin Constant le 24 brumaire 1799." *Annales révolutionaires* 13 (1921): 413–18.

JOURNALS WITH ARTICLES BY OR ABOUT BENJAMIN CONSTANT

Note the collections by Ephraim Harpaz: *Benjamin Constant: Receuil d'Articles, 1817–1820. Le Mercure, La Minerve et La Renommée*, 2 vols. (Geneva, 1972); *Benjamin Constant: Receuil d'articles, 1795–1817* (Geneva, 1978); and *Benjamin Constant; Receuil d'articles, 1820–1830* (forthcoming).

"L'ambigu ou variétés littéraires et politiques, 1804–18." *Christian Examiner* 10 (1831); 17 (1834).

Le constitutionnel, journal politique et littéraire, 1815–17, 1827.

Le courrier français, journal du commerce, politique et littéraire, 1819–30.

Edinburgh Review 24 (1814–15); and 26 (1816).

Journal du commerce, de politique et de littérature, 1817–19.

Journal des débats, 1814–30.

Journal de Paris, 1811–27.

Le mercure de France, journal politique, littéraire et dramatique, 1789–1820.

Le mercure de France au XIX siècle XXXI, 1830.
La minerve française 1817–20.
Le moniteur universel ou gazette nationale, 1789–1830.
Nouvelles politiques, nationales et étrangères, 1792–97.
La renommée, 1818–20.
Le Républicain français, 1795.
La sentinelle, 1795.
Le temps, journal des politiques, scientifiques, littéraires et industriels, 1829–30.

ANONYMOUS WORKS ON BENJAMIN CONSTANT

Adresse à tous les amis de la France sur la brochure de Benjamin Constant "Des causes de la contre-révolution en Angleterre." 1799.
A MM les députés des départements. 1829.
A MM les membres de la Chambre des Députés. 1829.
A MM les membres de la Chambre des Députés au sujet de la proposition de M. B. Constant tendant à rendre libres les professions d'imprimeur de libraire. 1830.
Combat des six. 1829.
Consultation pour M. B. Constant. 1822.
Critique raisonné dans laquelle on signale les fautes d'orthographe, de construction, de solécismes, les barbarismes, les néologismes, les imprissions impropres et inconvénients dont est remplie la brochure que vient de publier M. B. Constant sur la "Dissolution de la Chambre" par un auteur de la pureté de langage. 1820.
De la loterie et des maisons de jeu. Lettre à M. B. Constant. 1822.
Lettre à M. B. Constant au sujet de l'attentat de Saumur. 1820.
Lettre à M. B. Constant sur celle qu'il a écrit à M. Ch. Durand, insérée dans le livraison de la Minerve française, auteur de l'écrit intitulé, "L'impartial." 1818.
Lettre à M. B. Constant sur l'obligation d'improviser dans les assemblées législatives.
Lettre à M. B. Constant et Manuel membres de la Chambre des Députés en réponse à quelques passages des discours qu'ils ont prononcé sur la traité des noirs dans la séance du 27 juin 1821. 1821.
Lettre à M. Esmangart, conseiller d'état, préfet du département du Bas Rhin, par un saucissier de Strasbourg en réponse à un article inséré dans le journal ministériel du département au sujet d'un banquet offert à M. B. Constant. 1827.
Lettre d'un républicain du département de la Gironde à un de ses amis à Bordeaux sur le discours prononcé par B. Constant au cercle constitutionnel du Palais Royal de 9 ventôse. 1798.

*Le cri d'un ultra ou le vade-mecum de l'électeur honnête homme suivi de
"Quelques mots sur les élections de 1818." 1818.*
M. B. *Constant, est-il français, est-il éligible? 1818.*
M. B. *Constant de Rebecque Suisse d'origine, est-il ami de la Charte?
1818.*
Note historique et biographique sur B. Constant député de France. 1830.
Note sur la note de M. B. Constant de Rebecque. 1817.
*Ordre du convoi funèbre de B. Constant, commençant par de mots "Le
convoi de B. Constant." 1830.*
*Quelques mots à M. le vicomte de Chateaubriand et à M. B. Constant par
M. le marquis de Paris. 1818.*
Sur l'ouvrage de M. B. Constant intitulé "Des élections prochaines." 1817.
Trois têtes dans un bonnet ou MM Constant, Jay et Guizot. 1820.
Vie patriotique de B. Constant dédié à la jeune France. 1830.

RELATED ORIGINAL WORKS IN THE NINETEENTH AND TWENTIETH CENTURIES

Acton, John Emerich. *Essays on Freedom and Power.* Edited by
Gertrude Himmelfarb. New York, 1948.
————. *Lectures on Modern History.* London, 1906.
————. *Lectures on the French Revolution.* London, 1910.
————. *The History of Freedom and Other Essays.* London, 1907.
Adams, John. *A Defense of the Constitutions of Government of the United
States of America.* London, 1787.
Adams, John Quincy, "Publicola" (1791). In *The Writings of John Quincy
Adams,* edited by W. C. Ford. 7 vols. New York, 1913–17.
Bagehot, Walter. *The English Constitution.* London, 1867.
Bailleul, Jacques Charles. *Doctrines religieuses et politiques, seules propres
à terminer ou à prévenir les révolutions et à concilier les esprits.* Paris,
1824.
————. *Sur les écrits de Benjamin Constant relatifs à la liberté de presse et
à la responsibilité des ministres.* Paris, 1817.
Barante, Prosper de. *Des communes et de l'aristocratie.* Paris, 1821.
————. *La vie politique de Royer-Collard, ses discours et ses écrits.*
2 vols. Paris, 1861.
————. *Mélanges historiques et littéraires.* 3 vols. Paris, 1835.
————. *Questions constitutionnelles.* Paris, 1849.
————. "Réflexions sur les oeuvres politiques de Jean-Jacques Rousseau"
and "De la souveraineté." In *Etudes littéraires et historiques.* 2 vols.,
1:275–351, 352–62. Paris, 1859.
————. *Souvenirs du Baron de Barante, 1782–1866.* 8 vols. Paris,
1890–1901.

Barras, Paul F. *Mémoires de Barras*. Edited by George Duruy. 4 vols. Paris, 1895–96.

Barthelémy-Saint-Hilaire, Jules. *Victor Cousin, sa vie et sa correspondance*. 3 vols. Paris, 1895.

Bentham, Jeremy. *Deontology or the Science of Morality*. 2 vols. London, 1834.

————. *Works*. 11 vols. London, 1843.

Béranger, Pierre Jean de. *Ma biographe*. Paris, 1860.

Beyle, Henri (Stendhal). *Courrier anglais*. 5 vols. Paris, 1935–36.

Blackstone, Sir William. *Commentaries on the Laws of England*. 4 vols. Oxford, 1768–69.

Blanc, Louis. *The History of Ten Years 1830–1840 or France under Louis Philippe*. 2 vols. London, 1844.

Bonald, Louis G. A., Vicomte de. *Essai analytique sur les lois naturelles de l'ordre social dans la société ou du pouvoir, du ministre et du sujet dans la société*. 1800.

————. *Législation primitive considérée dans les derniers temps par les seules lumières de la raison*. 1802.

————. *Oeuvres complètes de M. de Bonald*. 3 vols. Paris, 1959.

————. *Théorie du pouvoir politique et religieux dans la société civile, démontrée par le raisonnement et par l'histoire*. 1796.

Boulainvilliers, Comte de. *Histoire de l'ancien gouvernement de la France*. Paris, 1727.

Boulay de la Meurthe, Antoine. *Essai sur les causes qui en 1649 amenèrent en Angleterre à l'établissement de la République*. Paris, 1799.

Boyer-Fonfrède, F. B. *Des avantages d'une constitution libérale*. Paris, 1814.

Broglie, Duc Victor de. *Souvenirs, 1785–1870*. 4 vols. Paris, 1886.

Buchez, P. J. B., and Roux, P. C. *Histoire parlementaire de la révolution française*. 40 vols. Paris, 1834–1938.

Chateaubriand, François Auguste René, Vicomte de. *De Bonaparte et des Bourbons et de la nécessité de se rallier à nos princes légitimes pour le bonheur de la France et celui de l'Europe*. 1814.

————. *De la monarchie selon la Charte*. 1816.

————. *Essai historique, politique et moral sur les révolutions anciennes et modernes considérées dans leurs rapports avec la révolution française*. 1797.

————. *Le génie du Christianisme et défense du génie du Christianisme*. 1802.

————. *Mémoires d'outre tombe*. 6 vols. Paris, 1898–1900. See Robert Baldrick, ed., *The Memoirs of Chateaubriand*. New York, 1961.

————. *Oeuvres complètes*. 28 vols. Paris, 1826–31, and 12 vols. Paris, 1870.

Cheron, Fr. *Sur la liberté de la presse. Réponse à un article inseré dans le Journal des débats le 13 juillet et réflexions sur la brochure de M. Benjamin Constant de Rebecque et sur d'autres écrits relatifs à cette question.* Paris, 1914.

Clausel de Coussergues, Jean Claude. *Considérations sur l'origine, la rédaction, la promulgation et l'exécution de la Charte.* Paris, 1830.

————. *De la souveraineté du peuple et du serment demandé aux membres des collèges électoraux.* Paris, 1830.

Clermont-Tonnerre, Stanislas de. *Oeuvres complètes.* 4 vols. Paris, 1795.

————. *Recueil des opinions de Stanislas de Clermont-Tonnerre.* 4 vols. Paris, 1791.

Coessin, F. G. *De l'esprit de conquête et de l'usurpation dans le système mercantile en réponse à l'ouvrage de M. B. Constant de Rebecque sur l'esprit de conquête et de l'usurpation par le système guerrier dans l'état actuel de la civilisation européenne.* Paris, 1822.

Comte, Auguste. *Système de politique positive.* 4 vols. Paris, 1912.

Condorcet, Marquis de. *Outlines of an Historical View of the Progress of the Human Mind.* Baltimore, 1802.

————. "Première mémoire sur l'éducation." In *Oeuvres.* 12 vols., vol. 8. Paris, 1847–49.

Coste. *Opinions prononcés dans la Chambre des Députés durant les sessions de 1818, 1819, 1820, 1821 par M. B. Constant.* Paris, 1822.

Coulmann, J. *Notice sur Benjamin Constant lue à la séance générale de la Société de la morale chrétienne.* Paris, 1831.

————. *Reminiscences.* 3 vols. Paris, 1862–69.

Crapelet, G. A. *Observations sur la proposition de M. B. Constant relative à la suppression des brevets d'imprimeur et de libraire.* Paris, 1830.

Daunou, Pierre. "De la religion publique ou réflexions sur un chapitre du Contrat Social de Jean Jacques Rousseau." *Journal Encyclopédique* 1 and 2 (1794).

————. *Essai sur les garanties individuelles qui réclame l'état actuel de la société.* Paris, 1819.

De Ferron, Henri. *Théorie du Progrès.* 2 vols. Paris, 1867.

Destutt de Tracy, Antoine. *Commentaire sur l'Esprit des Lois de Montesquieu.* Paris, 1819.

Diderot, Denis. *Pensées philosophiques.* Geneva, 1956.

Dunoyer, Charles. *L'industrie et la morale considérée dans leurs rapports avec la liberté.* Paris, 1825.

————. *Oeuvres.* 3 vols. Paris, 1870.

Dupont de Nemours, Pierre-Samuel. *De l'origine et des progrès d'une science nouvelle.* Paris, 1768.

Durkheim, Emile. *Suicide.* Translated by J. A. Spaulding and G. Simpson. Glencoe, Ill., 1951.

Duvergier de Hauranne, J. M. *Réponse à M. B. Constant.* Paris, 1818.

Duvergier de Hauranne, Prosper. *Histoire du gouvernement parlementaire en France, 1814–1848.* 10 vols. Paris, 1857–71.

———. "M. Charles de Rémusat." *Revue des deux mondes* 12 (1875): 315–69.

Eckstein, B. F. *Réponse aux attaques dirigées contre lui par M. B. Constant.* Paris, 1827.

Fadeville, Th. *B. Constant jugé par ses discours et ses écrits.* Paris, 1824.

The Federalist, New York, 1971.

Ferguson, Adam. *An Essay on the History of Civil Society.* London, 1767 and 1773.

Ferrand, Antoine-François-Claude. *L'esprit de l'histoire.* 4 vols. Paris, 1802.

———. *Le rétablissement de la monarchie.* Paris, 1793.

Fichte, Johann Gottlieb. *Der Geschlossene Handelsstaat.* Tübingen, 1800.

Filangieri, Gaetano. *The Science of Legislation.* London, 1816.

France, Anatole. "Le journal de Benjamin Constant." In *La vie littéraire.* 4 vols. Paris, 1889–92.

Fustel de Coulanges, Numa-Denis. *The Ancient City: A Study of the Religion, Laws and Institutions of Greece and Rome.* New York, 1956.

Godart. *Premier appel aux sifflets ou petit rapport au public sur le grand M. B. Constant.* Paris, 1821.

Godwin, William. *An Enquiry Concerning Political Justice and Its Influence on General Virtue and Happiness.* 2 vols. New York, 1926.

Goyet, Ch. *A MM Hardouin, Lafayette, B. Constant, Picot-Desormaux.* Paris, 1819.

———. *Lettre à M. B. Constant le 12 août 1820.* Paris, 1820.

———. *Lettres à M. B. Constant.* Paris, 1821.

Green, Thomas Hill. "Liberal Legislation and Freedom of Contract" (1881). In *Works of Thomas Hill Green,* edited by R. L. Nettleship, 3 vols., 3:365–86. London, 1885–88. See John R. Rodman, ed., *The Political Theory of T. H. Green, Selected Writings.* New York, 1964.

Guizot, François. *Democracy and Its Mission.* London, 1848.

———. *Du gouvernement de la France depuis la Restauration et du ministère actuel.* Paris, 1820.

———. *Du gouvernement représentatif et de l'état actuel de la France.* Paris, 1820.

———. *Histoire générale de la civilisation en Europe.* Paris, 1828.

———. *Historical Essays and Lectures.* Edited by Stanley Mellon. Chicago, 1972.

———. *History of the Origin of Representative Government in Europe.* London, 1861.

_____. *Mémoires pour servir à l'histoire de mon temps*. 8 vols. Paris, 1858–67.

Hello, G. G. *Essai sur le régime constitutionnel ou introduction à l'étude de la Charte*. Paris, 1827.

Helvétius. *De l'esprit*. Paris, 1758.

Herder, Johann Gottfried von. *Outlines of a Philosophy of the History of Man*. New York, 1966.

Hobbes, Thomas. *Leviathan*. London, 1914.

Hugo, Victor. *Journal d'un révolutionnaire de 1830–1848*. Edited by Henri Guillemin. Paris, 1954.

Humboldt, Wilhelm von. *The Limits of State Action*. Edited by J. W. Burrow. Cambridge, 1969.

James, William. *The Varieties of Religious Experience: A Study in Human Nature*. New York, 1923.

Jefferson, Thomas. "First Inaugural Address" (March 4, 1801). In *A Compilation of the Messages and Papers of the Presidents*, compiled by James D. Richardson, 1:309–12. New York, 1897.

Jouslin de la Salle, A., *Lettres à M. B. Constant sur le procès de Wilfrid-Regnault*. Paris, 1818.

Kant, Immanuel. "On a Supposed Right to Lie from Altruistic Motives." In *Critique of Practical Reason and Other Writings in Moral Philosophy*, pp. 346–50. Edited by L. W. Beck. Chicago, 1949.

Laboulaye, Edouard. "Benjamin Constant." *Revue nationale et étrangère* 5 (1861): 321–57, 489–533; 6 (1861):6–43, 161–210, 481–513; 7 (1861):5–27, 321–64.

_____. "Benjamin Constant et les Cent Jours." *Revue nationale et étrangère* 25 (1866): 385–411; 26 (1866–67): 55–77, 161–79, 404–31.

_____. "La liberté antique et la liberté moderne." In *L'état et ses limites: Suivis d'essais politiques*. Paris, 1871.

Lafayette, le Marquis de. *Mémoires, correspondance et manuscrits du général Lafayette*. 6 vols. Paris, 1837–38.

Lamartine, Alfonse de. *Cours familier de littérature: Un entretien par mois, 1856–1869*. 28 vols. Paris, 1866–69.

Lammenais, Félicité Robert de. *De la religion considérée dans ses rapports avec l'ordre politique et civil*. Paris, 1825.

_____. *Essai sur l'indifférence en matière de religion*. Paris, 1817.

Lanjuinais, Jean de. *Constitutions de la nation française avec un essai de traité historique et politique sur la Charte*. 2 vols. Paris, 1819.

_____. *Examen du huitième chapitre du Contrat Social de Jean-Jacques Rousseau*. Paris, 1825.

Lerminier, J. L. *De l'influence de la philosophie du XVIII siècle sur la législation et la sociabilité du XIX siècle*. Paris, 1833.

————. *Philosophie du droit.* Paris, 1835.

Lettres de Claude-Ignace de Barante à son fils Prosper sur Mme de Staël, de Mme de Staël à Claude-Ignace de Barante, de Prosper de Barante à son père, de Prosper de Barante à Mme de Staël (1804–1815). Clermond-Ferrand, 1929.

Leverrier, A. *Epitre à M. B. Constant.* Paris, 1929.

Lezay, Adrien de. "Des causes de la révolution et de ses résultats." *Journal d'économie publique, de morale et de politique,* 1797.

Lieber, Francis. "Anglican and Gallican Liberty" (1849). In *Miscellaneous Writings.* 2 vols., 2:371–88. Philadelphia, 1881.

————. *Civil Liberty and Self-Government.* 2 vols. Boston, 1853.

Locke, John. *Treatise of Civil Government.* New York, 1937.

Lolme, Jean Louis de. *The Constitution of England.* London, 1775.

Loyson, Ch. *Guerre à qui la cherche.* Paris, 1818.

————. *Lettre à M. B. Constant, l'un des rédacteurs de la minerve.* Paris, 1819.

Mably, Gabriel Bonnet de. *De la législation ou principes des lois.* 2 vols. Amsterdam, 1776.

————. *Observations sur l'histoire de France.* 6 vols. Paris, 1788.

Mackintosh, Sir James. *Memoirs of the Life of the Right Honorable Sir James Mackintosh 1767–1832.* 2 vols. London, 1835.

————. *The Miscellaneous Works of the Right Honorable Sir James Mackintosh.* 3 vols. Philadelphia, 1847.

————. *Vindiciae Gallicae. Defense of the French Revolution and Its English Admirers against the Accusations of the Right Honorable Edmund Burke.* Dublin, 1791.

Madison, James. "Vices of the Political System of the United States" (1787). In *The Writings of James Madison,* edited by Gaillard Hunt. 9 vols. 2:361–69. New York, 1901.

Maine, Sir Henry. *Ancient Law; Its Connection with the Early History of Society and Its Relation to Modern Ideas.* London, 1861.

Maistre, Joseph de. *Considérations sur la France.* 1796. English translation by Richard A. Lebrun. London, 1974.

————. *Essai sur le principe générateur des constitutions politiques et des autres institutions humaines (1808–1809).* 1814. See the edition in English by Elisha Greifer (Chicago, 1959).

————. "Etude sur la souveraineté." In *Oeuvres inédites du Comte Joseph de Maistre.* Paris, 1870.

————. *Oeuvres complètes.* 14 vols. Lyons, 1884–86. See Jack Lively, *The Works of Joseph de Maistre.* New York, 1965.

Mallet du Pan, Jacques. *Considérations sur la nature de la révolution française et sur les causes qui en prolongent la durée.* Brussels, 1793. English translation, *Considerations on the Nature of the French Revolution and on the Causes which Prolong the Duration.*

Introduction by Paul Beik. New York, 1974.

———. *Correspondance inédite de Mallet du Pan avec la Cour de Vienne (1794–1798)*. 2 vols. Paris, 1884.

———. *Correspondance politique pour servir à l'histoire du républicanisme française*. Hamburg, 1796.

———. "Du degré d'influence qu'a eu la philosophie française sur la révolution," le 20 mars 1799. *Mercure britannique; ou notices historiques et critiques sur les affaires du temps*. 5 vols., 2:342–70. London, 1798–99.

Mao Tse-tung. "Combat Liberalism." In *Selected Works*. 5 vols., 2:32–33. Peking, 1965.

Marigne, A. M. *Benjamin Constant en réponse à l'article inséré dans le Journal des débats d'aujourd'hui (le 21 avril 1814) sous le titre "Des Révolutions de 1660 et 1688."* 1814.

Mill, John Stuart. *On Liberty*. London, 1859.

———. *Considerations on Representative Government*. London, 1861.

Mirabeau, Marquis de. *L'ami des hommes*. Paris, 1756.

Molé, Louis-Mathieu, Comte de. *Essais de morale et de politique*. Paris, 1806.

Montesquieu, Charles de Secondat, Baron de. *The Spirit of the Laws*. Translated by Thomas Nugent. New York, 1949. See also the edition of David W. Carrithers (Berkeley, 1977), and selections by Melvin Richter, *The Political Theory of Montesquieu* (New York, 1977).

Montlosier, François. *De la monarchie française depuis son établissement jusqu' à nos jours*. 3 vols. Paris, 1814.

Möser, Justus. *The Modern Taste for General Laws Is a Danger to Our Common Liberty* (1772). In Karl Mannheim, "Conservative Thought," *Essays on Sociology and Social Psychology*. New York, 1953.

Mounier, Jean Joseph. *Considérations sur les gouvernements et principalement sur celui qui convient à la France*. Paris, 1789.

———. *Recherches sur les causes qui ont empêché les Français de devenir libres et sur les moyens qui leur restent pour acquérir la liberté*. Paris, 1792.

Napoleon Bonaparte. *Letters of Napoleon*. Edited by J. M. Thompson. Oxford, 1934.

Pagès, J. P. "Benjamin Constant." In *Dictionnaire de la conversation et de la lecture*. Paris, 1835.

———. *De la responsibilité ministerielle et de la nécessité d'originer le mode d'accusation et de jugement des ministres*. Paris, 1818.

Paine, Thomas. *The Age of Reason*. London, 1794.

———. *The Rights of Man*. London, 1791. Everyman edition, London, 1915.

Pharon, J. *Notice sur B. Constant*. Paris, 1830.

Prevost, Pierre. *L'économie des anciens gouvernements comparée à celle des gouvernements modernes.* Berlin, 1783.

Price, Richard. *Observations on the Nature of Civil Liberty, the Principles of Government.* London, 1776.

Priestley, Joseph. *An Essay on the First Principles of Government and of the Nature of Political, Civil, and Religious Liberty.* London, 1768.

Rabbe. *Notice sur B. Constant.* Paris, 1827.

Real, P. T. *Indiscrétions, 1798–1830: Souvenirs anecdotiques et politiques.* Paris, 1835.

Rémusat, Charles de. *Correspondance de M. de Rémusat pendant les premières années de la Restauration.* 6 vols. Paris, 1884–86.

———. "De l'esprit de réaction: Royer-Collard et Tocqueville." *Revue des deux mondes* 35 (1861): 777–813.

———. *L'Angleterre au XVIIIᵉ siècle.* 2 vols. Paris, 1856.

———. *Mémoires de ma vie.* 5 vols. Paris, 1858–67.

Ripley, George. *Philosophical Miscellanies, Translated from the French of Cousin, Jouffroy, and Benjamin Constant.* Boston, 1838.

Romilly, Sir Samuel. *Memoirs of the Life of Sir Samuel Romilly, 1757–1818.* 3 vols. London, 1840.

Rousseau, Jean-Jacques. *The First and Second Discourses.* Edited by Roger D. Masters and Judith R. Masters. New York, 1964.

———. *The Government of Poland.* Edited by Willmore Kendall. New York, 1972.

———. *Lettres écrites de la Montagne.* Amsterdam, 1764.

———. *The Miscellaneous Works of Mr. Jean-Jacques Rousseau.* 5 vols. London, 1767.

———. *Oeuvres complètes.* Edited by Bernard Gagnebin and Marcel Raymond. 3 vols. Paris, 1959–64.

———. *On the Social Contract with Geneva Manuscript and Political Economy.* Edited by Roger D. Masters and Judith R. Masters. New York, 1975.

———. *The Social Contract.* Translated by Maurice Cranston. London, 1968.

Sainte-Beuve, Charles Augustin. "Benjamin Constant et Madame de Charrière." In *Portraits littéraires.* 3 vols., 3:185–285. Paris, 1864.

———. "Benjamin Constant: Son cours de politique constitutionnel." *Nouveaux lundis.* 13 vols., 9:135–60. Paris, 1871.

———. "Un dernier mot sur Benjamin Constant." In *Portraits contemporains.* 5 vols., 5:275–300. Paris, 1871.

Saint-Marc Girardin, François A. *Jean Jacques Rousseau: Sa vie et ses ouvrages.* 2 vols. Paris, 1875.

Saint René Taillandier, René. *Lettres inédites de J. C. L. de Sismondi, de Bonstetten, Mme de Staël et Mme de Souza à la comtesse d'Albany.* Paris, 1863.

Saint-Simon, Henri de. *L'industrie.* Paris, 1816.

———. *Oeuvres.* 47 vols. Paris, 1865–78.

Sarran, J. *Démenti formel connue à MM Manuel et B. Constant sur un incident élevé à la Chambre des Députés le 26 avril et 31 janvier, 1822.* Paris, 1822.

Say, Jean Baptiste. *Traité d'économie politique.* 2 vols. Paris, 1817.

Sieyès, Joseph. *Qu'est-ce que le Tiers Etat?* Paris, 1789. English translation, *What Is the Third Estate?*, edited by S. E. Finer. London, 1963.

Simonde de Sismondi, Jean Charles L. *Epistolario.* Edited by Carlo Pelligrini. 3 vols. Florence, 1933–54.

———. *Etudes sur les constitutions des peuples modernes.* Paris, 1836.

———. *Examen de la constitution française.* Paris, 1815.

———. *Histoire des républiques italiennes du Moyen Age.* 10 vols. Paris, 1840.

———. *Nouveaux principes d'économie politique.* 2 vols. Paris, 1819.

Smith, Adam. *An Inquiry into the Nature and Causes of the Wealth of Nations.* 2 vols. London, 1776.

Somerville, William C. *Letters from Paris on the Causes and Consequences of the French Revolution.* Baltimore, 1822.

Spencer, Herbert. *The Man versus the State.* Edited by Donald G. Macrae. London, 1969.

———. *The Principles of Sociology.* 3 vols. London, 1876–96.

———. *Social Statics.* London, 1851.

Staël, Germaine de. *Considérations sur les principaux événements de la révolution française.* 1817. English translation, *Considerations on the Principal Events of the French Revolution.* 2 vols. New York, 1818.

———. *De l'Allemagne.* Paris, 1810.

———. *De l'influence des passions sur le bonheur des individus et des nations.* Paris, 1796.

———. *Des circonstances actuelles qui peuvent terminer la révolution et des principes qui doivent fonder la République en France* (1799). Edited by John Vienot. Paris, 1896. See also Edouard Herriot, *Un ouvrage inédit de Madame de Staël. Les fragments d'écrits politiques de 1799.* Paris, 1904.

———. "Dix années d'exil." In *Mémoires de Mme de Staël.* Paris, 1861.

———. *Lettres de Madame de Staël à Benjamin Constant.* Paris, 1928.

———. *Lettres sur les écrits et le caractère de Jean Jacques Rousseau.* [Paris?] 1788.

———. *Oeuvres complètes de Mme la Baronne de Staël.* 20 vols. Paris, 1820–21.

———. *Portrait d'Atilla.* Paris, 1814.

———. *Réflexions sur la paix intérieure.* Paris, 1795.

Taine, Hippolyte-Adolphe. *The Origins of Contemporary France.* Vol. 1, *The Ancien Regime.* New York, 1885.

Talleyrand-Périgord, Charles Maurice de. *Mémoires complètes et authentiques de Charles Maurice de Talleyrand.* 5 vols. Paris, 1967.

Thiers, Adolphe. *Histoire du consulat et de l'empire.* 21 vols. Paris, 1874.

Tocqueville, Alexis de. *Democracy in America.* Introduction by Phillip Bradley. 2 vols. New York, 1946.

————. "Etat social et politique de la France depuis 1789 or Political Science and Social Condition of France." *London and Westminster Review,* April 1836.

————. *Oeuvres complètes.* Edited by J. P. Mayer. 13 vols. Paris, 1951—

————. *Oeuvres complètes.* Edited by Gustave de Beaumont. 9 vols. Paris, 1864–66.

————. *Oeuvres et correspondance inédites.* 2 vols. Paris, 1861.

————. *The Old Regime and the French Revolution.* Translated by Stuart Gilbert. New York, 1955.

————. *Recollections.* Edited by J. P. Mayer. London, 1948.

Torombert, H. *Principes du droit politique, mis en opposition avec ceux du Contrat Social.* Paris, 1825.

Turgot, Anne Robert Jacques. "Discours sur les avantages que l'établissement du Christianisme a procurés aux genre humain." In *Démonstrations évangéliques,* edited by Abbé Jacques-Paul Migne, vol. 10. Paris, 1843.

————. *Oeuvres.* 9 vols. Paris, 1818–21.

Vico, Giambattista. *The New Science* (1744). Ithaca, 1968.

Vigny, Alfred, Comte de. *Le journal d'un poète (le 12 décembre 1830).* Paris, 1867.

Villers, Charles. *Philosophie de Kant.* Metz, 1801.

Vitrolles, Baron de. *Du ministère dans le gouvernement représentatif.* Paris, 1815.

Secondary Sources

Acomb, Frances D. *Mallet du Pan (1749–1810); A Career in Political Journalism.* Durham, 1973.

Acocella, Giuseppe. "Constituzione liberale e democrazia totalitaria nella critica Benjamin Constant al Contratto sociale." *Filosofia* (1976): 67–100.

Actes du Congrès Benjamin Constant à Lausanne, Octobre, 1967. Geneva, 1968.

Alexander, I. W. "La morale ouverte de Benjamin Constant." In *Studi in onore di Carlo Pellegrini,* pp. 395–410. Turin, 1963.

Anderson, Frank M. *The Constitutions and Other Select Documents Illustrative of the History of France, 1789–1901.* Minneapolis, 1901.

Arendt, Hannah. *The Human Condition.* Garden City, 1959.

———. *The Origins of Totalitarianism.* New York, 1951.

———. "What Is Freedom?" In *Between Past and Future,* New York, 1968.

Aron, Raymond. "La définition libérale, Alexis de Tocqueville et Karl Marx." *European Journal of Sociology* 15 (1964): 159–89.

———. *Main Currents in Sociological Thought.* New York, 1965.

Asse, Eugene. "Benjamin Constant et le Directoire." *Revue de la révolution* 15 (July 1889): 337–56; and 16 (Oct. 1889): 105–25.

Bach, Woldemar. *Benjamin Constant und die Politik, 1767–1802. Eine psychologische-historische Studie.* Leipzig, 1936.

Baelen, Jean. *Benjamin Constant.* Beyrouth, 1941.

———. "Benjamin Constant et la question sociale." *Lettres d'humanité* 13 (1954): 125–54.

———. *Benjamin Constant et Napoléon.* Paris, 1965.

———. "Positions générales de Benjamin Constant en matière politique et sociale." In *Actes du Congrès,* pp. 23–30. Geneva, 1968.

Bagge, Dominicq. *Les Idées politiques sous la Restauration.* Paris, 1952.

Baker, Keith M., ed. *Condorcet: From Natural Philosophy to Social Mathematics.* Chicago, 1975.

Baldensperger, Ferdinand. "Benjamin Constant condottieri du parlementarisme." *Le correspondant,* 25 Nov. 1930, pp. 494–506.

Barbé, Maurice. *Etude historique des idées sur la souveraineté en France de 1815 à 1848.* Paris, 1904.

Barbey d' Aurevilly, J. "Oeuvres politiques de Benjamin Constant." *Le constitutionnel,* Feb. 1875.

Barrès, Maurice. "Méditation spirituelle sur Benjamin Constant." In *Un homme libre,* pp. 92–107. Paris, 1894.

Barthélemy, Joseph. *L'introduction du régime parlementaire en France sous Louis XVIII et Charles X.* Paris, 1904.

Bartholini, Fernand. *Introduction à la politique de Benjamin Constant.* Paris, 1964.

Barthou, Louis. "Benjamin Constant contre les discours écrits." *Revue de France* 1 (Jan. 1933): 39–51.

Bastid, Paul. *Benjamin Constant et sa doctrine.* 2 vols. Paris, 1966.

———. *Les institutions politiques de la monarchie parlementaire française.* Paris, 1954.

———. *Sieyès et sa pensée.* Paris, 1939.

———. "Tocqueville et la doctrine constitutionnelle." In *Alexis de Tocqueville: Livre du centénaire, 1859–1959,* pp. 45–56. Paris, 1961.

Beik, Paul H. *The French Revolution Seen from the Right.* Philadelphia, 1956.

Berger, Morroe. *Madame de Staël on Politics, Literature and National Character*. London, 1964.

Berlin, Isaiah. *Four Essays on Liberty*. Oxford, 1969.

————. "Montesquieu." *British Academy Proceedings* 40 (1956): 267–96.

Berr, Michel. *Eloge de Benjamin Constant*. Paris, 1836.

Berthauld, M. "Deux individualistes: Benjamin Constant et Daunou." In *Mémoires de l'Académie des sciences de Caen*, 1863, pp. 172–209.

Berthoud, Dorette. *Constance et grandeur de Benjamin Constant*. Lausanne, 1944.

Blennerhasset, Charlotte J. "The Doctrinaires." In *Cambridge Modern History*. 13 vols., 10:40–70. Cambridge, 1907.

————. *Madame de Staël et son temps (1766–1817)*. 3 vols. Paris, 1890.

Bobbio, Norberto. "Della liberta dei moderni comparate a quella dei posteri." In *Politica e cultura*, pp. 160–94. Turin, 1955.

Bonnefon, Joseph. *Le régime parlementaire sous la Restauration*. Paris, 1905.

Bonno, Gabriel. *La constitution britannique devant l'opinion française de Montesquieu à Bonaparte*. Paris, 1932.

Bouglé, C. *Du sage antique au citoyen moderne*. Paris, 1921.

————. "La philosophie politique de Benjamin Constant." *Revue de Paris* 2 (1 March 1914): 209–24.

Bourget, Paul. "Benjamin Constant." In *Le livre du centenaire du Journal des débats*, pp. 144–49. Paris, 1889.

Bowers, Hilda. *Les idées religieuses de Benjamin Constant*. Paris, 1950.

Bowman, Frank. "B. Constant, Germany and De la religion." In *Romanische Forschungen*, pp. 77–108. 1962.

Bressler, Henri. *Benjamin Constant et les femmes*. Geneva, 1973.

Bruford, W. H. *The German Tradition of Self-Cultivation*. Cambridge, 1975.

Bryson, Gladys. *Man and Society: The Scottish Inquiry of the Eighteenth Century*. Princeton, 1945.

Burdeau, Georges. *Traité de science politique*. 7 vols. Paris, 1949–57. Vol. 5, *L'état libéral et les techniques politiques de la democratie gouvernée*.

Caillet, Emile. *La tradition littéraire des Idéologues*. Philadelphia, 1933.

Calogero, C. "La liberta degli antichi e la liberta dei moderni." In *Saggi di etica e di teoria del diritto*, pp. 56–73. Bari, 1947.

Cappadocia, E. "The Liberals and Madame de Staël in 1818." In Richard Herr and Harold Parker, eds., *Ideas in History Presented to Louis Gottschalk by His Former Students*. Durham, 1965.

Carcassonne, Elie. *Montesquieu et le problème de la constitution française au XVIIIe siècle*. Paris, 1927.

Carey, E. G. "The Liberals of France and Their Reaction to the Development of Bonaparte's Dictatorship, 1799–1804." Ph.D. dissertation, University of Chicago, 1945.

Carré, J. M. *Les écrivains français et le mirage allemand.* Paris, 1947.

Cassirer, Ernst. *The Philosophy of the Enlightenment.* Boston, 1951.

_____. *The Question of Jean Jacques Rousseau.* Introduction by Peter Gay. New York, 1954.

_____. *Rousseau, Kant, Goethe.* Princeton, 1947.

Castille, Hippolyte. *Benjamin Constant.* Paris, 1857.

Centenaire de Benjamin Constant, 1767–1830. Discours prononcé à la séance commemorative du 14 juin 1930 à l'Aula de l'Université de Lausanne. Lausanne, 1930.

Champion, E. *Les idées politiques et religieuses de Fustel de Coulanges.* Paris, 1903.

Chevallier, Jean Jacques. *Les grandes oeuvres politiques de Machiavel à nos jours.* Paris, 1849.

_____. *Histoire des institutions politiques de la France moderne (1789–1945).* Paris, 1958.

_____. "Montesquieu ou le libéralisme aristocratique." *Revue internationale de la philosophie* 9 (1955): 330–45.

Clark, John P. *The Philosophical Anarchism of William Godwin.* Princeton, 1977.

Clerq, Victor de. "La pensée religieuse de B. Constant." *La vie catholique,* 27 Dec. 1930.

Cobban, Alfred. *A History of Modern France.* 2 vols. London, 1957 and 1961.

_____. *In Search of Humanity: The Role of the Enlightenment in Modern History.* London, 1960.

Cohen, Marshall. "Berlin and the Liberal Tradition." *Philosophical Quarterly* 10 (1960): 216–28.

Cordey, Pierre. *Mme de Staël et Benjamin Constant sur les Bords du Léman.* Lausanne, 1966.

Cordie, Carlo. *Benjamin Constant oeuvres choisies.* Milan, 1946.

_____. *Ideali e figure d'Europe.* Pisa, 1954.

Cotta, S. *Gaetano Filangieri e il problema della legge.* Torino, 1954.

Courtney, Cecil P. "La pensée politique de Benjamin Constant." In *Actes du Congrès Benjamin Constant,* pp. 31–39. Geneva, 1968.

_____. "Témoin et interprète de son temps," *Europe.* March 1968, pp. 126–33.

Cranston, Maurice. *Freedom.* New York, 1967.

_____. "Liberalism." In *The Encyclopedia of Philosophy.* 8 vols., 3:458–61. New York, 1967.

Croce, Benedetto. "Constant e Jellinek. Intorne al differenze tra la liberta degli antichi e quella dei moderni." In *Etica e politica*, pp. 294–301. Bari, 1945.

————. *History as the Story of Liberty*. London, 1941.

————. *History of Europe in the Nineteenth Century*. New York, 1933.

Cruikshank, John. *Benjamin Constant*. New York, 1974.

Cumming, Robert D. *Human Nature and History: A Study of the Development of Liberal Political Thought*. 2 vols. Chicago, 1969.

David, Madeleine. "Vue comparée des idées de Herder et de Benjamin Constant sur l'étude des religions." *Numen. International Review for the History of Religion* 3 (Jan. 1956): 14–27.

Declareuil, J. "De l'esprit de conquête ou Benjamin Constant cosmopolite, pacifiste, anti-militariste." *Revue du droit public et de la science politique* 26 (1919): 471–504.

Dedieu, Joseph. *Montesquieu et la tradition politique anglaise en France: Les sources anglaises de l'Esprit des Lois*. Paris, 1902.

Deguise, Pierre. *Benjamin Constant: De la perfectibilité de l'espèce humaine*. Lausanne, 1968.

————. "Benjamin Constant depuis deux siècles." *Europe*, March 1968, pp. 38–48.

————. *Benjamin Constant méconnu: Le livre de la religion*. Geneva, 1966.

————. "La doctrine politique de Benjamin Constant." *Romanic Review* 58 (1967): 200–203.

————. "Etat présent des études sur Benjamin Constant." *L'information littéraire* 9–10 (1957–58): 139–50.

————. "Inédites de Benjamin Constant." *Revue de Paris* 7–12 (Aug. 1963): 91–106.

De Jouvenel, Bertrand. *Power: The Natural History of Its Growth*. New York, 1949.

————. *Sovereignty: An Inquiry into the Political Good*. Chicago, 1957.

De Lanzac de Laborie, Léon. "L'amitié d'Alexis de Tocqueville et de Royer Collard." *Revue des deux mondes* 58 (15 Aug. 1930): 876–911.

————. *Un royaliste libérale en 1789: Jean Joseph Mounier, sa vie politique et ses écrits*. Paris, 1887.

De Lauris, Georges. *Benjamin Constant et les droits individuels*. Paris, 1903.

Delbouille, Paul. *Genèse, structure et destin d'Adolphe*. Paris, 1971.

Del Corral, Luis D. *El liberalismo doctrinario*. Madrid, 1943.

————. "Tocqueville et la pensée politique des Doctrinaires." In *Alexis de Tocqueville Livre du centenaire, 1859–1959*, pp. 57–70. Paris, 1960.

D'Entrèves, Alexander Passerin. "Mallet du Pan." *Occidente* 7 (1951): 371–403.

————. "Mallet du Pan: Swiss Critic of Democracy." *Cambridge Journal* 1 (1947): 99–108.

————. *The Notion of the State.* Oxford, 1967.

Derré, Jean. *Lammenais, ses amis et le mouvement des idées à l'époque romantique, 1824–1834.* Klincksieck, 1962.

De Salis, Jean-R. *Sismondi, la vie et l'oeuvre d'un cosmopolite philosophe, 1773–1842.* Paris, 1932.

Descotes, Maurice. *La légende de Napoléon et les écrivains français du XIX siècle.* Paris, 1967.

Des Granges, Charles M. *Le romantisme et la critique; La presse littéraire sous la Restauration, 1815–1830.* Paris, 1907.

Dicey, Albert V. *Introduction to the Study of the Law of the Constitution.* 8th ed. London, 1926.

Dodge, Guy H. *The Political Theory of the Huguenots of the Dispersion.* New York, 1947 and 1972.

————, ed. *Jean-Jacques Rousseau: Authoritarian, Libertarian?* Lexington, Mass., 1971.

Dodu, Gaston. *Le parlementarisme et les parlementaires sous la révolution (1789–1799).* Paris, 1911.

Dolmatowsky, Aron. *Der Parlementarismus in der Lehre Benjamin Constant.* Tübingen, 1907.

Droz, Jacques. *Histoire des doctrines politiques en France.* Paris, 1948.

DuBos, Charles. *Grandeur et misère de Benjamin Constant.* Paris, 1946.

Dugas, Ludovic. *Les grandes timides: Jean-Jacques Rousseau, Benjamin Constant, Chateaubriand, Stendhal, Merimée.* Paris, 1922.

Duguit, Leon. "The Law and the State." *Harvard Law Review* 31 (1917–18): 1–185.

Dumont-Wilden, Louis. *La vie de Benjamin Constant.* Paris, 1930.

Dunning, William A. *A History of Political Theories from Rousseau to Spencer.* New York, 1920.

Duverger, Maurice. "Démocratie libérale et démocratie totalitaire." *La vie intellectuelle* 2 (July 1948): 56–70.

————. *Droit constitutionnel et institutions politiques.* Paris, 1955.

Duzer, Ch. von. *The Contribution of the Ideologues to the French Revolution.* Baltimore, 1935.

Ehrenberg, Victor. *The Greek State.* New York, 1964.

Elkington, Margery E. *Les relations de société entre l'Angleterre et la France sous la Restauration, 1814–1830.* Paris, 1929.

Ettlinger, Joseph. *Benjamin Constant: Der Roman Eines Lebens.* Berlin, 1909.

Europe: Numéro spécial de la revue consacré à Benjamin Constant. Paris, 1968.

Fabre-Luce, Alfred. *Benjamin Constant.* Paris, 1939.

Faguet, Emile. *Le libéralisme.* Paris, 1902.

————. *Politiques et moralistes du dix-neuvième siècle.* Paris, 1888.

Fargher, R. "Retreat from Voltairianisme, 1810–1815." In *The French*

Mind: Studies in Honor of Gustave Rudler, pp. 220–37. Oxford, 1952.

Fasnacht, George E. *Acton's Political Philosophy.* London, 1952.

Fay, Eliot G. "The Man Who Hesitated for Fifteen Years." *French Review* 27 (1954): 323–33.

Ferrero, Guglielmo. *The Principles of Power.* New York, 1942.

Fink, Beatrice C. "Benjamin Constant and the Enlightenment." In Harold E. Pagliaro, *Studies in Eighteenth-Century Culture,* 3:67–81. Cleveland, 1973.

―――. "Benjamin Constant on Equality." *Journal of the History of Ideas* 33 (April-June 1972): 307–14.

―――. "The Idea-World of Benjamin Constant as Expressed in His Political Philosophy." Ph.D. dissertation, University of Pittsburgh, 1966.

Folman, Marcel. *Le secret de Benjamin Constant, sa maladie, sa vie intérieure.* Geneva, 1959.

Ford, Franklin. *Robe and Sword.* Cambridge, 1953.

Fox-Genovese, Elizabeth. *The Origins of Physiocracy.* Ithaca, 1976.

Franck, Adolphe. "Idées de Benjamin Constant sur la religion." *Revue politique et littéraire* 5 (1968): 170–78, 434–38, 442–45.

Friedrich, Carl J. *Constitutional Government and Democracy: Theory and Practice in Europe and America.* Boston, 1950.

―――. *The Philosophy of Hegel.* New York, 1954.

―――. *Transcendental Justice: The Religious Dimension of Constitutionalism.* Durham, 1964.

Gall, Lothar. *Benjamin Constant, Seine politische Ideenwelt und der Deutsche Vormärz.* Wiesbaden, 1963.

Gautier, Paul. *Madame de Staël et Napoléon.* Paris, 1902.

Genequand, Raymond. *Benjamin Constant, homme religieux.* Geneva, 1928.

George, Paul. "Montesquieu and De Tocqueville and Corporate Individualism." *American Political Science Review* 16 (1922): 10–21.

Girard, Alain. "Benjamin Constant et le livre de la religion devant la critique." *Revue d'histoire littéraire de la France* 66 (1966): 115–26.

―――. *Le journal intime.* Paris, 1963.

Girard, William. "Du transcendentalisme considérée essentiellement dans sa définition et ses origines françaises." *University of California Publications in Modern Philology* 4 (1913–16): 351–498.

Glachant, V. *Benjamin Constant sous l'oeil du guet.* Paris, 1906.

Glotz, Gustave. *The Greek City and Its Institutions.* New York, 1928.

Godet, Philippe. *Madame de Charrière et ses amis (1740–1805).* Geneva, 1906.

Goldstein, Doris. *Trial of Faith: Religion and Politics in Tocqueville's Thought*. New York, 1975.

Gonnard, Philippe. "Benjamin Constant au début de la Restauration (1817–1820)." *Revue politique et parlementaire* 76 (1913): 512–34.

———. "Benjamin Constant et le groupe de la minerve." *Revue politique et littéraire* 1 (8 Feb. 1913): 181–86 and (15 Feb. 1913): 209–12.

Gordon, H. Scott. "Laissez-Faire." In *International Encyclopedia of the Social Sciences*. 16 vols., 8: 546–49. New York, 1968.

Gougelot, Henri. *L'idée de liberté dans la pensée de Benjamin Constant. Essai critique historique*. Melun, 1942.

Gouhier, Henri. *Benjamin Constant*. Paris, 1967.

Gribble, Fr. "Benjamin Constant." *Fortnightly Review* 81 (1907): 117–27.

Gruner, Shirley M. "Political Historiography in Restoration France." *History and Theory* 8 (1969): 346–65.

Guillemin, Henri. *Benjamin Constant muscadin, 1795–1799*. Paris, 1958.

———. *Madame de Staël, Benjamin Constant et Napoléon*. Paris, 1959.

Guillois, Antoine. *Le salon de Madame Helvétius, Cabanis et les Idéologues*. Paris, 1894.

Gwyn, William B. *The Meaning of the Separation of Powers*. New Orleans, 1965.

Gwynne, G. E. *Madame de Staël et la révolution française: Politique, philosophie, littérature*. Paris, 1969.

Halévy, Elie. *The Growth of Philosophical Radicalism*. Boston, 1955.

Hallowell, John H. "Liberalism and the Open Society." In *The Open Society in Theory and Practice*, edited by Dante Germino and Klaus von Beyme, pp. 121–41. The Hague, 1974.

Hamburger, Joseph. "Mill and Tocqueville on Liberty." In *James and John Stuart Mill, Papers of the Centenary Conference*, edited by John M. Robson and M. Laine. Toronto, 1976.

Harpaz, Ephraim. *L'école libérale sous la Restauration. Le mercure et la minerve, 1817–1820*. Geneva, 1968.

Hasselrot, Bengt. *Nouveaux documents sur Benjamin Constant et Mme de Staël*. Copenhagen, 1952.

Hawkins, R. L. *Newly Discovered French Letters of the Seventeenth, Eighteenth, and Nineteenth Centuries*. Cambridge, 1933.

Hayek, Friedrich von. *The Constitution of Liberty*. Chicago, 1960.

———. *Law, Legislation and Liberty: A New Statement of the Principles of Justice and Political Economy*. Vol. 1, *Rules and Order*; vol. 2, *The Mirage of Social Justice*; vol. 3, *The Political Order of a Free People*. Chicago, 1973–79.

———. "The Principles of a Liberal Social Order." In *Studies in Philosophy, Politics and Economics*, pp. 160–77. Chicago, 1967.

Herold, Christopher J. *Mistress of an Age: A Life of Madame de Staël.* Indianapolis, 1958.

Herriot, Edouard. *Madame Récamier et ses amis.* Paris, 1905.

Hiestand, Jean. *Benjamin Constant et la doctrine parlementaire.* Paris, 1928.

Himmelfarb, Gertrude. *Lord Acton: A Study in Conscience in Politics.* New York, 1952.

————. *On Liberty and Liberalism: The Case of John Stuart Mill.* New York, 1974.

Hofmann, Etienne. "Benjamin Constant à la veille des Cent-Jours, L'article du 19 mars 1815 dans le Journal des débats." *Etudes de lettres,* July-Sept. 1978.

Hogue, Helen H. S. *Of Changes in Benjamin Constant's Books on Religion.* Geneva, 1964.

Holdheim, William W. *Benjamin Constant.* London, 1961.

Holmes, Stephen T. "Aristippus In and Out of Athens." *American Political Science Review* 73 (March 1970): 113–28.

————. "Transformations of Legitimacy." Ph.D. dissertation, Yale University, 1976.

Hulliung, Mark. *Montesquieu and the Old Regime.* Los Angeles, 1977.

Hytier, Jean. *Les romans de l'individu.* Paris, 1928.

Jacqueline, René. "Les Cent Jours et le régime parlementaire." *Revue de droit public et de la science politique en France et à l'étranger* 7 (1897): 193–200.

Jasinski, Beatrice W. *L'engagement de Benjamin Constant: Amour et politique, 1794–1796.* Paris, 1971.

Jeanson, F. "Benjamin Constant ou l'indifférence en liberté." *Les temps modernes* 3 (1948): 2128–53.

Jellinek, Georg. *Allgemeine Staatslehre.* Berlin, 1929.

Kaufman, A. S. "Professor Berlin on Negative Freedom." *Mind* 71 (1962): 241–44.

Kelly, George. "Liberalism and Aristocracy in the French Restoration." *Journal of the History of Ideas* 26 (1965): 522–30.

Kerchove, Arnold de. *Benjamin Constant ou le libertin sentimental.* Paris, 1950.

Kettler, David. *The Social and Political Thought of Adam Ferguson.* Columbus, 1965.

King, Preston. *Fear of Power: An Analysis of Anti-Statism in Three French Writers: Tocqueville, Proudhon, Sorel.* London, 1967.

Kohn, Hans. *Making of the Modern French Mind.* New York, 1955.

Kossman, E. "De Doctrinairen tijdens de Restauratie." *Tijdschrift voor Geschiedenis* 64–65 (1951–52): 123–67.

Krafft, A. *Homage à Benjamin Constant.* Lausanne, 1956.

Lakoff, Sanford A. *Equality in Political Philosophy*. Cambridge, 1964.

La Lombardière, Jacqueline de. *Les idées politiques de Benjamin Constant*. Paris, 1928.

La Luz-Leon, J. *De historia di un alma Benjamin Constant. Donjuanismo intellectuel*. Habens, 1937.

Lehmann, William G. *Adam Ferguson and the Beginnings of Modern Sociology*. New York, 1936.

Lenzer, Gertrud, ed. *Auguste Comte and Positivism: The Essential Writings*. New York, 1975.

Léon, Paul L. *Benjamin Constant*. Paris, 1930.

Leroy, Maxime. *Histoire des idées sociales en France*. 3 vols. Paris, 1947–54.

Levaillant, Maurice. *Les amours de Benjamin Constant*. Paris, 1958.

Lewis, James M. "The Religious Thought of Benjamin Constant." Honors dissertation, Harvard University, 1970.

Lindsay, A. D. "Individualism." In *Encyclopedia of the Social Sciences*, 7: 674–80. New York, 1930–33.

Lively, Jack. *The Social and Political Thought of Alexis de Tocqueville*. Oxford, 1962.

Loeve-Weimars. "Lettres sur les hommes d'état de la France: Benjamin Constant." *Revue des deux mondes*, 1 Feb. 1833, pp. 225–63.

Loewenstein, Karl. *Political Reconstruction*. New York, 1946.

Loirette, G. "Montesquieu et son influence sur la doctrine politique de Benjamin Constant." In *Actes Académie nationale des sciences, belles-lettres et arts de Bordeaux*, pp. 61–79. 1952.

Longchamp, F. "De l'Esprit de conquête par Benjamin Constant: Bibliographie raisonnée." *Bulletin de bibliophile* (1937): 486–94, 533–41.

Lopez-Michelson, Alfonso. *El padre Bohemio de un liberalismo gurgues, ensayo sobre Benjamin Constant*. Bogata, 1934.

Lukes, Steven. *Individualism*. Oxford, 1972.

MacCullum, G. C., Jr. "Negative and Positive Freedom." *Philosophical Review* 76 (July 1967): 312–34.

Macfarlane, L. J. "On Two Concepts of Liberty." *Political Studies* 14 (1966): 77–81.

Macpherson, C. B. "Berlin's Division of Liberty." In *Democratic Theory*, pp. 95–119. Oxford, 1973.

———. *The Political Theory of Possessive Individualism: Hobbes to Locke*. Oxford, 1962.

"Madame de Staël et Benjamin Constant." *Revue d'histoire littéraire de la France* 66 (Jan.-March 1966).

Manning, D. J. *Liberalism*. New York, 1976.

Mansfield, Harvey C., Jr. *The Spirit of Liberalism*. Cambridge, 1978.

Manuel, Frank. *The New World of Henri Saint-Simon.* Cambridge, 1956.
————. *The Prophets of Paris.* Cambridge, 1962.
Marcuse, Herbert. *One Dimensional Man: Studies in the Ideology of Advanced Industrial Societies.* Boston, 1964.
————. "Repressive Tolerance." In Robert P. Wolff, ed., *A Critique of Pure Tolerance,* pp. 81–123. Boston, 1965.
Marion, H. "Individualisme." *La grande encyclopédie* 20: 723. Paris, n.d.
Marx, P. *Evolution des régimes représentatifs vers le régime parlementaire de 1814 à 1816.* Paris, 1929.
Masters, Roger D. *On the Social Contract Jean Jacques Rousseau.* New York, 1978.
Mathiez, A. "La place de Montesquieu dans l'histoire des doctrines politiques du XVIIIe siècle." *Annales historiques de la révolution française* 7 (1930): 97–112.
Matteucci, Mario. "Sul pensiero religioso di Benjamin Constant." *Saggi e ricerche di letterature francese* 7 (1966): 139–200.
Matteucci, Nicola. *Il liberalismo in un mondo in transformazione.* Bologna, 1972.
————. *Jacques Mallet du Pan.* Naples, 1956.
————. "Mallet du Pan, genevois et européen." *Bulletin de la société d'histoire et d'archéologie de Genève* 11 (1957): 153–68.
Maunier, René. "Benjamin Constant historien des sociétés et des religions." *Revue de l'histoire des religions* 101–4 (1930–31): 93–113.
Mayer, Jacob Peter. *Political Thought in France from the Revolution to the Fifth Republic.* London, 1961.
————. *Prophet of the Mass Age: A Study of Alexis de Tocqueville.* London, 1939.
McIlwain, Charles H. *Constitutionalism and the Changing World.* New York, 1939.
Medd, Patrick. *Romilly: A Life of Sir Samuel Romilly.* London, 1968.
Meek, Roland, trans. and ed. *Turgot on Progress, Sociology, and Economics.* London, 1973.
Meister, Konrad. *Benjamin Constant und die Freiheit.* Zurich, 1954.
Melchior de Molènes, Charles. "Un grand parlementaire: Benjamin Constant." *Revue politique et parlementaire* 68 (Oct. 1966): 79–89.
————. "Pour le bicentenaire de Benjamin Constant." *Res publica* 10 (1968): 683–93.
Mellon, Stanley. *The Political Uses of History: A Study of Historians in the French Restoration.* Palo Alto, 1958.
Merriam, Charles E. *The History of the Theory of Sovereignty since Rousseau.* New York, 1910.
Michel, Henri. *L'idée de l'état: Essai critique sur l'histoire des théories*

sociales et politiques en France depuis la Révolution. Paris, 1896.

Michon, Louis. *Le gouvernement parlementaire sous la Restauration.* Paris, 1905.

Mims, Edwin. "Henri Benjamin Constant de Rebecque (1767–1830)." *Encyclopedia of the Social Sciences,* 4: 241–42. New York, 1931.

――――. *The Majority of the People.* New York, 1941.

Mirkine-Guetzivitch, B. "Le gouvernement parlementaire sous la Convention." *Cahiers de la révolution française,* No. 6 (1937), pp. 66ff.

Monchaux, André. *L'Allemagne devant les lettres françaises de 1814 à 1835.* Toulouse, 1955.

Monod, Albert. *De Pascal à Chateaubriand; Les défenseurs français du Christianisme de 1670 à 1802.* Paris, 1916.

Morel, Louis. "L'influence germanique chez Benjamin Constant. Benjamin Constant à la Cour de Brunswick." *Revue d'histoire littéraire de la France* 22 (1915): 86–112.

――――. "L'influence germanique chez Madame de Charrière et chez Benjamin Constant." *Revue d'histoire littéraire de la France* 18 (1911): 838–64 and 19 (1912): 95–125.

Mortier, P. *Benjamin Constant l'homme et l'oeuvre.* Paris, 1930.

Mortier, Roland. "Benjamin Constant et les lumières." In *Clarté et ombres du siècle des lumières. Etudes sur le XVIIIe siècle littéraire,* pp. 144–56. Geneva, 1969.

Moulin, L. "On the Revolution and the Meaning of the Word Individualism." *International Social Science Bulletin* 7 (1955): 181–85.

Mueller, I. W. *John Stuart Mill and French Thought.* Urbana, 1956.

Munteano, Basil. "*Episodes kantiens en Suisse et en France sous le Directoire.*" *Revue de littérature comparée* 15 (July-Sept. 1935): 387–454.

――――. *Les idées politiques de Madame de Staël et la constitution de l'an III.* Paris, 1931.

Muret, Charlotte. *French Royalist Doctrine since the Revolution.* New York, 1933.

Nef, John U. *War and Human Progress: An Essay on the Rise of Industrial Civilization.* Cambridge, 1950.

Neppi Modona, Leo. "Quelques réflexions sur le commentaire Benjamin Constant à la Scienza della legislazione de Filangieri." *Europe,* March 1968, pp. 57–63.

Nesmes-Desmarets, Robert de. *Les doctrines politiques de Royer-Collard.* Paris, 1908.

Ngo Dinh Tu. "The Political Philosophy of François Guizot." Ph.D. dissertation, Harvard University, 1969.

Nichols, James H., Jr. "On the Proper Use of Ancient Political Philosophy:

A Comment on Stephen Taylor Holmes's 'Aristippus In and Out of Athens.'" *American Political Science Review* 62 (March 1979): 129–33.

Nicolson, Harold. *Benjamin Constant*. London, 1949.

Nisbet, Robert. *The Sociological Tradition*. New York, 1966.

————. *Twilight of Authority*. New York, 1975.

Oechslin, Jean Jacques. *Le mouvement ultra-royaliste sous la Restauration. Son idéologie et son action politique, 1814–1830*. Paris, 1960.

Oliver, Andrew. *Benjamin Constant écriture et conquête de moi*. Paris, 1970.

Omedeo, Adolpho. "Benjamin Constant et la liberte come ideale et come metode." In *Sull' eta della restaurazione*, pp. 197–209. Turin, 1976.

————. *La cultura francese nell' et a della restaurazione*. Milan, 1946.

Ortega y Gasset, José. *Invertebrate Spain*. New York, 1937.

————. *La révolte des masses*. Paris, 1961.

Painter, George. *Chateaubriand*. Vol. 1. New York, 1978.

Palmer, R. R. "Man and Citizen: Applications of Individualism in the French Revolution." In *Essays in Political Theory Presented to George H. Sabine*, pp. 130–52. Ithaca, 1948.

Pangle, Thomas L. *Montesquieu's Philosophy of Liberalism: A Commentary on the Spirit of the Laws*. Chicago, 1973.

Pappé, H. O. "Sismondi's System of Liberty." *Journal of the History of Ideas* 40 (April-June 1979): 251–66.

Parker, Harold. *The Cult of Antiquity and the French Revolutionaries: A Study in the Development of the Revolutionary Spirit*. Chicago, 1937.

Passerin, Ettore. "Gaetano Filangieri e Benjamin Constant." *Humanitas* 7 (Dec. 1952): 1110–22.

Passmore, John R. *The Perfectibility of Man*. London, 1970.

Peel, John David Y. *Herbert Spencer: The Evolution of a Sociologist*. London, 1971.

Pellegrini, Carlo. *Da Constant a Croce*. Pisa, 1958.

————. *Madame de Staël; Il gruppe cosmopolita di Coppet; L'influenza della sue idee critiche*. Florence, 1938.

Petric, Daniel S. *Le groupe littéraire de la Minerve française, 1818–1820*. Paris, 1927.

Picavet, François. *Les Idéologues: Essais sur l'histoire des idées et des théories scientifiques, philosophiques, religieuses etc en France depuis 1789*. Paris, 1891.

————. *La philosophie de Kant en France de 1773–1814*. Paris, 1927.

Plamenatz, John. "Liberalism." *Dictionary of the History of Ideas*, 3: 36–61. New York, 1973.

————. *Readings from Liberal Writers*. New York, 1965.

Pocock, J. G. A. "Civic Humanism and Its Role in Anglo-American

Thought." *Il pensiero politico* 1 (1968): 172–89.

Poggi, Gianfranco. *Images of Society: Essays on the Sociological Theories of Tocqueville, Marx, and Durkheim*. Stanford, 1972.

Poisson, Jacques. *Le romantisme et la souveraineté*. Paris, 1931.

Pollin, Burton B., ed. *Benjamin Constant, de la justice politique. Traduction inédite de l'ouvrage de William Godwin, Enquiry Concerning Political Justice*. Quebec, 1972.

Popper, Karl. *The Open Society and Its Enemies*. 2 vols. New York, 1966.

Postgate, Helen B. *Madame de Staël*. New York, 1968.

Poulet, Georges. *Benjamin Constant par lui-même*. Paris, 1968.

Pouthas, Charles H. *Guizot pendant la Restauration; Préparation de l'homme de l'état, 1814–1830*. Paris, 1923.

Pozzo di Borgo, Olivier. "Un libéral devant une dictature." *Revue d'histoire littéraire de la France* 66 (1966): 94–114.

Radiguet, Leon. *L'Acte additionnel aux constitutions de l'empire du 22 avril, 1815*. Caen, 1911.

Raico, Ralph. "Benjamin Constant." *New Individualist Review* 3 (1965): 45–54.

Rawson, Elizabeth. *The Spartan Tradition in European Thought*. Oxford, 1969.

Reboul, Pierre. *Le mythe anglais dans la littérature française sous la Restauration*. Lille, 1962.

Rémond, René. *La droite en France de 1815 à nos jours*. Paris, 1954.

Rendall, Jane. *The Origins of the Scottish Enlightenment, 1707–1776*. New York, 1979.

Reynaud, Louis. *L'influence allemand en France aux XVIIIe et XIXe siècle*. Paris, 1922.

Richter, Melvin. "Comparative Political Analysis in Montesquieu and Tocqueville." *Comparative Politics* 1 (1969): 129–60.

———. "Despotism." *Dictionary of the History of Ideas*. 2:1–18. New York, 1973.

———. *The Political Theory of Montesquieu*. New York, 1977.

———. *The Politics of Conscience: T. H. Green and His Age*. Cambridge, 1964.

———. "The Uses of Theory: Tocqueville's Adaptation of Montesquieu." In *Essays in History and Theory: An Approach to the Social Sciences*, pp. 74–102. Cambridge, 1970.

Riesman, David. *Individualism Reconsidered*. Glencoe, Ill., 1954.

———. *The Lonely Crowd*. New Haven, 1950.

Rod, Edouard. "Les idées politiques de Benjamin Constant. A propos d'un livre nouveau." *Bibliothèque universelle et revue suisse* 34 (1904): 449–75.

Romieu, Andre. *Benjamin Constant et l'esprit européen*. Paris, 1933.

Röpke, Wilhelm. *Civitas Humana: A Human Order of Society.* London, 1948.

————. *The Social Crisis of Our Time.* Chicago, 1950.

Rosenblum, Nancy. *Bentham's Theory of the State.* Cambridge, 1978.

Roulin, Alfred. *Oeuvres de Benjamin Constant.* Paris, 1957.

Roussel, Jean. *Jean-Jacques Rousseau en France après la Révolution, 1795–1830.* Paris, 1972.

Rudler, Gustave. *Benjamin Constant, député de la Sarthe (1819–1822).* Le Mans, 1913.

————. "Benjamin Constant et son ralliement à l'empire." *Revue de Paris* 6 (15 Dec. 1930): 832–47.

————. *Bibliographie critique des oeuvres de Benjamin Constant.* Paris, 1908.

————. "Un chapitre de la tragi-comédie académique. Les candidatures de Benjamin Constant." *Bibliothèque universelle et revue suisse* 98 (1920): 29–38, 189–202.

————. "Comment un règne se prépare. Benjamin Constant et le Palais Royal." *Mélanges de littérature, d'histoire et de philologie offerts à Paul Laumonier par ses élèves et ses amis,* pp. 507–14. Paris, 1935.

————. *La jeunesse de Benjamin Constant, 1767–1794. Le disciple du XVIII siècle, utilitarisme et pessimisme Mme de Charrière.* Paris, 1909.

————. "Un portrait littéraire de Sainte-Beuve. Notes historiques et critiques." *Revue d'histoire littéraire de la France* 12 (1905): 177–203.

————. "Robespierre et les Jacobins dans la correspondance de Benjamin Constant." *Annales révolutionnaires* 3 (1910): 92–103.

Ruggiero, Guido de. *The History of European Liberalism.* London, 1927.

————. "Liberalism." *Encyclopedia of the Social Sciences.* 15 vols., 9:435–41. New York, 1930–33.

Sabine, George H. *A History of Political Theory.* Revised by Thomas T. Thorson. New York, 1973.

————. "The Two Democratic Traditions." *Philosophical Review* 61 (Oct. 1952): 451–74.

Saltet, Mathieu. *Benjamin Constant historien de la religion.* Geneva, 1905.

Salvadori, Massimo. *The Liberal Heresy: Origins and Historical Development.* New York, 1978.

Sartori, Giovanni. *Democratic Theory.* New York, 1965.

Schapiro, John S. *Liberalism and Its Meaning and History.* New York, 1958.

————. *Liberalism and the Challenge of Fascism: Social Forces in England and France, 1810–1870.* New York, 1949.

Schermerhorn, Elizabeth W. *Benjamin Constant: His Private Life and His*

Contribution to the Cause of Liberal Government in France, 1767–1830. London, 1924.

Schlatter, Richard. *Private Property: The History of an Idea.* New Brunswick, N.J.: 1951.

Schwartz, Fritz, ed. *Benjamin Constant. Reise durch die deutsche Kultur.* Potsdam, 1919.

Scott, Franklin D. "Benjamin Constant's Project for France in 1814." *Journal of Modern History* 7 (1935): 41–48.

————. *Bernadotte and the Fall of Napoleon.* Cambridge, 1935.

————. "Propaganda Activities of Bernadotte, 1813–1814." In Donald C. McKay ed., *Essays in the History of Modern Europe,* pp. 16–30. New York, 1936.

Sévéry, William de. *La vie de société dans le pays de Vaud à la fin du dix-huitième siècle.* 2 vols. Lausanne, 1912.

Shklar, Judith N. *After Utopia: The Decline of Political Faith.* Princeton, 1957.

————. *Men and Citizens: A Study of Rousseau's Social Theory.* Cambridge, England, 1969.

Shumway, Anna E. *A Study of the Minerve française (February 1818–March 1820).* Philadelphia, 1934.

Signornini, Alberto. "Constant e la liberte dei moderni." *Storia e politica* 2 (1963): 115–28.

Simon, Walter. *French Liberalism, 1789–1848.* New York, 1972.

Soltau, Roger. *French Liberal Thought in the Nineteenth Century.* New Haven, 1931.

Stadler, Peter von. "Politik und Geschichtschreibung in der franzöischen Restauration 1814–1830." *Historische Zeitschrift* 180 (Oct. 1955): 265–96.

Starzinger, Vincent E. *Middlingness: Juste Milieu Political Theory in France and England, 1815–1848.* Charlottesville, 1965.

Stewart, John H., ed. *The Restoration Era in France, 1814–1830.* New York, 1968.

Stocker, Arnold B. *Constant ou la névrose compensée.* Geneva, 1941.

Strauss, Leo. *Liberalism Ancient and Modern.* New York, 1968.

————. *Natural Right and History.* Chicago, 1953.

Suter, Jean F. "L'idée de légitimité chez Benjamin Constant." In *Institut internationale de philosophie politique. Annales de philosophie,* 7: 181–93. Paris, 1957.

Swart, Koenraad W. *The Sense of Decadence in Nineteenth Century France.* The Hague, 1964.

Switzer, Richard. *Chateaubriand.* New York, 1971.

Talmon, Jacob L. *The Origins of Totalitarian Democracy.* Boston, 1952.

————. *Political Messianism: The Romantic Phase.* London, 1966.

Tambour, E. "Benjamin Constant à Luzarches." *Revue de l'histoire de Versailles et de Seine-et-Oise* 7 (1906): 5–23, 158–72, 248–61, 317–35.

Taylor, Keith, ed. *Saint-Simon: Selected Writings on Science, Industry and Social Organizations.* New York, 1975.

Tenenbaum, Susan. "The Social and Political Thought of Mme de Staël." Ph.D. dissertation, City University of New York, 1976.

Texte, Joseph. *Les relations littéraires de la France avec l'étranger de 1789 à 1848.* Paris, 1899.

Thompson, Patrice. "A propos d'une récente publication des écrits politiques de Benjamin Constant par M. Pozzo di Borgo: La politique, la religion et la doctrine de la perfectibilité humaine." *Revue des sciences humaines,* Jan.–March 1965, pp. 129–45.

————. "Constant et les vertus révolutionnaires." *Europe,* March 1968, pp. 49–62.

Thureau-Dangin, Paul. *Le parti libéral sous la Restauration.* Paris, 1876.

Touchard, G. "Un publiciste italienne au XVIIIᵉ siècle." *Revue historique de droit français et étranger* 25 (1901): 19–46, 490–525, 744–66.

Touchard, Jean. *Histoire des idées politiques.* 2 vols. Paris, 1959 and 1962.

Tronchon, Henri. *La fortune intellectuelle de Herder en France.* Paris, 1920.

Truman, David. *The Governmental Process.* New York, 1956.

Turnell, Martin. "Introduction to the Study of Benjamin Constant." *The Nineteenth Century and After* 144 (July-Dec. 1948): 31–41.

Ullmann, Helene. *Benjamin Constant und seine Beziehungen zum deutschen Geistesleben.* Marburg, 1915.

Vallois, Maximilien. *La formation de l'influence kantienne en France.* Paris, 1935.

Vile, M. J. C. *Constitutionalism and the Separation of Powers.* Oxford, 1967.

Villers, Robert. "La Convention pratiqua-t-elle le gouvernement parlementaire?" *Revue de droit publique* 67 (April-June 1951): 375–89.

Wach, Joachim. "The Role of Religion in the Social Philosophy of Alexis de Tocqueville." *Journal of the History of Ideas* 7 (1946): 74–90.

Wagner, Fritz. *Der liberale Benjamin Constant; Zur Geschichte seines politischen Wesens.* Munich, 1932.

Watkins, Frederick. *The Political Tradition of the West: A Study in the Development of Modern Liberalism.* Cambridge, 1948.

Wernli, A. *Le thème de la liberté dans l'itinéraire spirituel de Benjamin Constant.* Zurich, 1968.

Wiltshire, David. *The Social and Political Thought of Herbert Spencer.* New York, 1978.

Wittmer, L. *Charles de Villers: Un intermédiaire entre la France et l'Allemagne, et un précurseur de Mme de Staël.* Paris, 1908.

Wolff, Robert P. "Beyond Tolerance." In *A Critique of Pure Tolerance,* pp. 3–52. Boston, 1965.

————. *The Poverty of Liberalism.* Boston, 1968.

Woloch, I. *Jacobin Legacy.* Princeton, 1970.

Wolowski, L. "Mémoires sur le Cours politique constitutionnel de Benjamin Constant." *Séances et travaux de l'Académie des sciences morales et politiques,* April-June 1862, pp. 105–36.

Zampogna, Domenico. *Benjamin Constant et Belle de Charrière.* Messina, 1969.

Zanfarino, Antonio. *La liberta dei moderni nel constitutionalismo di Benjamin Constant.* Milan, 1961.

Zeitlin, Irving M. *Liberty, Equality and Revolution in Alexis de Tocqueville.* Boston, 1971.

Zeldin, Theodore. "English Ideals in French Politics during the Nineteenth Century." *Historical Journal* 2, no. 1 (1959): 40–58.

Index